The Southwest in American Literature and Art

The **S**outhwest in

David W. Teague

American Literature and Art

The Rise of a Desert Aesthetic

The University of Arizona Press

Tucson

Published in cooperation with the Center for American Places,
Harrisonburg, Virginia.

The University of Arizona Press
© 1997 David W. Teague
All rights reserved
∞ This book is printed on acid-free, archival-quality paper.
Manufactured in the United States of America
02 01 00 99 98 97   6 5 4 3 2 1

Library of Congress Cataloging-in-Publication Data
Teague, David W., 1964–
The Southwest in American literature and art : the rise of a
desert aesthetic / David W. Teague.
    p.   cm.
"Published in cooperation with the Center for American Places,
Harrisonburg, Virginia."
Includes bibliographical references and index.
ISBN 0-8165-1783-5 (cloth : alk. paper). — ISBN 0-8165-1784-3
(paper : alk. paper)
1. American literature—Southwestern States—History and
criticism.   2. American literature—19th century—History and
criticism.   3. American literature—20th century—History and
criticism.   4. Geographical perception in literature.
5. Southwestern States—In literature.   6. Southwest, New—In
literature.   7. Southwestern States, in art.   8. Southwest, New, in
art.   9. Deserts in literature.   10. Aesthetics, American.
11. Deserts in art.   I. Title.
PS277.T43   1997
810.9′3279—dc21   97-4816
CIP

British Library Cataloguing-in-Publication Data
A catalogue record for this book is available from the British Library.

Contents

List of Illustrations   vii

Preface   ix

Acknowledgments   xi

1 Introduction   3

2 A Barren Wild   13

3 Imaginative Men   51

4 The Desert in the Magazines   91

5 A Desert Paradox   127

6 Early Voices   147

7 In Beauty It Is Finished   159

Notes   171

References   189

Index   203

Illustrations

Emanuel Leutze's *Westward the Course of Empire Takes Its Way*   18

Frontispiece from Powell's *The Exploration of the Colorado*   36

Fire in Camp, from John Wesley Powell's "Cañons of the Colorado"   38

The Rescue, from John Wesley Powell's "Cañons of the Colorado"   39

Jack Hillers's Grand Canyon photograph *Side Cañon*   42

Thomas Moran's painting *The Chasm of the Colorado*   44

Detail from Powell's topographic map of Utah's Green River   46

Timothy O'Sullivan's photograph *Rhyolite Columns*   53

Frederic Remington's painting *A Cavalryman's Breakfast on the Plains*   63

Remington's painting *On the Southern Plains in 1860*   67

Remington's sculpture *The Wounded Bunkie*   69

Remington's sculpture *The Stampede*   71

The initial illustration from "The Bride Comes to Yellow Sky"   84

Mary Hallock Foote's illustration for William Smythe's "Ways and Means in Arid America"   124

Preface

This book is about a part of the world I have loved since I first encountered it when I was five—the arid United States. At that dimly remembered stage of my life, I rode in the back seat of a station wagon behind my parents to visit my cousins in Los Alamos, New Mexico. We began our trip in Arkansas, where I did almost all of my growing up near Little Rock amid creeks, jungly vines, water moccasins, and mud. We lived in the region between the Mississippi Delta and the ridges that, fifty miles to the north, become the Ozark Mountains. We must have approached Los Alamos by way of a set of relatives living in San Antonio, Texas, because I remember driving north through El Paso and Las Cruces rather than west through Oklahoma City and Tucumcari. In Truth or Consequences, New Mexico, while my father gassed up our white Chevy II with the turquoise top, I watched the small dust clouds people raised with their underslung bootheels as they walked in front of the sky, the rocks, the clean, dry horizon of New Mexico—a very long horizon to my forest-and-beanfield way of seeing. In deep-green Arkansas, I'm sure people were engaged daily in making their small gestures on the face of the landscape, too, but in Arkansas I couldn't see those gestures. I first noticed people suiting posture to place during that visit to the desert.

Since then the question of how people can learn to suit themselves better to their place on earth has become more crucial than any five-year-old could have imagined. And now I would like to contribute to the search for an answer to this question. In making my contribution, I have looked most often to books because books are what I love the most of all human things. I have looked to books about the desert because the desert was where I stood when I first grasped how fundamentally ill-at-ease most human beings are in the landscapes they inhabit. And I have also turned to individual works of art and to other media, such as magazines and scientific reports, in which words and pictures about the desert were first made known to the citizens of the United States.

My goal as I undertook this study, an impossibly high goal, has been to recover the clarity of that five-year-old's perception, and although such recovery is, of course, impossible, what follows is my attempt.

Acknowledgments

For the fact of this book's existence, I thank Alan Howard, who kept me at this task; Jerome McGann—may a part of his grace and intelligence have rubbed off on me and may it surface here; and Michael Branch, Cheryll Glotfelty, Scott Slovic, Allison Wallace, Dan Philippon, Sean O'Grady, Ralph Black, Terrell Dixon, William Howarth, Zita Ingham, Tom Lyon, Ian Marshall, Kent Ryden, Mary Ellen Bellanca, and the rest of the Association for the Study of Literature and Environment and the community it embraces—you have kept me afloat. My special thanks go to George F. Thompson, President of the Center for American Places in Harrisonburg, Virginia, for his fine work in directing this project to its completion.

The Southwest in American Literature and Art

Chapter **1**

It seems a gigantic statement for even nature to make, all in one mighty stone word, apprehended at once like a burst of light, celestial color its natural vesture, coming in glory to mind and heart as to a home prepared for it from the very beginning. Wildness so godful, cosmic, primeval, bestows a new sense of the earth's beauty and size. —John Muir, "The Grand Canyon"[1]

Introduction

This book is a study of various imaginative representations of the desert in the United States. Its focus is on a series of watershed years during which the nation at large acquired an aesthetic appreciation of the arid western lands it had traditionally vilified.[2] Until about the mid-1890s, deserts were powerful icons of howling wilderness for citizens of the United States. They were incomprehensible to the collective imagination of the "civilized" portion of the country because they were places where accustomed modes of geography, agriculture, industry, and commerce did not obtain. But by 1910 deserts had become associated with the very height of American culture. They were developing into the aesthetic wonderlands that gave rise to the nature writing of Mary Austin, the art of Georgia O'Keeffe, the photographs of Alfred Stieglitz, and the essays of Joseph Wood Krutch. The work of some of the most important contemporary American writers is a legacy of these two decades: Edward Abbey, N. Scott Momaday, Rudolfo Anaya, Leslie Marmon Silko, Charles Bowden, Gloria Anzaldúa, and Terry Tempest Williams write in a tradition that finds much of its early definition in the desert writing and desert art of the turn of the twentieth century.

As with any seemingly sudden and profound change, however, the closer one looks at this radical evolution in desert perspectives, the less sudden—the less isolated from the rest of history—it appears. The years 1890 to 1910 saw a series of events that constitute what Henry Steele Commager has identified as the single defining cultural watershed in United States history. During these twenty years the nation's citizens witnessed, among other things, the perceived closing of their western frontier, the emergence of the former colonies as an international power, and the rise of American multinational corporations. These developments necessitated a comprehensive reassessment of American culture and character.[3] However, as Commager warns, "with all such watersheds the topography is blurred."[4] Cultural changes such as the one I discuss in this book do not exhibit clearly defined outlines or boundaries. They exist within cultural and historical contexts that extend far forward and backward in time.

Thus, not all the works of art and literature I examine in this study date from the central period in question, 1890 to 1910. Chapter 2 begins with a discussion of Zebulon Pike and his reaction in 1809 to the region that is present-day New Mexico, and it then presents a survey of the history of Anglo American perceptions of the desert as they evolved through the nineteenth century. Beginning with Frederic Remington and Stephen Crane, figures whose writing represents the beginning of the watershed years in the 1890s, my examination of artists and writers becomes more detailed. The turn of the twentieth century represents such a rich era of desert writing and desert art that its artistic production requires close analysis. And just as chapter 1 traces the long prelude to the rise of the "aesthetic desert," chapter 6 traces its legacy in the work of contemporary artists such as Silko, Momaday, and Anzaldúa.

Furthermore, just as no discrete time period could adequately contain such a profound cultural change as the United States' rapprochement with its arid western landscapes, neither could any single cultural narrative. Although I address primarily what might be called the mainstream artistic production of the United States—imaginative treatments of the arid regions produced and consumed primarily by middle- and upper-class Americans—a strictly mainstream perspective would be inadequate to characterize fully the United States' changing relationship to its arid regions at the turn of the century. Civilizations other than the current Eurocentric American one have long existed on the western deserts, and as the work of contemporary writers and artists implies, still different civilizations will arise in the future, civilizations whose roots will lie not only in our culturally central and traditionally valued Euro-American past and present but also in our Hispanic and indigenous pasts and presents, which the United States has historically been slow to acknowledge in its literature, arts, and cultural criticism.

Before I address such issues, however, I must address a more basic one: the definition of the desert land under consideration here. Despite my rather broad application of the term, no one portion of land in this country is identifiable as "the desert." *Desert* is an elusive term, in large part because the idea is so hard to define that, as Patricia Limerick has noted, "Deserts have made fools of the wisest people."[5]

The deserts of the United States are many and varied. Nevertheless, I do not employ the precise regional nomenclature of geographers and biologists—Chihuahuan, Sonoran, Great Basin, or Mojave, among others—because in large measure such ecological distinctions were not an issue for the writers and artists I examine. Nor have I found it expedient to employ a strictly geographical definition, for deserts have tended to appear, at different times and in the minds of different people, over much of North America. As John Warkentin has shown, the Great American Desert, according to many nineteenth-century Canadians, extended far into Saskatchewan,[6] and contemporary ecologists are well aware that the boundaries of North American deserts are currently expanding rapidly enough to make some bioregional maps of the West inaccurate shortly after they are prepared.[7]

In this book, my use of the term *desert* is a conceptual one. The deserts discussed in this study represent as much an ideological as a geographical construct. Following Peter Wild, I will simply take *desert* to mean "a place where habits learned in humid areas are bound to fail."[8] *Desert* is a term defined by the needs of U.S. citizens largely of northwestern European descent, the name of a place that will not easily yield to traditional cultural imperatives such as farming, industrial production, or pastoral art. A desert is, as Mary Austin suggested, a region where "not the law, but the land sets the limits."[9]

Thus, the desert's boundaries and its definitions have changed as the United States has interacted with it. *Desert* has necessarily been a word plastic in meaning. The *Oxford English Dictionary* traces the evolution of the term from a descriptor of any "uninhabited and uncultivated tract of country . . . including forest land" to a word describing waterless and treeless areas. In Judeo-Christian thought, as Limerick observes, "the word *desert* did in fact carry the meaning of a deserted place, or wilderness," to the extent that the Puritan leader Cotton Mather thought of his tangled green New England landscape as a "'Squalid, horrid American Desert.'"[10] So, too, did Michael Wigglesworth when, in describing the wild North America of the seventeenth century in "God's Controversy with New England," he saw the edge of the desert—"a waste and howling wilderness"—in the forest that surrounded his Massachusetts village.[11] In his *Exploratory Travels through the Western Territories of North America*, published in 1811, Zebulon Pike labeled the Great Plains and everything west of the Mississippi as the Great American Desert.[12] And now, nearly two hundred years later, the United States is left with much more limited areas of wild desert land in the West and Southwest, where aridity has to an extent kept industrial civilization at bay.[13] Deserts, which occur primarily in West Texas, New Mexico, Arizona, Utah, Nevada, and southern California, resist whatever the United States would do to the natural world.[14]

In order to approach the desert thus defined, I deal with creative texts, works of visual art, and other aesthetic re-creations of the arid landscape, tracing the recent relationship between human imagination and the nonhuman desert world. The written aesthetic responses of early explorers who came to the desert "wilderness" are enlightening, because, as Yi-Fu Tuan has noted in *Topophilia,* the "visitor's evaluation of wilderness is essentially aesthetic."[15] By the turn of the twentieth century, when the citizens of the United States were no longer simply visitors to the region, aesthetic responses had become even more compelling. As Paul Ward English and Robert C. Mayfield hold, "the aesthetic landscape is a symbolic creation designed with care, whose form reflects a set of human attitudes . . . [and] the thinking of a people about the world around them."[16]

I focus primarily on the written record because I assume, along with Joseph Meeker, that "[i]f the creation of literature is an important characteristic of the human species, it should be examined carefully and honestly to discover its influence upon human behavior and the natural environment—to determine what role, if any, it plays in the welfare and survival of mankind and what insight it offers into human relationships with other species and the world around us."[17] According to Tuan, studying human beings' "perception, attitude, and value" regarding the physical environment will "prepare us, first of all, to understand ourselves," which is vital if humans are to learn a more tenable orientation toward the nonhuman world.[18] I examine the literature of desert landscapes because such literature has been and will continue to be a vehicle for propagating our culture's beliefs about nature, a reflection of the perception, attitude, and value to which Tuan refers. And, because I am interested here in imaginative treatments of the landscape, true geography—physical, cultural, and otherwise—tends to remain a function of the imaginative figures in this book. While Homer Aschmann, Dan Flores, and other scholars have studied the landscape itself, I generally turn my attention instead to the succession of images that has been laid down upon it.

Neil Evernden argues that cultures "use different conceptions of the idea of nature in order to achieve specific societal goals.[19] My study is essentially a test case of his thesis. It looks at a specific culture (progressive America at the turn of the twentieth century), and at a part of the natural world readily identifiable to that culture (the arid Southwest), and it asks what part the component of that culture called literature has played in defining the two entities.

I thus assume that the literature I examine has an environmental impact. Lawrence Buell asserts in his book *The Environmental Imagination* that "the environmental crisis involves a crisis of the imagination the amelioration of which depends on finding better ways of imagining nature and humanity's relation to it," and that "[a]esthetics can become a decisive force for or against environmental change."[20] Annette Kolodny maintains that "fundamental change can occur only within the mind. If we seriously contemplate any meaningful reordering of our relations with our landscape, then we need . . . a better grasp of the ways in which language provides clues to the underlying motivations behind action; provides clues, if you will, to our deepest dreams and fantasies."[21] Or, as she has put it more directly in *The Land before Her,* "our actions in the world . . . are shaped by the paradigms in our head."[22] Certainly the relationship of the literary production of the United States to its objective treatment of landscape is, in many instances, clearly drawn, as when Theodore Roosevelt, who had been one of the leading literary arbiters of the arid West, shepherded through Congress the Reclamation Act of 1902, which would forever shape the approach Americans would take to the desert.

The relationship between imagination and practice works in the other direction as well. Narratives such as Thomas Jefferson's description of the mythic yeoman farmer and his lifeways—narratives and lifeways that have been broadly disseminated through mainstream American culture—are symbiotically related, because, as Mary Austin observed in studying the original inhabitants of New Mexico and Arizona, such exigencies of the physical world as raising crops affect a culture's collective imagination. This is especially the case when a culture tries to raise crops under arid conditions. "Corn is a town-builder," Austin wrote, "a maker of policies, mother of inventions. Out of its necessities were drawn architecture, philosophical systems, and the material of drama."[23] The existence of such connections encourages me to hope that, by examining some of the ways in which the United States has imagined arid nature in the past, I may be able to suggest a more tenable environmental practice for the future.[24]

It is important to be aware that in this book I am addressing only a selection of the myriad ways in which citizens of the United States have approached arid lands, proceeding as Limerick does in *Desert Passages,* by synecdoche.[25] Further, those familiar with the work of Gerald Vizenor, Ishmael Reed, Raymond Paredes, Walter Ong, Simon Ortiz, Janice Mirikitani, and other influential critics and authors working outside the confines of traditionally anthologized American literature will be aware that I give desert literature from Hispanic, Native American, African American, and Asian traditions very short shrift or no shrift at all. There is a reason for my narrowly construed canon of desert texts. The texts that were influential among the chiefly white, chiefly male, chiefly middle- and upper-class Americans whose vision largely shaped our present environmentally precarious tradition in the deserts of the United States requires explication simply because they have been so influential. These are the kinds of privileged narratives that dictate any culture's perception of its landscape, as Kolodny discusses in her introduction to *The Land before Her,*[26] and they require attention in part because they have obscured, if only temporarily, other cultural traditions at large on the desert landscape at the same time that Americans have overrun the ecosystem.

In general, I have chosen texts that exemplify one of the most pervasive and persistent elements of the United States' collective approach to the environment, one that is more evident in the deserts than in more humid climes: its tendency toward what Lawrence Buell has called environmental doublethink. Buell argues that the United States' chronic condition of being "at once a nature-loving and resource-consuming nation . . . is sustained by acts of compartmentalization made habitual by the way our sensibilities are disciplined."[27] Nowhere was there more intellectual and conceptual work done to compartmentalize American sensibilities than in the aesthetic revaluing of the desert at the turn of the twentieth century.

The turn-of-the-century figurative responses to the deserts I discuss in depth in this book—among them Stephen Crane's "The Bride Comes to Yellow Sky," Frederic Remington's art and sculpture, John C. Van Dyke's *The Desert,* and the desert essays and articles that appeared in popular monthly magazines between 1890 and 1905—exemplify the contradictory attitudes Americans developed toward the nonhuman arid world during this time. To these writers, the deserts, which were some of the last "wild" and "natural" places remaining to the nation at the time, seemed largely uninhabited, largely unexplored, and largely "unreclaimed" even though, according to Frederick Jackson Turner, a report based on the 1890 census had declared that the frontier no longer existed in the United States.[28] As they do today, the deserts presented a good deal of empty space to the eyes of Americans who had boarded trains in New York City, Philadelphia, and Chicago, so they served as the last opportunity these people had to decide what to think about wilderness before it disappeared.

As John Muir's hopeful description of the Grand Canyon in the epigraph that begins this introduction implies, there seemed to have been something "from the very beginning" in the American mind and heart that promised to be receptive to the desert. Muir's intuition about his peers' minds and hearts has proved correct; a group of his contemporaries successfully created a brand new myth, the myth of the cowboy, and set it in motion across the deserts. Others struggled mightily and finally succeeded in making the "wastelands" fructify through irrigation. And a small, very literate segment of American society managed, in a self-conscious self-education in natural aesthetics, to learn to value the sparse beauty of the desert for its own sake.

Given the culture of late Victorian America, this last negotiation might be considered the most remarkable. The concept of a wasteland, a place that will not produce in abundance without irrigation, has traditionally been nothing short of odious to European Americans, who are generally, as David Potter argued, a "people of plenty." But there were Americans living during the watershed decade of the 1890s, on the cusp between Victorian and modern America, who learned to value the desert and to understand that nature need not serve humans in order to be valuable.[29]

That understanding, that "new sense of the earth's beauty" to which Muir referred, is a complex legacy that Americans would do well to understand, primarily because it provides, as I argue in chapter 5, a central thread for the developing nexus of cultural, geographical, and environmental negotiations centered in the desert cultures of the United States. Despite the different traditions in which they worked, there are many similarities between, for instance, writers like John C. Van Dyke and Mary Austin at the turn of this century and Gloria Anzaldúa and Leslie Marmon Silko at its end. While contemporary scholars of American Indian and Hispanic literature continue to enhance our understanding of those portions of Anzaldúa's and Silko's traditions that our culture has long overlooked, I hope, by including their work in my study, to suggest ways in which the various literary monuments that have arisen on the arid lands of North America over the past several hundred years might find common ground.

Admittedly, I work from within a European American tradition, but from this perspective I examine responses to something neither Anglo Americans, American Indians, nor Hispanic Americans can ever fully claim: the desert. In the challenges it has presented to human imagination of all kinds, the desert provides an environmental constant with which human cultures must continually come to terms and through which environmental challenges and cultural differences are mediated.

American culture's struggle to come to terms with its arid regions proves truly enlightening, just as Mary Austin predicted. "The profoundest implications of human experience are never stated rationally," she observed, "never with explicitness, but indirectly in what we agree to call art forms, rhythms, festivals, designs, melodies, objective symbolic substitutions." And the study of these indirect articulations of human experience on the landscape, Austin suggested, would be no easy task: "The business of assembling such a set of symbols for the expression of its deeper reactions is, to a people newly come to a country, likely to be a long one."[30] It is on this long "business of assembling" that I hope to shed some light.

Chapter **2**

The country presents a barren wild of poor land, scarcely to be improved by culture. —Zebulon Pike[1]

A Barren Wild

Although indigenous cultures have existed in the desert regions of what is now the United States for some 30,000 years, and some Spanish and Mexican cultures have existed there for 400 years, the desert was, until the decade of the 1890s, a nearly impossible place for most citizens of the United States to live. It was sparsely populated and vaguely was understood by English-speaking people. It was too dry and too hot for a culture brought from the eastern United States and before that from Europe, and the arid version of nature it presented to those white Americans who bothered to visit it was so strange as to be unrecognizable. As Mary Austin described their situation, "The topography of the country [could] not be expressed in terms invented for such purpose in a low green island by the North Sea."[2]

The process by which the United States came to understand and to appropriate its deserts was long and difficult. The land put several obstacles, both physical and psychological, in the path of the expanding nation, obstacles that effectively kept a large population of settlers out of it for nearly half a century after its initial exploration. The first and most obvious was that the deserts were deadly. It was impossible to live in them, or even move across them, in the ways settlers were used to back in the humid East. That is why they were called deserts—their population of "civilized" people was distressingly small in the eyes of people of European descent, who, as Henry Nash Smith observed in his book *The Virgin Land,* generally believed that "civilization depended on agriculture."[3] From Zebulon Pike's earliest published assessments of the arid regions in 1811 until well after the railroads came through in the 1880s, simply surviving the deserts for an extended period presented a challenge that the vast majority of Anglo Americans could not meet.

In addition to their physical hostility, the arid regions of the West presented a second, psychological obstacle. There was, and to a degree there still is, a deep distrust of desert places in the Anglo American mind. As members of a Judeo-Christian culture, the people of the United States knew from Exodus and Deuteronomy that desert wilderness was a place of punishment and atonement for a "stiffnecked people." Created by God as an expression of his wrath, the desert was a landscape of "brimstone, and salt, and burning, that it is not sown, nor beareth, nor any grass groweth therein, like the overthrow of Sodom, and Gomorrah, Admah, and Zeboim, which the Lord overthrew in his anger, and in his wrath" (Deuteronomy 29:23). Deserts constituted a purgatorial if not hellish realm. Hell's Canyon and El Jornada del Diablo were not names given in the spirit of fun in which they are now taken. Americans knew that God had forced his own children, when they transgressed, to endure the desert for forty years—the desert known as the wilderness of Sinai, or the wilderness of Sin (Exodus 17:1)—and they knew that the self-same landscape lurked on the arid margins of their civilization. There was thus a moral dimension to early perceptions of the desert. The deserts had been made wastelands because those associated with them had displeased God.

This perception deepened and grew more complex as the nineteenth century passed. The people who would civilize the entire continent, and who were certain that their project had God's blessing, were faced in the second half of the nineteenth century with the fact that the desert stood directly in their way. Not just the stigma of desert places but the desert itself hindered the nation's achievement of its Manifest Destiny, because most Anglo Americans had no idea of how to settle it. And although the dark view of desert wilderness imported from ancient Israel was rather a minor consideration compared to the real logistical and economic hardships that the desert inflicted on settlers and developers, the conflation of the two responses to the desert produced a profound suspicion of arid lands. In antiquity the desert had been made a punishment for sin; in the age of the Republic of the United States, it hindered the spread of goodness in the form of civilization, Christianity, and a market economy.

Anglo Americans were used to seeing moist, green, usually pastoral landscapes, and were generally suspicious of any other kind. Robert Thacker, in his book *The Great Prairie Fact and Literary Imagination,* has documented the difficulties encountered by U.S. settlers in the "transformation of the prairie from 'virgin land' to 'home place.'" Essentially, Thacker argues, "the prairie has offered vistas ever at odds with the western European notion of 'landscape.' It was, and ever is, unlike any landscape conventionally thought pleasing."[4] Deserts, like prairies, offered wide-open spaces at odds with conventional landscape tastes, but if anything they were more unsettling to explorers and settlers than the prairie, which at the very least usually had grass covering it.

The enduring popularity of the Hudson River School of painting during the mid nineteenth century—beginning approximately with Thomas Cole's arrival on the cultural scene in 1825[5]—attests to a fairly large American audience which, according to H. T. Tuckerman in his *Book of the Artists* (1867),

> has watched the advent and discharge of a thunder cloud, in summer, among the White Mountains or the Hudson Highlands, [and which] will appreciate the perfect truth to nature, in the impending shadow of the portentous mass of vapor, as it falls on tree, rock, sward, and stream; the contrasted brilliancy of the sunshine playing on the high ridge above[,] the strata of the latter, as well as the foliage and foreground of the whole landscape, are thoroughly and minutely American in their character.[6]

Rich green landscapes, not dry white or red or yellow ones, were truly American in character.

As David Bjelajac has shown, such prominent Americans as William Ware balked when confronted with spare, rocky landscapes. In 1852, nearly three decades after he had first seen Washington Allston's painting *Elijah in the Desert,* Ware "continued to struggle with his recollection of the painting's ambiguous treatment of the biblical subject and the apparently arbitrary forms of the wilderness landscape."[7] Part of Ware's objection to the desert piece arose from the fact that he simply did not like the scenery surrounding Elijah, for in painting dead trees and bare rocks, "Mr. Allston neglected the general truth of nature, to single out and depict a subordinate particular, and that particular having no beauty or charm of its own—though certainly possessing a sort of savage grandeur—simply a piece of natural history and nothing more. . . . And, to make it a principal object in a great work of art, is to degrade the art to the rank of a print in Goldsmith's Animated Nature."[8] The fecund Hudson Highlands might have been, as Tuckerman claimed, the general type of American nature, suitable for great art, but deserts were not; they were freaks of nature better suited to the specialized inquiries of naturalists than to the canvases of great artists.

Emmanuel Leutze's twenty-by-thirty-foot painting, *Westward the Course of Empire Takes Its Way,* commissioned in 1861 for the west stairway of the U.S. Capitol, demonstrates the degree to which this concept of America overcoming the desert became institutionalized in American culture. In the frame of Leutze's grand scene of North American conquest appear "faint grisaille vignettes," one of which is entitled "Moses Leading the Israelites through the desert."[9] On the steps of the Capitol, the task of overcoming the desert becomes no less than a subtext of the nation's Manifest Destiny.

To members of a culture whose most basic definition of itself involved, as David Potter has argued, the idea that Americans are indeed a people of plenty appropriately inhabiting a countryside of natural wealth—revealed endlessly in glowing descriptions of a temperate climate, rich natural resources, and general fecundity[10]—the desert was unfamiliar and even ran counter to the nation's natural impulse toward abundance. Deserts represented a kind of evil.

Deserts appeared unpromising, intimidating, forbidding and evil because, as John Berger has shown, "The way we see things is affected by what we know or what we believe."[11] The Anglo Americans' predisposition for verdant landscapes, which allowed them as a group to comprehend and enjoy such visual cues as the looming green timber and vapor-shrouded rivers of the eastern United States while they shuddered at the sight of bright dusty deserts, is a human trait that George Nelson has called visual literacy.[12] The appreciation of landscapes is a learned response, one that requires a fairly sophisticated iconography—in the case of the Hudson River valley an iconography of the rich natural abundance of tall timber and running rivers. Anglo Americans could not comfortably look at sparse landscapes.

Those who are visually literate are able to put together images into a coherent narrative. In Nelson's sense of the term, people are visually illiterate in the world of twentieth-century art if they stare blandly and smile distractedly at abstract expressionist paintings, possessing "no vocabulary of value, and very probably no idea that nonverbal languages exist."[13] Similarly, nineteenth-century Americans such as Zebulon Pike and those who followed him possessed no vocabulary of value with which to describe the arid landscapes they saw in the West. According to David Emmons, those "who traveled and commented upon the plains were, in subtle and often unconscious ways, programmed by the society from which they came, and to which they reported."[14] Thus the arid regions of the new United States often overtaxed the vocabularies of early explorers. Joni Louise Kinsey notes in her study of Thomas Moran that since "the time of Coronado and Columbus, New World explorers had expressed frustration with the inadequacy of words to convey the extraordinary appearance of landscape."[15]

These new English-speaking arrivals on the plains of New Mexico and the bajadas of Arizona coped with the radical change in nature's appearance by developing a bifurcated set of responses to it. On the one hand, the desert demanded a new descriptive vocabulary because it represented a new landscape to be explored and settled, and its would-be exploiters needed practical figures with which desert concerns could be articulated before the exploitation could be undertaken. On the other hand, the desert demanded a new imaginative, aesthetic, and literary vocabulary because it looked like no place the citizens of the United States had seen before, and it invariably struck them with wonder. Both new vocabularies were hard to come by, for as Harold Rosenberg has observed, "People carry their landscapes with them, the way travelers used to cart along their porcelain chamber pots. The stronger their sense of form the more reluctant they are to part with either."[16] Most Americans were used to grass, trees, and rivers; their imaginations balked at the features of this land to which they were not accustomed.

Still, despite these conceptual and perceptual difficulties, newly arriv-

Emanuel Leutze's *Westward the Course of Empire Takes Its Way* (Westward Ho!) gives a tangible form to America's dreams of conquest in the desert. (Courtesy of the Architect of the Capitol)

ing explorers and settlers did develop a set of categories with which to see it and a language adequate to describe it: a desert literacy. Beginning with the zero point of Zebulon Pike's bleak initial assessment, descriptions of the desert written in English became increasingly ambitious, increasingly optimistic, and increasingly apt. They were, in effect, tried on for size by Americans, who created and applied them in practical situa-

tions they encountered on the land. And as more and more white Americans came from the East, they experimented with more and more words.

What explorers and settlers first learned to say about the desert reflected the things they hoped to accomplish there. Over time, however, their language came to reflect the new set of practical approaches they developed in order to thrive in the harsh and rugged landscape. By conceiving of the desert as a series of rational problems to be solved or practical challenges to be met and overcome, Anglo Americans were able to create for themselves the illusion of control over the landscape. The desert world would be made subject to reason. The fearful, incomprehensible things in it, such as the killing aridity and the apparently infinite barrenness, could be overcome by the exercise of rationally administered human will. The wilderness would be forced to succumb to reason, for, according to Max Horkheimer and Theodor Adorno's construction of Enlightenment rationality, "[i]n the most general sense of progressive thought, the Enlightenment has always aimed at liberating men from fear and establishing their sovereignty." Further, this sovereignty would manifest itself as a clear understanding of the nonhuman realm, because the "program of the Enlightenment was the disenchantment of the world."[17] Knowledge, in the practical application of Yankee ingenuity, would be precisely the tool to use in subduing the alien, enchanted landscape of the western deserts.

By approaching the desert from two directions—imaginatively re-inventing their language for use in the desert and practically re-inventing the face of the desert to fit their language—Anglo Americans coming to arid lands were able to hedge their bets psychologically; they gave themselves two routes by which to come to terms with the desert. If it was sometimes difficult to appreciate the beauty of a parched landscape, to think of it as a garden, or if its appearance was downright terrifying, then there was always the alternative—to appreciate the land's potential utility.

Pike, Frémont, Magoffin, and Manly

Early explorers and travelers exhibited signs of distress, sometimes at deep levels, brought on by their exposure to the desert, so they seldom saw anything practically or aesthetically redeeming in it. Zebulon Pike, one of the first white Americans to write about the Southwest, saw no future there for civilized people. He could not imagine human life as he understood it existing in the desert. Pike responded positively to the mountainsides and river bottoms of New Mexico, but he reported in his *Exploratory Travels through the Western Territories of North America* (1811) that "all the rest of the country presents to the eye a barren wild of poor land, scarcely to be improved by culture."[18] In his eyes, as E. N. Feltskog has suggested, "the wilderness of desert and mountain seemed to bar the triumphant expansion of American history and progress."[19] For thirty years, few Americans seriously challenged Pike's assessment, and many explorers endorsed it. Indeed, according to Feltskog for "the two generations of Americans who discovered [the deserts] in the pages of Nuttall and Bradbury, Pike and Edwin James, Cooper and Irving and Cullen Bryant and a thousand newspaper-letters and traveler's guides, the Desert *was* the Great West, a constant limit to American expansion and a proof—if proof were needed—that even an empty landscape might be cursed with primal barrenness."[20]

John C. Frémont, exploring the region in 1843–44, found the Great Basin Desert to be of "dreary and savage character"[21] and, in reporting its inward-draining rivers,[22] expressed doubt about its future productivity.[23] The idea of the desert as irrigated breadbasket, the artificially watered counterpart of the natural garden of the East, would not arise for two generations, for as Henry Nash Smith has shown, "[i]n order to establish itself in the vast new area of the plains . . . the myth of the garden had to confront and overcome another myth of exactly opposed meaning, although of inferior strength—the myth of the Great American Desert."[24]

Even travelers who were somewhat more self-contained, who did not feel obligated to ponder such daunting concerns as the possibility of propagating American culture across the landscape, experienced difficulty in confronting its otherworldliness. Susan Shelby Magoffin was, according to Howard Lamar, "a pert, observant young lady of wealth and fashion," but she felt discomfort when she confronted the open spaces of New Mexico in 1846.[25] Distanced somewhat by her gender from the essentially male contemporary enthusiasm for western travel, she accompanied her husband on a trading expedition from Independence, Missouri, to Brownsville, Texas, by way of Santa Fe.[26] Over the course of her journey, lacking for the most part a masculine interest in conquering the difficult desert terrain, Magoffin began to display the kind of mental exhaustion many early travelers from the lush East felt after having to face the barrenness of New Mexico day after day.

Magoffin made an enthusiastic start when she left Independence on June 11, 1846, expressing an impatience with the trees of eastern Kansas because she wanted to see open spaces. "As we proceeded from this thick wood of oaks and scrubby underbrush," she relates, "my eyes were unable to satiate their longing for a sight of the wide spreading plains."[27] The novelty of the plains quickly wore off, however, and the landscape began to oppress her. By early July, Magoffin had begun looking for analogs in her own experience to help her grasp the landscape and had begun trying out new metaphors in the Southern Plains. Facing a storm, she resorted in her journal to the conceit of the now-familiar "prairie sea": "The vivid and forked lightning quickly succeeded by the hoarse growling thunder impresses one most deeply of his own weakness and the magnanimity of his God. With nothing before or near us in sight, save the wide expanse of Prairie resembling most clearly in the pale light of the moon, as she occasionally appeared from under a murky cloud and between the vivid lightning, the wide sea."[28] The effort of always having to work to describe the landscape told on Magoffin. By February 1847 she was psychologically exhausted and could no longer enjoy sights that she admitted were beautiful but barren. The river bottoms, with their lush green vegetation, had provided her imagination some respite from the barren landscape during the summer and fall, but they were no comfort to her in winter. She had been away from the green to which she is accustomed for too long, and so she had to green the landscape in her imagination in order to come to terms with it:

> *Fray Cristobal* [the last watering point for travelers on the trail before the Jornada del Muerto]. . . At present I can say nothing of its beauties—the bleak hill sides look lovely enough and feel cold enough. In the summer season though I suspect it is quite attractive; the River bottom is then green; the cottonwoods are leaved; the stream, though at all times dark and ugly, is more brisk and lively in its flow and these now unattractive sand-hills serve as a variation in the scene; with all I guess it is not so disagreeable.[29]

A combination of mental and physical exhaustion brought on by the rigors of traveling in arid country seem to have soured Magoffin's perception of the Southwest.

In her disappointment Magoffin was not unusual. She was one of a long line of desert travelers who had been disappointed, or worse, by their experiences with the landscape. For William Manly and his party, crossing the Mojave Desert three years after Magoffin's trek through New

Mexico, the desert was impossible not only to the point of disillusionment but ultimately to the point of death. It was Manly's traveling party, many of whom perished of thirst, that gave Death Valley its name.[30]

Manly was a remarkably strong man and was capable of a remarkably bright outlook on life. In 1849 he actually escaped Death Valley twice: after walking out the first time, he and a companion collected water and supplies and hiked a hundred miles back into the desert to rescue the remnants of their party of forty-niners, thus struggling out of Death Valley once again.

While Manly recounts his experience in twice meeting the challenge of escaping from the valley, he presents himself as a man engaged with the landscape, immersed in it and in his effort to bring himself and his companions out alive. He had no time to despair at the bleakness of the desert as Magoffin had done. Had Manly's attention not remained fixed on the challenge presented by the land around him and had he not read it correctly, he and all his friends would have died in the desert. The Lewis Manly of *Death Valley in '49* exists in a rational, passionless relationship with the landscape, a one-dimensional interaction predicated solely on the desire to escape the country alive.

Manley's approach to the land was pragmatic. The desert comes across as a worthy adversary that he only barely defeats. Indeed, his description of his close engagement with the physical world of the Mojave often betrays a grudging admiration for it. With his party trapped behind the Panamint Range dying of thirst, Manly's task was to scout a way out. But his reaction to the scene went beyond practicality:

The range we had been traveling nearly paralell [*sic*] with seemed to come to an end here where this snow peak stood, and immediately north and south of this peak there seemed to be a lower pass. . . . In the morning I concluded to go to the summit of that pass and with my glass have an extensive view. . . .

Next morning I reached the summit about nine o'clock, and had the grandest view I ever saw. I could see north and south almost forever. . . . A few miles to the north and east of where I stood, and somewhat higher, was the roughest piece of ground I ever saw. It stood in sharp peaks and was of many colors, some of them so red that the mountain looked red hot. I imagined it to be a true volcanic point, and had never been so near one before, and the most wonderful picture of grand desolation one could ever see.[31]

Both in 1849 when he first surveyed the scene and forty-five years later in 1894 when he committed his narrative to paper, Manly's imagination was engaged by the possibilities of the landscape. He was thrilled by the grand and wonderful vistas, and he became so excited in recounting his emotions that a sense of the beauty of the landscape shown through.

Nevertheless, once Manly escaped Death Valley his aesthetic relationship with the landscape came to an end. At the point in Manly's memoir where he delivers his party from the Mojave, he inserts one of the most impassioned condemnations of arid land in American literature, a philippic predicated on the fact that the desert does not provide enough water to support the sort of travel Manly and his party had meant to undertake and which goes on to attribute an aesthetic and moral dimension to the landscape in order to make the curse more comprehensive. No longer thrilled by the challenge of the desert, Manly cannot see it as beautiful:

> We were out of the dreadful sands and shadows of Death Valley, its exhausting phantoms, its salty columns, bitter lakes and wild, dreary sunken desolation. If the waves of the sea could flow in and cover its barren nakedness, as we now know they might if a few sandy barriers were swept away, it would be indeed, a blessing, for in it there is naught of good, comfort or satisfaction, but ever in the minds of those who braved its heat and sands, a thought of a horrid Charnel house, a [corner of] the earth so dreary that it requires an exercise of strongest faith to believe that the great Creator ever smiled upon it as a portion of his work and pronounced it "Very good."[32]

Writing in 1894, when the rest of the country was enthusiastic about "reclaiming" arid land, Manly continued to see it as a landscape deserving nothing less than divine retribution because of its hostility to Anglo American habits—in this case the habit of overland travel by ox-drawn wagon.

Irving, Gregg, and Greeley

Other Americans who came to the desert from humid regions were not so severely used by the landscape and were able to respond to it in terms less extreme. In 1835, Washington Irving, like Pike twenty-five years before him and Manly fourteen years after him, saw the region as a stumbling block to the advancement of American civilization. The landscape Irving describes in his *Tour on the Prairies* and his *Rocky Mountains* was, to be precise, actually the Southern Plains, not what we today think of as the western deserts. The plains are not as dry as the Sonoran or Chihuahuan Deserts, but they nevertheless represent a transition between the lushness of the Mississippi Valley and the aridity of the Southwest, and to Irving they looked relatively barren. In his eyes, the dry plains were indeed a "desert," a place that stultified the human character. Such a barren place must, in his eyes,

> ever remain an irreclaimable wilderness, intervening between the abodes of civilization, and affording a last refuge to the Indian. Here, roving tribes of hunters, living in tents or lodges, and following the migrations of the game, may lead a life of savage independence, where there is nothing to tempt the cupidity of the white man. . . . [S]hould they continue their present predatory and warlike habits, they may, in time, become a scourge to the civilized frontiers on either side of the mountains; as they are at present a terror to the traveller and trader.[33]

Despite this dim view of the landscape and the people living in it, taken from a rather grand historical perspective predicated on his assumptions about the progress of civilization, Irving is at other moments capable of finding redeeming features in the region. From a more immediate, less worldly perspective—namely, camping on the ground—Irving was prepared to perceive the landscape's difficulty as an attractive feature. It held potential as a kind of proving ground for young Americans, a place valuable in its harshness, a place to which America could send her young men for a "tour on the prairies [which] would be . . . likely to produce that manliness, simplicity, and self-dependence most in unison with our political institutions."[34]

Still, the strangeness, aridity, and difficulty that Irving valued as tests of character for young Americans had been, and continued to be, more problematic for writers who ventured farther into the desert and saw more of it. Certainly Pike, Magoffin, and Manly did not have the luxury of seeing the Southern Plains or the deserts as recreational areas. Irving's experience on the "irreclaimable" high plains illustrates a sort of arid-land appreciation formula: one's ability to see redeeming features in a parched landscape is inversely proportional to the likelihood that one will suffer and die there.[35] Those like Irving who came into such places better prepared to survive than had Manly, Magoffin, or even Pike were able to see more of the practical value in the landscape.

Josiah Gregg, approaching the plains and deserts of New Mexico in the 1830s and early 1840s not as a country in which to hunt and explore but as one in which to carry on trade, articulates more clearly what Irving had in mind when he suggested that the United States send its young men on a formative tour of the prairies. Gregg, like Magoffin, joined a trading expedition traveling on the Santa Fe Trail, in his case in 1831. And like many who would follow his example in the second half of the nineteenth century, Gregg hoped that his health, which had declined as he made his way in the frontier settlements of the late 1820s as a lawyer and teacher, would be improved by a change of climate.[36]

Gregg did improve his health by moving, and in signing on as a pioneering trader in the unsettled lands of the West and recording his experiences in these lands, he found his vocation. Gregg proved to be gifted at articulating his experience of unknown regions in language citizens of the young United States found accessible. *The Commerce of the Prairies* became popular in large measure because Gregg used, if he did not originate, effective metaphors for representing the unfamiliar region.

In what would become a standard Anglo American response to arid landscapes, for instance, Gregg described the Southern Plains and the northern sections of the Chihuahuan Desert as a spectacular challenge to the people who crossed it—mainly a logistical challenge, but also a conceptual one. At times the two elements found expression together, as when Gregg employed the "prairie ocean" image to describe the country and his mode of navigating it. He said that the Southern Plains "may be truly styled the grand 'prairie ocean'; for not a single landmark is to be seen for more than forty miles—scarcely a visible eminence by which to direct one's course. All is as level as the sea, and the compass was our surest, as well as principal guide."[37] The landscape required a conceptual leap—in order to find his way, Gregg had to think of his party as explorers abroad on the featureless ground's nearest analog, the ocean.

Descriptions of himself and his companions engaged in demonstrations of practical skill appear often in *The Commerce of the Prairies*. Gregg constantly halts the progress of his travel narrative in order to include arcane, if interesting, practical details of his traveling. Out on a "'prairie expanse,'" he informs his readers that "[b]eing compelled to keep a reckoning of our latitude, by which our travel was partly governed, and the sun being now too high at noon for the use of the artificial horizon, we had to be guided entirely by observations of the meridian altitude on the moon, planets, or fixed stars. At Gypsum creek our latitude was 36° 10'— being the utmost northing we had made."[38] The quintessential self-made American (a self-taught surveyor and schoolteacher who had built a quadrant out of wood at age eleven and who was endlessly fascinated by the rational structure of the world), Gregg found that his logical, practical approach to the Great American Desert enabled him to thrive on it.

But despite his success in the Santa Fe trade, Gregg echoed Pike in his concern over the possibility of succeeding at more complex human endeavors in the desert. Building a culture there seemed unlikely to him. He was afraid that, due to its isolation from the rest of the country and its lack of navigable water, New Mexico would always remain a barren wilderness because, he said, it

> possesses but few of those natural advantages, which are necessary to anything like rapid progress in civilization. Though bounded north and east by the territory of the United States, south by that of Texas and Chihuahua, and west by Upper California, it is surrounded by chains of mountains and prairie wilds, extending to a distance of 500 miles or more, except in the direction of Chihuahua, from which its settlements are separated by an unpeopled desert of nearly two hundred miles— and without a single means of communication by water with any other part of the world.[39]

Gregg does not mean just commerce when he uses the word *civilization* here; he means culture as well. Gregg laments, "There is no part of the civilized globe, perhaps, where the Arts have been so much neglected, and the progress of Science so successfully impeded as in New Mexico."[40] Further, due to the simple fact of its hostility to civilization, Gregg concluded that the other human endeavors undertaken in this desert—language, medicine, law, architecture, agriculture, manufacturing, and transportation—must always be undertaken on a much less sophisticated level than in more hospitable places.[41]

In addition, experiencing the desert relatively early in the nations's history, Gregg, like Magoffin, found the very appearance of arid landscape daunting. Empty vistas were not attractive to eyes used to trees and rivers. Approaching Santa Fe, Gregg uncharacteristically indulged in an aesthetic judgment while recording a physical description of the landscape over which he experienced "weary travel" for several days: "We . . . emerged into an open plain or *mesa* which was one of the most monotonous I had ever seen, there being not a break, not a hill or valley, nor even a shrub to obstruct the view."[42] This monotonous landscape disturbed Gregg so profoundly that he resorted to fantasy, combining an imaginative with a practical conception of the landscape in order to convince himself and his readers that one day it would be both economically and aesthetically redeemed:

> The high plains seem too dry and lifeless to produce timber; yet might not the vicissitudes of nature operate a change likewise on the seasons? Why may we not suppose that the genial influences of civilization—that extensive cultivation of the earth—might contribute to the multiplication of showers, as it certainly does of fountains? . . . Then may we not hope that these sterile regions might yet be thus revived and fertilized, and their surface covered one day by flourishing settlements to the Rocky Mountains?[43]

The idea that rain follows the plow may have been fanciful, but given the large-scale irrigation that now goes on in the region, Gregg's vision of multiplying "fountains" was remarkably prescient.

In addition to his concern with meeting the practical exigencies of the desert, Gregg also begins the process of its aesthetic redemption in one passage in his book. On the Southern Plains he experienced a sublime moment. After his party's "weary travel" across the monotonous open landscape, Gregg relates that

> the picturesque valley of the Canadian burst once more upon our view, presenting one of the most magnificent sights I had ever beheld. Here rose a perpendicular cliff, in all the majesty and sublimity of its desolation;—there another sprang forward as in the very act of losing its balance and about to precipitate itself upon the vale below. A little further on a pillar with crevices and cornices so curiously formed as eas-

ily to be mistaken for the work of art; while a thousand other objects grotesquely and fantastically arranged, and all shaded in the sky-bound perspective by the blue ridge-like brow of the *mesa* far beyond the Canadian, constituted a kind of chaotic space where nature seemed to have indulged in her wildest caprices. . . . [I]t was altogether impossible to determine whereabouts the channel of the Canadian wound its way among them.[44]

For a brief moment, before turning his attention to the mundane task of finding the river channel in this landscape, Gregg experienced the sublime of Immanuel Kant and Edmund Burke.

Sublime landscapes are, to use Kant's formulation, "contrapurposive for our power of judgment, incommensurate with our power of exhibition, as it were violent to our imagination," sights that threaten to overwhelm the cognitive capabilities of human observers.[45] Given their vastness and their incomprehensibility to humid-land Americans, desert landscapes such as the one Gregg described were and are capable of doing exactly that. But as Kant was careful to indicate, landscapes themselves are not sublime; only human perceptions of a landscape may be sublime. The sublimity Gregg experienced is a function of cognition in which "the mind is induced to abandon sensibility and occupy itself with ideas containing a higher purposiveness,"[46] which is exactly what Gregg contemplated as he took in the scene—the "majesty and sublimity of its desolation," and the "wildest caprices" of nature.

Beyond this traditional sublime, Gregg experienced one of two distinct sublime responses that Anglo Americans typically reported upon coming into the arid West, as described by Barbara Novak. Gregg's was an experience of Novak's "older sublime," which evokes feelings of dread and overwhelming awe, as in Longinus and Kant. Not until after Gregg's time did Anglo Americans began to experience a "newer, more tranquil sublime," which evoked sensations of peace and universal tranquillity, and also of a proprietary national pride in the grandeur of the landscape. Although later explorers like John Wesley Powell and Clarence Dutton would see the country in just such attractive terms, the landscape was still too strange and threatening for Gregg and his contemporaries to experience positive, or even proprietary, feelings for it.[47]

Sublime reactions to the desert—of the older type—are the first aesthetic reactions Anglo Americans reported having. Such reactions do not involve an identification with the landscape or an embrace of it, as perceptions of its beauty would later do. The perception of sublimity necessarily involves a certain distance from the subject, the sort of conceptual aloofness early desert explorers liked to maintain in the face of unfamiliar landscapes. Sublime experiences involve the first entry in Edmund Burke's definitive list of sublime qualities: terror.

A landscape perceived as sublime, Kant wrote, "cannot be contained in any sensible form but concerns only ideas of reason, which, though they cannot be exhibited adequately, are aroused and called to mind by this very inadequacy, which cannot be expressed in sensibility."[48] Landscapes outside the rational, beneficent green world to which easterners were accustomed were then prime subjects of sublime experience. Not until the turn of the twentieth century, when more Americans learned to accept the perceived desolation of arid regions as a part of the rational world, did desert landscapes become widely seen as beautiful and therefore approachable. Still, the experience of the desert's sublimity as reported by Gregg was a first step in coming to terms with arid landscapes. It is his emotional response to the land's appearance that matters.

Sublime experiences go hand in hand with newly encountered landscapes. Elizabeth McKinsey describes such a process occurring in Georgian England. By the mid eighteenth century, Englishmen, in the course of building the British Empire, had begun to come across strange natural phenomena, much like Americans would do during the next century as they built their own empire. Such experiences with unfamiliar nature, for which Addison, Burke, and Kant borrowed the name sublime from Longinus the rhetorician, led to what McKinsey describes as "a new capacity to appreciate the beauty and grandeur of potentially terrifying natural objects—mountains, volcanoes, storms at sea—[which] replaced old attitudes of disdain and fear long before there was language to describe the new feeling adequately."[49]

In the meantime, however, this desert landscape, which often received less than ten inches of rain a year and most of that during periods of high transevaporation, appeared so desolate to many Americans coming to it from the forests of the East that they reacted to it with disgust. To writers such as Horace Greeley, parts of the desert appeared not just lifeless but devoid of any redeeming qualities whatsoever. In 1859, looking at the valley of the Humboldt, Greeley saw a land that made him wish

> only to record [his] opinion that the Humboldt, all things considered, is the meanest river of its length on earth. Rising in the Humboldt Mountains, hardly one-hundred and fifty miles west of Salt Lake, it is at first a pure stream—or rather streams, for there are two main branches—but is soon corrupted by its alkaline surroundings, and its water, for at least the lower half of its course, is about the most detestable I ever tasted. I mainly chose to suffer thirst rather than drink it. . . . It is certainly not a pleasure to ride, night and day, along such a stream, with the heat intense, the dust a constant cloud, and the roads all gullied, and ground into chuckholes; but then, who would stay in such a region one moment longer than he must?[50]

According to Greeley, in this desert,

> famine sits enthroned, and waves his scepter over a dominion expressly made for him. . . . The sagebrush and greasewood, which cover the high, parched plain on either side of the river's bottom, seem thinly set, with broad spaces of naked, shining, glaring, blinding clay between them; the hills beyond, which bound the prospect, seem even more naked. Not a tree, and hardly a shrub, anywhere relieves their sterility. . . . As the only considerable stream in the Great Basin that pursues a general east and west direction, the Humboldt may continue for years to be traveled; but I am sure no one ever left it without a sense of relief and thankfulness.[51]

This was not God's country, Greeley noted, but Famine's.

Nevertheless, although he did not articulate it (not having the words to do so), Greeley's reaction was not all bitter. He felt, as had Gregg, the sublimity of the landscape. A range of desert mountains (probably the Humboldt Range) moved him to compose a detailed and graceful description so carefully put together that it implied a genuine attraction to this place "where mountains rise behind mountains, range behind range, rank above rank, till the summits of the farthest that may be seen are flecked with snow."[52] Greeley had not encountered such scenery before. There was no desert landscape tradition for precedent, because the Hudson

River School painters had generally dictated landscape taste in America, and he had no single word to describe mountains arranged like this.[53] Suspicious of what he could not contain in his language, he dismissively tagged this landform, which had come across in his prose as sublime, "a chaos or jumble of mountains."

But Greeley's grim assessment of the landscape moderates at times. Casting around for a way to articulate the expansive effect this country had on him, he hit on a solution that would serve writers well for the next forty years. He could not appreciate the scenery, but he could see agricultural possibilities in it, so in lieu of discussing Nevada's sublimity, he described its economic potential. In the valley of the Carson, which is arid but susceptible to irrigation, Greeley predicted:

> The time will ultimately come—it may or may not be in our day—when two or three great dams over the Carson will render the irrigation of these broad, arid plains on its banks perfectly feasible; and then this will be one of the most productive regions on earth. . . . And when the best works shall have been constructed, and all the lights of science and experience brought to bear on the subject, it will be found that nearly everything that contributes to human or brute sustenance can be grown actually cheaper by the aid of irrigation than without it.[54]

Greeley expressed the hugeness of the desert landscape as a huge economic potential. His practical impulse seems to have overshadowed his poetical one, and in fact poetical impulses toward desert landscapes were not yet a part of the cultural lexicon.

John Wesley Powell

John Wesley Powell faced a challenge similar to Greeley's when he entered the arid regions to explore the Colorado River and the Grand Canyon in 1869: to describe a landscape for which he at first had no words. While Irving, Gregg, and even Greeley tended to see the desert on only one level, as a thing that raised specific and even interesting practical questions—how to get across it, how to make it fruitful—Powell also thought about the desert in more imaginative terms. His desert writings, even his government reports, lean toward literature.

Often Powell's scientific reports, especially his *Exploration of the Colo-*

rado River of the West, show a higher regard for unity and colorful language—for making the desert an attractive and exciting place—than the government reports that had come before it. Wallace Stegner notes that Powell conflated different voyages down the river in order to make the scientific reports of different places he explored in different years flow into each other more smoothly. Indeed, with its "empurpled descriptions written from a crag above the Gate of Lodore and from the camp at the mouth of the Yampa, . . . the whole first half of the *Exploration* indicates a literary intent."[55]

More interesting than Powell's regard for unified structure is his regard for language. His voice, crying from the desert, was not only the rational, scientific voice of a government surveyor, it was also a voice that performed heroic feats for the American public. Through aesthetic treatments of the desert landscape, through adventure tales describing his exploits there, and finally, later in his career, through his public relations material, Powell set forth a political program of sustainable development for the region.

Describing the beginning of his descent of the Colorado in a letter "he would send out to the *Chicago Tribune* if and when he had the chance,"[56] Powell employed simile and a touch of hyperbole to dramatize himself and his landscape, the Grand Canyon:

> When I came down at noon, the sun shone in splendor on its vermilion walls shaded into green and gray when the rocks are lichened over. The river fills the channel from wall to wall. The cañon opened like a beautiful portal to a region of glory. Now, as I write, the sun is going down, and the shadows are setting in the cañon. The vermilion gleams and the rosy hues, the green and gray tints, are changing to sombre brown above, and black shadows below. Now 'tis a black portal to a region of gloom.
>
> And that is the gateway through we enter [in] our voyage of exploration tomorrow—and what shall we find?[57]

This tone—composed of equal parts of respect for the natural entity he is about to confront, high regard for his ambition to confront it, and attention to language—runs through the *Exploration* from the first. The Grand Canyon itself becomes the Great Unknown, for down it Powell and his men "have an unknown distance yet to run; and unknown river yet to explore." Of his party's position, he melodramatically relates, "What falls there are, we know not; what rocks beset the channel, we know not; what walls rise over the river, we know not. Ah, well! we may conjecture many things."[58] The descent of this river in the desert is a practical exercise in crossing difficult ground.

But it is also a transcendental endeavor. Powell's descriptions of the Canyon reflect a dualism. At one level, the dry, sharply eroded rocks present a nearly insurmountable barrier to human progress across the landscape. When Powell perceives them this way, he describes the ground precisely and rationally because the ground is in fact a problem to be solved. When Powell and his party come to "a bad place," they must scout a way around it. Powell describes such a difficult stretch of river:

> Now there is a bed of basalt on this northern side of the cañon, with a bold escarpment, that seems to be a hundred feet high. We can climb it, and walk along its summit to a point where we are just at the head of the fall. Here the basalt is broken down again, so it seems to us, and I direct the men to take a line to the top of the cliff, and let the boats down along the wall. . . . I climb the cliff, and pass along to a point just over the fall, and descend by broken rocks, and find that the break of the fall is above the break of the wall, so that we cannot land; and that still below the river is very bad, and that there is no possibility of a portage.[59]

This is remarkable landscape, although it is not an attractive one, because the necessity of addressing practical concerns overwhelms any impulse to see figuratively. There is a lot to do in this canyon (the first of which is to get out of its black basalt alive) before the opportunity of creating metaphors about it will arise.

But other days are different. On August 15, 1869, Powell wrote,

> we find smooth water.
>
> Clouds are playing in the cañon to day. Sometimes they roll down in great masses, filling the gorge with gloom; sometimes they hang above, from wall to wall, and cover the cañon with a roof of impending storm; and we can peer long distances up and down this cañon corridor, with its cloud roof overhead, its walls of black granite, and its river bright with the sheen of broken waters. Then, a gust of wind sweeps down a

side gulch, and, making a rift in the clouds, reveals the blue heavens, and a stream of sunlight pours in. Then, the clouds drift away in the distance, and hang around crags, and peaks, and pinnacles, and towers, and walls, and cover them with a mantle, that lifts from time to time, and sets them all in sharp relief. Then, baby clouds creep out of side cañons, glide around points, and creep back again, into more distant gorges. Then, clouds, set in strata, across the cañon, with intervening vista views, to cliffs and rocks beyond. The clouds are children of the heavens, and when they play among the rocks, they lift them to the region above.[60]

Powell enlists the very rocks in this early example of a sublime transport in the desert. The intransigent basalt, which would hinder his progress and his imagination on August 28, has not yet appeared. Here the rock is black granite arranged sublimely in crags, peaks, pinnacles, towers, and walls, all of which, when shrouded in cloudbanks, seem to ascend to heaven.

If this sensibility seems somewhat expansive for a government document, it was. *The Exploration of the Colorado River* was not originally composed as a government report. Powell published early versions of it in *Scribner's* well before he submitted it to the U.S. Geological Survey, and the fantastic element of the narrative that was calculated to excite the readers of high-brow *Scribner's* made the transition from magazine article to report intact. Neither the picture of Powell dangling from the height of a cliff while grasping Lieutenant Bradley's underwear with his one good arm nor the picture of the expedition's camp going up in flames appear in *Exploration,* but similarly enhanced prose does.[61] Powell saw fit to present several circulation-boosting passages of purple prose from his magazine articles to Congress, having only reworked his verb tenses. Compare the passage above from *Exploration* with its original incarnation as copy for *Scribner's*:

> Clouds were playing in the cañon that day. Sometimes they rolled down in great masses, filling the gorge with gloom; sometimes they hung above from wall to wall, covering the cañon with a roof overhead.[62]

Still, for all his enthusiasm and imagination, Powell knew that most Americans were not prepared to call this landscape beautiful. Midway

The frontispiece from John Wesley Powell's *The Exploration of the Colorado* demonstrates Powell's grasp of the emotional, sublime, and even lurid qualities of the landscape he was exploring and documenting.

through his series of *Scribner's* articles he bluntly initiated an object lesson in the appreciation of desert canyons. "Let us understand these cañons," he invites the reader, and then for approximately the next thirty-six column inches interrupts his chronological narrative with a narrative structured by landscape, describing Gray Cañon, the Orange Cliffs, Labyrinth Cañon, the Book Cliffs, and so on, stopping briefly to warn that, despite his own love for it, "the desert has no bird of sweet song, and no beast of noble mien." Part of his lesson seems aimed directly at those who would refer to a desert range as Horace Greeley had sixteen years before, as a "chaos or jumble of mountains."[63]

Powell takes pains to give his readers their best chance to appreciate this landscape. His descriptions are consistently careful and detailed, and he does not hide the fact that the region is barren of life, even of soil: "The landscape everywhere away from the river is of rock, a pavement of rock with cliffs of rock, tables of rock, plateaus of rock, terraces of rock, crags of rock, buttes of rock, ten thousand strangely carved forms; rocks everywhere, and no vegetation, no soil, no sand."[64] The landscape, harsh as it is, calls for a special sensibility, the sensibility Horace Greeley lacked as he struggled to understand Nevada. Greeley, looking at the Humboldt Range but not seeing its beauty, could indeed have been among the intended audience for Powell's piece, for Powell admonished those who would come to the desert looking for more of what was back east:

> When speaking of [these rocks], we must not conceive of piles of bowlders or heaps of fragments, but a whole landscape of naked rock with giant forms carved on it, cathedral-shaped buttes towering hundreds or thousands of feet, cliffs that cannot be scaled, and cañon walls that make the river shrink into insignificance, with vast hollow domes and tall pinnacles, and shafts set on the verge overhead, and all the rocks, tinted with buff, gray, red, brown, and chocolate, never lichened, never moss-covered, but bare, and sometimes even polished.[65]

Powell realized that there was little chance that this landscape would appeal to his readers as it had to him. The didactic tone of the passage, along with Powell's resort to an unwieldy rhetoric of cumulative description in an attempt simply to capture the grandeur of the canyon in a catalog, further indicate Powell's suspicion that even should his audience—Americans of the humid East—actually see the Grand Canyon, they would

FIRE IN CAMP.

These lurid images from John Wesley Powell's series of articles entitled "Cañons of the Colorado" demonstrate that the desert titillated adventurers as much as it intrigued scientists. (*Scribner's* 39 [1875]: 304–5)

most likely see incidental piles of erosional detritus instead of a sublime landscape. Powell works carefully, even poetically here, employing detailed descriptions and urgent rhythms, all the while sounding something like a lecturer on landscape appreciation as he attempts to make a place for the desert in the collective imagination of the United States.

It is in passages like these, despite the somewhat awkward presentation, that Powell gets at what Gregg in 1844 had not: the arid regions' facility for evoking the newer, more positively inflected American sublime that Novak has described. Powell's is one of those projections of an aesthetic view onto nature, Novak argues, that "augmented the American's

THE RESCUE.

sense of his own unique nature, his unique opportunity, and could indeed foster a sense of destiny."[66] From Powell's perspective the large, dramatically weathered features of the Southwest are imposing, sublime, and therefore impressive occasions for patriotic pride. They are no longer terrifying, as they had been in the eyes of travelers like Gregg.

But another John Wesley Powell existed apart from the enthusiastic advocate of the beauty of desert regions. In addition to the *Scribner's* articles, Powell wrote a much more scientifically rigorous series of articles for *Popular Science Monthly* which later became the second part of the *Exploration*. It was this sober, rational, scientific Powell who spoke in the *Report on the Arid Regions* and who headed the United States Geological and Geographic Survey of the Rocky Mountain Region. This is not the Powell who hung off a cliff by his assistant's underwear. He is distinctly not the poetic, literary Powell, not the adventurer. He is the Powell capable of seeing rocks in the channel of the Colorado merely as an obstruction to navigation. In this rational, scientific incarnation, Powell formulated the general approach (though, unfortunately for the ecosystem, not the actual method) by which Americans could make their homes on arid lands through the rest of the nineteenth century.

The manner in which Powell negotiated between these two poles of the aesthetic and the practical is suggested in his approach to the development in the region of the disciplines of landscape photography and painting, and in the roles he expected them to play in his explorations. According to Elizabeth C. Childs, Powell's use of images in publicizing his work in the Grand Canyon "charts the brief significant intersection of elite science and the fine arts in American culture after the Civil War."[67] On the one hand, "[e]xploration called for both the empiricist, who longed to complete the map of the land, and the theorist, who strove to explain land forms the new maps recorded," while on the other hand, "the rationale for doing photography at the Grand Canyon was in part commercial, and the interests and tastes of the eastern viewer-consumer helped shape the photographic enterprise."[68]

In 1872, Powell revised his approach to this audience by hiring Thomas Moran to accompany him on the 1873 expedition because Moran's painting "offered public celebration, commemoration, poetic commentary, and the aura of uniqueness in a way that survey photography could not."[69] With his funding at stake, Powell certainly needed these attributes. Thus, while Powell intended to solve scientific questions regarding geological processes at work through time by using images such as Jack Hillers's *Side Cañon,* he also intended to "sell" the Grand Canyon to the eastern public on several levels through such images as Moran's *The Chasm of the Colorado.*

The same sensitivity to the landscape that enabled Powell to capture the arid regions aesthetically also helped him to devise a way to appropriate them practically. He was enthusiastic about developing every square inch of land on the continent, and he even went so far as to call water left in riverbeds when irrigation facilities proved inadequate to remove it "surplus waters."[70] Still, the fact did not elude him that many portions of the West were very different from, and much more fragile than, the humid East to which he and other Anglo Americans were accustomed. His experience in the arid regions led him to question and ultimately to revise traditional American ideas about land use. In the mid 1870s, Powell foresaw that the federal government's homestead policy of granting individuals free land in 160-acre parcels would be unworkable in the arid West and that, in fact, for grazing land, "the farm unit should not be less than 2,560 acres."[71]

The special case of the desert landscape inspired Powell to implement fundamental changes in the way topographical maps were made. He came back from his survey of the arid regions with maps that were, according to Joel Makower, "geologic landmarks, concentrating for the first time on mineral and soil development as well as studying the catalysts for the chosen path of a river or formation of a mountain."[72] Powell, in his most impressive case of flying in the face of tradition, suggested that the water-monopoly capitalists of the frontier be put out of business by federal legislation insuring that "[t]he right to the water necessary to the redemption of an irrigation tract of a pasturage farm shall inhere in the land."[73] As do his more literary endeavors in the *Exploration of the Colorado River,* Powell's practical work in the desert shows an unprecedented ability to look at this landscape and grasp the implications of its aridity. His *Report on the Lands of the Arid Regions* is a landmark among the attempts of Anglo Americans to come to terms with the desert. Wallace Stegner called it "a sober and foresighted warning about the consequences of trying to impose on a dry country the habits that have been formed in a wet one."[74] Powell brought the desert into a conceptual space that was

Jack Hillers's Grand Canyon photographs for the 1873 Powell expedition, like *Side Cañon* shown here, provided an objective record of Powell's survey but also explored the aesthetic aspects of arid-land geology. (Courtesy of the Arizona Historical Society/Tucson; no. 73,084)

accessible to most Americans. He realized that Americans were unlikely to be capable of seeing their parched deserts as beautiful, but he also realized that they might be amenable to viewing the desert as a challenging place into which they could expand their civilization.

Powell, in his principal incarnation as government surveyor, approached the desert as a huge problem to be solved by the growing country, and he used every genre at his disposal, whether objective or figurative, in his effort to solve this problem. To his credit, sensitive to the desert environment as he was, he formulated a solution to the problem of aridity in the West that Americans look back on even now with admiration mixed with regret—admiration for its intelligence, and regret over the fact that it was and still is so widely ignored by the developing nation. Wallace Stegner called Powell's *Report on the Arid Regions* "one of the most important books ever written about the West."[75] Powell was one of the few Anglo Americans in whose mind the two distinct impulses toward the desert—the impulse to appreciate it and the impulse to develop it—complemented one another.

Clarence Dutton

Through the 1870s and 1880s, Captain Clarence Dutton would pursue Powell's projects, both the practical endeavor of surveying the arid West and the conceptual endeavor of developing an arid-land aesthetic. There is a continuity between the works of the two men. Captain Dutton worked under Powell—indeed, Stegner characterized him as "Powell's left hand," the man upon whom Powell looked as his "geological heir." Dutton was also Powell's literary heir: as a recipient of the Yale Literary Prize as an undergraduate and a popular lecturer in Washington, Dutton was skilled with language.[76] Like Powell's own work, Clarence Dutton's texts express two impulses: an inclination to see the desert as beautiful and a need to find it to be useful. But while Powell ultimately focused his interest on the practical challenge presented by isolation and aridity, Dutton gravitated toward the aesthetic approach to desert land. In literate and often literary prose, Dutton heightened the imaginative element of Powell's desert writing to "a refined and sometimes fevered pitch,"[77] drifting "constantly away from the meticulous and toward the suggestive."[78] Like Powell, Dutton consciously sought to teach his peers a way to appreciate

Perhaps even more than the Grand Canyon itself (which is a vast and changing complex of images), Thomas Moran's archetypal painting *The Chasm of the Colorado* has shaped the popular perception of western desert landforms. (Courtesy of the National Museum of American Art, Smithsonian Institution, lent by the Department of the Interior, Office of the Secretary)

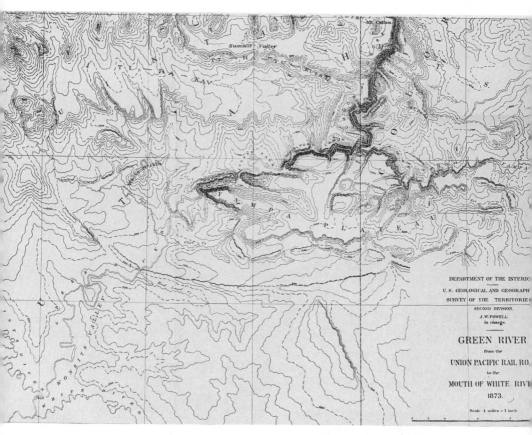

As seen in this detail from Powell's topographic map of Utah's Green River from *The Exploration of the Colorado,* Powell's maps work on both an aesthetic and a practical level because of the elegance with which they describe the arid landscapes he was exploring.

this unfamiliar landscape, but Dutton's concerns surfaced more often on an aesthetic than a practical level. Admittedly, Dutton's *Tertiary History* includes illustrations that reduce the Grand Canyon's fantastic formations to schematic erosion diagrams, but on the whole Dutton is much more likely to address Kantian sublimities than irrigation techniques or property rights. He is much more likely to rhapsodize.

The *Tertiary History,* printed by the Government Printing Office, is written in a visionary style. Transcendent moments often arise in it, as when Dutton describes the prospect from, fittingly enough, Point Sublime:

The space under immediate view from our standpoint, 50 miles long and 10 to 12 wide, is thronged with a great multitude of objects so vast in size, so bold yet majestic in form, so infinite in their details, that as the truth gradually reveals itself to the perceptions it arouses the strongest emotions. . . . As the mind strives to realize its proportions its spirit is broken and imagination is completely crushed.[79]

This is unequivocally the sublime of Kant, a sublime born not only of wonder but also of exhilaration and fear, a feeling that arises from the inability of the viewer's consciousness fully to comprehend what it confronts.

The sort of associations that the Grand Canyon provokes in Dutton resonate as well with other landscapes familiar to Anglo American culture. In keeping with the infernal attributes Anglo Americans had traditionally seen in desert landscapes, Dutton in his most creative moments saw in the Canyon a Miltonic struggle between sunlight and storm clouds. His clouds do not play, as Powell's had; they clash with the light from above. Dutton's passage not only illustrates the sort of dread that always lay beneath the surface of his impressions of the desert, it also indicates the sort of aesthetic disequilibrium into which the unaccustomed grandeur of the landscape threw its first Anglo explorers:

Late in the autumn of 1880 I rode along the base of the Vermilion Cliffs from Kanab to the Virgen, having the esteemed companionship of Mr. Holmes. We had spent the summer and most of the autumn among the cones of the Uinkaret, in the dreamy parks and forests of the Kaibab, and in the solitudes of intervening desert; and our sensibilities had been somewhat overtaxed by the scenery of the Grand Cañon. It seemed to us that all grandeur and beauty thereafter beheld must be mentally projected against the recollection of those scenes, and be dwarfed into commonplace by the comparison; but as we moved onward the walls increased in altitude, in animation, and in power. . . .

The next day was rarer still, with sunshine and storm battling for the mastery. Rolling masses of cumuli rose up into the blue to incomprehensible heights, their flanks and summits gleaming with sunlight, their nether surfaces above the desert flat as a ceiling, and showing, not the dull neutral gray of the east, but a rosy tinge caught from the reflected red of rocks and soil. As they drifted rapidly against the great barrier, the currents from below flung upward to the summits, rolled the vaporous masses into vast whorls, wrapping them around the towers and crest-lines, and scattering torn shreds of mist along the rock-faces. As the day wore on the sunshine gained the advantage. From overhead the cloud masses stubbornly withdrew, leaving a few broken ranks to maintain a feeble resistance. But far in the northwest, over the Colob, they rallied their black forces for a more desperate struggle, and answered with defiant flashes of lightning the incessant pour of sun-shafts.[80]

Dutton echoes the imagery Satan uses to describe his defeat by God in *Paradise Lost*, the

sulphurous hail
Shot after us in storm, o'erblown hath laid
The fiery surge, that from the precipice
Of heav'n received us falling, and the thunder,
Winged with red lightning and impetuous rage[81]

This is the scene that marks the end of Satan's initial rebellion against God, and it is one of our culture's archetypal images of struggle against the light, which ended in Satan's banishment, not coincidentally, to the desert: "yon dreary plain, forlorn and wild, / The seat of desolation," from which Satan continues his infernal plotting.[82] Such an association would not have been lost on Dutton, who had studied for the ministry at Yale before the Civil War altered his plans.

But the dread inspired in Dutton's language by the Canyon's weather is not derived solely from a culture-wide fear of violent storms and desert places. Dutton is out in the open, exposed to lightning, and he is at the bottom of a canyon that will fill with water should a substantial amount of rain fall. Although the spectacle of the storm thrills him for aesthetic reasons, it also excites him for very practical ones.

Dutton's response to the desert was one of the first in English to blur the distinction between the factual survey, which was the accustomed mode of writing about the desert through the 1870s and 1880s, and aesthetic treatments of the desert, which were to come at the turn of the twentieth century. He took note of the desert air, as did hundreds of later Americans who wrote about the desert, and he was forced to resort to metaphor in order to articulate what he saw: "The very air is then visible," he writes. "We see it, palpably, as a tenuous fluid, and the rocks behind it do not appear to be colored blue as they do in other regions, but reveal themselves clothed in colors of their own."[83]

Here, buried in Dutton's government report published in 1882, lies the sublime American desert of Mary Austin, Alfred Stieglitz, and Georgia O'Keeffe. And buried it was destined to remain until more Americans learned to see it. Despite his breathless expression of admiration for Point Sublime, Dutton did not expect other people to comprehend it readily, because scenery such as the parched Grand Canyon

> is not to be comprehended in a day or a week, not even in a month. It must be dwelt upon and studied, and the study must comprise the slow acquisition of the meaning and spirit of that marvelous scenery. . . . The study and slow mastery of the influences of that class of scenery and its full appreciation is a special culture, requiring time, patience, and long familiarity for its consummation. The lover of nature, whose perceptions have been trained in the Alps, in Italy, Germany, or New England, in the Appalachians or Cordilleras, in Scotland or Colorado, would enter this strange region with a shock, and dwell there for a time with a sense of oppression, and perhaps with horror.[84]

Dutton arrived at a conclusion that would be central to the effort to show Anglo Americans what their deserts looked like: that perceptions are a matter of training and thus that one's perceptions could in fact be trained to accommodate new and unfamiliar material.

Dutton's audience did not have a visual literacy capable of comprehending the desert as beautiful. Anglo America needed to be persuaded, as Dutton and Powell had been, that the landscape would bear close examination. Continuing the endeavor these two men had begun, writers and artists of considerable influence set out during the *fin-de-siècle* decade to persuade Americans exactly that.

Chapter **3**

These transcript from nature fellows who are so clever cannot compare with the imaginative men. —Frederic Remington[1]

Imaginative Men

Photographers such as Jack Hillers, who accompanied John Wesley Powell down the Colorado, and Timothy O'Sullivan, who accompanied Clarence King's surveying expeditions, were in many ways what Frederic Remington called "imaginative men," but they would have met with his disdain as "transcript from nature fellows" because their art tied them fairly closely to the objective observation of natural phenomena.[2] Just as Hillers's photographs were intended to provide evidence for Powell's version of geological history, O'Sullivan's were intended to codify in images other narratives about the Southwest. O'Sullivan traveled with Clarence King, whose expedition was meant to answer such questions as, Is it true there are diamond fields? And what about the great coal deposits? Is the land so fertile you can thrust down a cane and it will sprout leaves and branches? Can it take to the plow? Can it be sold, cultivated?[3] It was King's appointment as chief of the United States Geological Exploration of the Fortieth Parallel "in an attempt to answer the much-asked question of what sort of land was out there in the deep West" that brought O'Sullivan and his camera to the region.[4] When O'Sullivan first visited it, the landscape was widely regarded as "a wonderland made up of half-truths, myths, and legends, a land that rumbled and fired great geysers of hot water high into the air, of vast coal fields that had been burning since time began, of weird tribes that lived in apartments carved into the sides of sheer cliffs. And added were the usual tales of diamond mines, mountains of gold, and Coronado's legend of the Gilded Man."[5] Under King's direction, O'Sullivan's documentary photography debunked much of the fantastic rhetoric surrounding the region.[6] Nevertheless, his photographs retain something of an "imaginative bias," according to Naef and Wood, because O'Sullivan "was directed by both King and the geologist S. F. Emmons to make photographs that provided evidence for King's theory of 'catastrophism,' and Emmons's more sober principle of 'mechanical geology,' an outgrowth of King's thinking. Catastrophism had deep socioreligious implications, indeed was overtly anti-Darwinian in all its premises."[7] Still, apart from any subtle cultural biases they may betray, "it was [O'Sullivan's] pictures, obtained after great hardships and physical risks that helped to change the deep West from wonderland to reality."[8]

But Frederic Remington and his peers wanted the wonderland back. In the 1890s, fiction writers, painters, and poets—Remington's "imaginative men" (who were often women)—began in earnest to direct their creative energy to inventing new ways of conceiving of North American deserts, although the landscape itself was seldom the primary concern. To artists such as Remington, the desert was usually nothing more than an accidental part of a greater American fiction, the fiction of the Wild West.

Because Arizona, New Mexico, and parts of southern California and southern Colorado had resisted Anglo American civilization longer than most other parts of the country, they lent themselves to what Victorian America thrilled to think of as the semibarbaric enterprise of cattle ranching—semibarbaric by the standards of people like Frederic Remington, who were nonetheless fascinated by such romantic undertakings. Thus cowboys rode the West, and in Frederic Remington's work they rode the desert. Remington may or may not have consciously worked out this aspect of desert history for himself, but he recognized a potential Anglo American hero when he saw one, and he saw hundreds in Arizona. Thus Remington, along with Mark Twain before him and Owen Wister after him, represented the desert only as a backdrop for human activity, a stage upon which white explorers, cowboys, horse soldiers, and Indians

Timothy O'Sullivan's photograph *Rhyolite Columns* is an objective representation of a rock formation, but it also offers support for the theory of geological cata-strophism, to which his superior, Clarence King, subscribed. (Courtesy of the Na-tional Archives)

performed. In effect, Twain, Remington, and others helped to import the desert into the American consciousness through the back door. Americans learned to recognize it as the place they had seen in books and pictures behind soldiers and cowboys.

By the early 1890s, when large numbers of Americans from the East had gained access to desert land by train, it was, in a way, a familiar land-scape even to those who had never seen it, simply because people had seen so many Arizona cowboys in so many deserts in so many *Harper's Monthly* and *Harper's Weekly* stories and illustrations. The desert, in its incarnation as rangeland replete with cowboys and Indians, was a cross-cultural phenomenon. Its place in the Anglo American consciousness was negotiated at many levels in the work of anonymous dime novelists and some of the most acclaimed artists of the close of the nineteenth century.

Mark Twain

Mark Twain was one of the earliest Anglo American writers to concentrate on the desert. He began imagining the arid regions of Nevada and California in *Roughing It* (1872), employing a more complicated and human-centered perspective than any of the desert writers who had come before him. In *Roughing It*, the American desert played the role, as Patricia Nelson Limerick puts it, of a "geographical celebrity, and just being near it was an achievement."[9] The desert appeared as an important, if not a central, character in Twain's narrative, providing exciting circumstances and a colorful setting in which Twain's people pursued their tall-tale existences.

The innovation Twain brought to the desert was humor. He recounted his experiences—traveling across the very Humboldt Valley, in fact, that had so disgusted Horace Greeley—in a comic voice. Twain's voice is a literary manifestation of a kind of luxury. Traveling through the Great Basin Desert of Utah and Nevada in a stagecoach, he was in a position to create a more calmly considered and more thoroughly artificed version of the desert than anyone before him. His circumstances were different from those of earlier travelers. Unlike Pike, Powell, Magoffin, Manly, and most others who had written firsthand about the desert before him, Twain was never in any danger of succumbing to thirst, heat, or starvation. His perspective is a function of the desert appreciation formula evident in Washington Irving's work: the ability to enjoy the desert's redeeming features is inversely proportional to the hazards it presents.

In his stagecoach, Twain's character is free to direct his attention to more imaginative pursuits than scratching subsistence rations out of the land. He turns his eyes to the local color, which happens to be the color of the desert. At the beginning of the trek into the wilderness, the narrator, an "innocent" Mark Twain setting out across a romantic new western landscape, sets out to tell a humorous story. But this story is a carefully constructed narrative, the sort of thing Twain took great pains over, for, as he would later theorize, "there are several kinds of stories, but only one difficult kind—the humorous. . . . The humorous story depends on the *manner* of telling; the comic story and the witty story upon the matter."[10] By this definition, *Roughing It* is a humorous story and by virtue of its desert setting, an American one as well.

Roughing It is one of the first truly literary treatments of the desert in English, a carefully made comic narrative told in the voice of an innocent abroad in a western wonderland of his own imagining, a wonderland in which the romantic possibilities of the desert figure prominently. As it begins, and before he realizes that he will be invited along on the trip, Twain claims to be jealous of the odyssey his brother plans in the arid wilderness. He covets

> especially the long, strange journey [his brother] was going to make, and the curious new world he was going to explore. . . . Pretty soon he would be hundreds and hundreds of miles away on the great plains and deserts, and among the mountains of the Far West, and would see buffaloes and Indians, and prairie dogs, and antelopes, and have all kinds of adventures, and maybe get hanged or scalped, and have ever such a fine time, and write home and tell us all about it, and be a hero.[11]

The desert is a necessary part of Twain's narrative because it supplies a romantic space into which he can send his innocent abroad. It provides the point from which Twain's humor usually begins, a Romance in need of his realism. Thus the landscape, because of the unrealistic expectations it evokes in the naive narrator, provides the subject matter for the series of anecdotes that make up *Roughing It*. And since this is an American humor story in which, in Twain's formulation, "matter" is secondary to "manner," the desert itself is less important than the character who describes it.

Still, it is important to note that, although the landscape is often overshadowed by the personality of the narrator, it never quite disappears—at least not until the narrator embarks for Hawaii. The desert is more than a cipher in Twain's humorous formula, although critics as astute as Constance Rourke have failed to see the role landscape plays in Twain's humor. His humor, she posits, arises solely out of

> the variegated lot of migrants who could be seen anywhere in that period [of Twain's youth] moving along the river or toward the plains.
> In the compact encirclement of California with its renewal of pioneer life these elements flooded to the surface.[12]

As Rourke would have it, the important aspect of this landscape is its relative emptiness, which prompts a "renewal of pioneer life." Certainly the landscape is empty of humans, but there have always been significant entities other than humans abroad in the desert.

The Great Basin Desert itself, its dirt and dust, exerts an immediate physical influence on the narrator's body. Its alkaline salts attack his sinuses and throat, causing him to experience reactions to the desert landscape remarkably similar to the reactions experienced by Zebulon Pike, Susan Shelby Magoffin, Lewis Manly, and most of the other Anglo travelers who came before him. Often Twain hates the desert. Traveling across it, even inside a coach, was monotonous,

> And it was hot! and so close! and our water canteens went dry in the middle of the day and we got so thirsty! It was so stupid and tiresome and dull! . . . The alkali dust cut through our lips, it persecuted our eyes, it ate through the delicate membranes and made our noses bleed and *kept* them bleeding—and truly and seriously the romance all faded far away and disappeared, and left the desert trip nothing but a harsh reality—a thirsty, sweltering, longing, hateful reality![13]

But here Twain, his narrator safe if uncomfortable in a stagecoach, is turning pain into humor—taking the physical extremities into which the desert has thrust him as an occasion to speak in the humorous voice of the innocent who, ironically, at the outset of the journey had contemplated the romance of the desert. Now the romance is shattered, and in its place is the tone of the disappointed child, amusingly inappropriate in any Wild West.

Twain's anti-Romance set in the desert marks the beginning of a process by which many Anglo Americans inadvertently became aware of the arid regions of the West. Unlike Powell and Dutton, who endeavored to accustom their audiences to the desert landscape by presenting it directly and in sublime and even transcendent terms, Twain avoided pushing the landscape into the foreground. He was not, nor would his audience have been, interested in the region in and of itself. Instead, Twain puts people in motion across the desert, over which American commerce, in the form of stagecoaches and mining companies, had begun to exert control. Twain, like a second- or third-generation immigrant who can now rely on a new language in a new land well enough to deploy literary devices, presents the actions of desert dwellers in an entertaining narrative, using the landscape as the location for this classic local-color story. The harsh landscape thus behaves like a stage set: it is ever before the eye of the reader, but it is never the most important thing. There are always people engaged in roughing it on this desert, so although its soil can actually rise up and cause month-long nosebleeds, Twain supplies a painless way of dealing with those nosebleeds—a humorous anti-Romantic narrative that draws attention away from the fact that the un-artificed desert is a painful place.

Frederic Remington

Frederic Remington was neither the first nor, by most accounts, the most innovative visual chronicler of the desert West. Albert Bierstadt, Titian Peale, and Karl Bodmer, to name only a few artists, had painted it before him. Thomas Moran had accompanied Powell to the Grand Canyon in 1873 and from his experiences on that expedition generated hundreds of sketches and paintings, among them *The Chasm of the Colorado*, a seven-foot-high painting for which Congress had paid $10,000, and which hung in the Capitol. The paintings and sketches of such artists, Joni Kinsey has argued, enabled them to overcome the difficulties of presenting the land in a language that was not yet suited to the task. Still, because the nation's visual experience with arid landscapes was so limited, the work of early Anglo landscape painters in the West and Southwest tends to remain highly metaphorical and associative, representing, in Kinsey's words, "a visual synthesis of its time, reflecting contemporary events, scientific and technical developments, and an awareness of aesthetic ideals that had developed significantly since the 1850s."[14] Paintings like Moran's were composite views, amalgams not only of several different landscapes (the particular view of the Grand Canyon Moran represents in his *Chasm* does not exist anywhere but on his canvas) but also of personal associations and national preoccupations. As Kinsey has shown, the canvases of these painters tend to be complex iconographic compositions in which the landscape takes on shapes that already exist in the imaginations of the culture that conceives it.[15]

Thus, such artists worked within certain culturally defined boundaries. The most important one was that they tended to paint massive, sublime landscapes such as the Grand Canyon, which had precedents reaching back to Longinus, but were unable to make much of the bulk of the arid Southwest, which was much less dramatic. Frederic Remington, however, like Twain before him, made something of an end run around the "bleakness" of the deserts.

Remington saw the desert as a stage across which humans moved. He portrayed arid spaces not as places to be approached with a sense of humor, as Twain had done, nor, overtly at least, as the potential basis for an empire, but as places to be approached with a sense of heroism. By the mid-1890s, when Remington was publishing several stories and hundreds of illustrations in American magazines each year, there was nothing funny about the direction United States citizens had taken in the southwestern deserts. Remington's art showed serious work being undertaken there.[16]

In 1890 the superintendent of the census had declared that the concept of the frontier was no longer useful in describing the shape of the country,[17] a fact Frederick Jackson Turner noted in his 1893 essay "The Significance of the Frontier in American History." His often-quoted and often-disputed frontier thesis, which among other things held that "the existence of an area of free land, its continuous recession, and the advance of American settlement westward, explain American development,"[18] was profoundly influential throughout the decade in which he formulated it and for long afterward.[19] The ramifications of his thesis were also profoundly disturbing to the United States of the turn of the century. As Turner refined his thesis through the 1890s and into the twentieth century, the cost of running out of free land in the continental United States became apparent, for he posited that "American social development has been continually beginning over again on the frontier. This perennial rebirth, this fluidity of American life, this expansion westward with its new opportunities, its continuous touch with the simplicity of primitive society, furnish the forces dominating American character."[20] American development and American social development, both dependent as they were in Turner's formula upon unsettled territory, seemed likely to end soon after 1890.

For the generation of Americans facing this threat, Remington supplied a vital contemporary chronicle of one of the nation's few remaining pockets of wilderness. He saw a relatively wild Arizona when he traveled there as a young man in 1885 and 1886, and he remembered it long after he had settled down in the suburbs of New York City in middle age. Years later, after even the most intransigent deserts had begun to succumb—

after, for instance, the Santa Fe Railway had completed its spur to the rim of the Grand Canyon in 1901, effectively connecting it to Philadelphia, New York, and Boston—Remington continued to indulge his and his audience's nostalgia for the wilderness and the American character that the wilderness had produced.

Remington worked both personally and publicly to overcome the widespread pessimism about the direction that American character might take once "lighting out for the territories" became impossible. The project of "civilizing" the continent had, until it neared completion, provided leaders such as Theodore Roosevelt perfect opportunities to formulate, retrospectively, "the strenuous life," "the life of toil and effort, of labor and strife" and to apotheosize "the man who does not shrink from danger, from hardship, or from bitter toil, and who out of these wins the splendid ultimate triumph."[21] Unfortunately, the splendid ultimate triumph of having spread civilization from coast to coast, as the superintendent of the census implied Anglo Americans had done, had also involved exorcising danger, hardship, and bitter toil from the face of the continent. Civilization necessarily displaces toil, at least for the class of people to which Remington and Roosevelt belonged.

Remington was by no means alone in his anxiety. T. J. Jackson Lears notes that such fears pervaded Western civilization, for at the close of the nineteenth century "Europeans and Americans alike began to recognize that the triumph of modern culture had . . . promoted a spreading sense of moral impotence and spiritual sterility—a feeling that life had become not only overcivilized but also curiously unreal."[22] But there were imperialistic possibilities left in the world. For Americans, their West, along with some small colonial countries, such as the Philippines, still held the promise of a regenerative challenge. Roosevelt and his anxious peers were left looking at Remington's version of the Arizona desert, and at Cuba and the Philippines, for their self-definition.

For Remington in the late 1880s, the American ranch foreman in the barrens of northern Chihuahua was the type of man who appeared to be immune to the deleterious effects of civilization. Remington adored this sort of cowboy even if the cowboy was largely imaginary. He proudly recalled that "[i]n any association with these men of the frontier I have come to greatly respect their moral fibre and their character. Modern civilization, in the process of educating men beyond their capacity, often vulgarizes them."[23] So Remington painted upright cowboys who held out for as long as they could against what he considered to be the vulgarizing influences of modern civilization.

Although Remington recognized the worth of cowboys as cultural archetypes, he was not so naive as to think he could simply begin drawing them and convince his audience they were heroic figures. The cowboy, due to his dime-novel reputation, needed rehabilitation before he could be the subject matter for art. Remington recognized the problem inherent in his chosen subject: "When I began to depict the men of the plains, white and red, this Western business was new to art and we had the dread background of the dime novel to live down."[24]

As Remington tells it, he had set himself the task of both rehabilitating and preserving this American type from the time he first encountered it in 1885. In a 1905 reminiscence he attributed to himself a remarkably prescient desire to capture these men, and the open spaces that bred them, for posterity. Engaging to an extent in revisionary autobiography, he implies that it was this desire, not his contract with *Harper's Weekly*, that led him west to begin with: "I knew the railroad was coming—I saw men already swarming into the land. I knew the derby hat, the smoking chimneys, the cord-binder, and the thirty-day note were upon us in a resistless surge. I knew the wild riders and the vacant land were about to vanish forever, and the more I considered the subject the bigger the Forever loomed."[25] Remington's assessment of the Forever is a bleak one: "I saw the living, breathing end of three American centuries of smoke and dust and sweat, and I now see quite another thing where it all took place, but it does not appeal to me."[26]

As a hedge against such a dismal eternity, Remington drew, sculpted, and wrote about cowboys, soldiers, and occasionally Indians. In the eyes of his contemporaries, he did it better than anyone else. Theodore Roosevelt thought Remington the best artist in the nation. In a letter, he assured Remington that "It seems to me that you in your line, and Wister in his, are doing the best work in America today."[27] Roosevelt not only appreciated Remington's art, he also thought that Remington's prose constituted the very best treatment of the American West he had read. To Remington he wrote, "the very best will live and will make the cantos in the last Epic of the Western Wilderness before it ceased being a wilderness. Now, I think you are writing this 'very best.'"[28] By 1901, Remington had imposed the Arizona he had first visited in 1885 and had been re-creating in his art ever since upon the imagination of the most influential Americans.

But it is crucial to see that for Remington, as for Twain and Frederick Jackson Turner, the actual land, the desert itself, was little more than a stage upon which people moved. The arid stage was important, but it was important primarily as a wide-open backdrop for human undertakings. The deserts were incidental to cowboys and Indians and wildlife.

Remington himself did not initially like the land any better than had Greeley or Magoffin. He loved cowboys and cavalrymen, but he hated the desert. In fact, he dropped his first southwestern assignment for *Harper's Weekly*—recording the U.S. Army's pursuit of Geronimo—because he could not face the prospect of traveling through Arizona and Sonora. Some of his early responses to the desert appear in his journal for 1886:

> Let anyone who wonders why the troops do not catch Geronomo but travel through a part of Arizona and Sonora then he will wonder that they even try. Let him see the desert wastes of sand devoid of even grass, bristling with cactus, let the burning sirrocco fan a fever on his cheek, let the sun pour down white hot upon the blistering sand about his feet and it will be a plainer proposition. . . . In all the world there is no such cheerless place.[29]

Unlike Greeley and Magoffin, however, Remington was ultimately able to separate his reaction to the practical realities of the desert from his aesthetic response to it. Despite his inability and unwillingness physically to engage himself with the country by traveling through it with the soldiers, Remington did engage the landscape imaginatively. On a second trip to Arizona, in 1888, Remington kept a journal in which he not only narrated his activities but also recorded color notations. "In Arizona," he writes, "nature allures with her gorgeous color and then repells with the cruelty of her formation—waterless, barren, and desolate." Remington here is a living example of the person to whom Dutton had directed his Point Sublime description in 1882. In the desert, Dutton warned, "whatsoever might be bold and striking would at first seem only grotesque" and would become attractive only after dedicated observation. Remington proved to be just this sort of seer.[30]

Between his first publication in *Harper's Weekly* in 1882 and his death in 1909, Remington developed a perspective from which the desert looked beautiful. From his unique angle, which inevitably featured chaparral and colorful dust swirling around horses' hooves and stark mountains looming over the shoulders of cowboys, he also introduced his audience to the desert. Another entry in his 1886 journal suggests his angle of vision. One morning Remington "was awake early and saw the sun rise and day break—yellow, green, blue . . . lots of high color near the Earth—the soldiers stand about the camp fires and watch the breakfast cooking with a longing eye."[31] The desert itself, with its characteristic "high color" at sunrise, remains a tantalizing but unrealized aesthetic possibility, while soldiers with eyes longing for their breakfast take the central position in what becomes a narrative rather than a descriptive passage. The desert appears and it is colorful, but it is hidden behind a story about humans.

This journal entry made the transition to canvas virtually intact in Remington's *Cavalryman's Breakfast on the Plains* (c. 1890). The composition of the picture confronts the viewer with one of the desert's striking features: its breathtakingly swift recession of horizon. Remington forces the viewer to confront the vastness of visible space in the scene, a vertiginous sensation in a landscape with such clear air as the desert. The middle distance of the painting consists of a Wild West–sized herd of cavalry horses, hundreds of them. Over the heads of the nearest horses, a low mountain range is visible, but as the herd extends back toward the horizon, becoming less and less distinct, the horses' heads press directly into the eerily inflected lavender, blue, and yellow morning sky, making it palpably present in the scene, as if in the desert the sky reaches down around one's ears.

The open space in front of the herd, the bare ground, presents another desert effect: desolation. The space supports no life and consists only of stones, dead wood, and dust. Its interest lies in the people in it, because, despite the attention paid in its composition to the color effects of the sky and the deep perspective of the landscape, this is a narrative painting. The viewer's line of sight is low, about third-shirt-button-high on the central soldier, and the horizon line lies above the middle of the canvas, lengthening the foreground. From this angle, the nearest of four groups of soldiers looms out of the painting, each man watching the coffee with longing eyes.

Nearly a literal transcription of one of the journal entries from his Arizona days with the U.S. Cavalry, Frederic Remington's painting *A Cavalryman's Breakfast on the Plains* demonstrates his accustomed approach to desert landscape as the ground across which heroic mounted figures ride. (Courtesy of the Amon Carter Museum, Fort Worth, Texas; oil on canvas, ca. 1892, no. 1961.227)

This desert narrative represents Remington's customary oblique approach to the harsh land. It is a story of strong men facing desolation, constructing their everyday existence out of the bare dust and empty sky of some generic desert. The land itself, imaginatively emptied of any geographical identity besides wasteland, is represented as devoid of *any* vegetation whatsoever (an unlikely situation on the North American Continent, where all deserts support various kinds of vegetation, and many of them support thick ground cover so that totally empty areas are uncommon). It becomes a stylized backdrop for the rough-and-ready poses of soldiers who comb their hair, buckle their gunbelts, and smoke their pipes with amazing grace and balance, watching their breakfast boil as the wide desert swallows up their horses. Their poses are as stylized as a stage actor's.

By the early 1890s, Remington was seeing things in the desert that earlier seers had not—striking colors and unaccustomed perspectives—but he did not make much besides background material of them. For the most part during the 1890s, that is all the desert was to Anglo America—the backdrop for human undertakings. Matthew Baigell argues that the generic quality of Remington's work arose out of a dream, one he shared in part with Frederick Jackson Turner and in whole with Theodore Roosevelt. Remington dreamed that Americans had grown into their present heroic shape through encounters with the challenging West and that he, by concentrating on its still more challenging desert portions, could through his work preserve that noble history for America's posterity. The nonhuman world is not fully articulated in his work because it does not need to be. In fact, paying great attention to details other than human ones could never have been a part of Remington's project. Baigell notes that "Remington's frontier really has no location. He usually indicated landscape features with schematically rendered details—some underbrush, a distant mountain. More precise definition of background details would have imposed reality on the dream."[32]

Still, despite his intensely focused vision of the heroic arid West, Remington could not keep background details at bay indefinitely. By the early 1890s, cowboys were endangered, most Indians were on reservations, and in 1892 Remington himself was hired by *Harper's* to illustrate Richard Harding Davis's feature series entitled "The West from a Car Window"—a literary event that itself could have signaled the end of the West. It did signal the advent of the West as tourist attraction.

Throughout the 1890s, Remington's subject matter, strangely enough, suffered "an unnoticed erosion."[33] By the end of the decade, the desert Southwest that Remington had reproduced almost endlessly in his work had changed dramatically, becoming crisscrossed by railroad tracks and mining roads, and dotted with towns and cities. Nonetheless, his art of this period does not acknowledge the disappearance of its subject. In lieu of an admission of loss, Remington's art struggles to make present what has already gone.

The progress of Remington's career parallels the progress of America's nostalgia for its lost West. First, his subjects became increasingly popular as the deserts became decreasingly wild from the time Geronimo first appeared in *Harper's Weekly* until Remington's death in 1909. His success opened several cultural venues to him, initially supplying him with an audience for his magazine illustrations and after that supplying him with an audience for work done in "higher" genres, his painting and sculpture. By 1909 his illustrations, paintings, and bronzes had become cultural icons.

Second, Remington's technique became increasingly sophisticated. Remington consciously pushed himself to overcome what he saw as the stigma of being "just an illustrator."[34] He worked to learn the techniques of the best painters and sculptors of his time to gain access to a "higher" audience. Very late paintings such as *Shoshonie* (1908) represent a studied and fashionably impressionistic approach to the desert landscape, replacing his usual reliance on narrative to give structure to his work with a sophisticated concern for light and color.

Curiously, in transforming himself from illustrator to neo-impressionist and in expanding his range of venues to include the Metropolitan Museum in addition to *Harper's Weekly*, Remington redirected his approach to the land he had been drawing all along.[35] The desert, having served for nearly twenty years as an afterthought, the stage upon which cowboys and soldiers played out the heroic dreams of white America, became more fully developed in Remington's canvases as he developed his style. At times near the end of his career, arid landscapes became subjects in their own right; indeed, some of Remington's later works present no human figures at all.

In part, this convergent development of style and landscape awareness arises from the practical constraints of magazine illustration. As Remington noted in his journal, and as Powell and Dutton had noted before him, the dramatic visual effects of arid lands are functions of color and shadow—the "high color near the Earth" Remington saw at sunrise as he camped with soldiers in Arizona. But in the early stages of his career, in the 1880s when he was drawing illustrations for popular weeklies and monthlies, he usually worked in black and white in order to facilitate reproduction of his work by engravers, who carved his images in wood to be printed in black and white. The pictures had to be kept as simple as

possible. It was necessary that lines be definite so that they could be easily copied. Shadows and small details were difficult to reproduce, and color
illustrations were rare because they were prohibitively expensive. As well,
since monochrome illustrations cannot rely on juxtapositions of color to
convey visual drama, contrasts between light and dark must be heightened. Hence, a painting such as *Marching in the Desert* is not only painted
in grisaille, or black and white, but it is also stark in its contrasts, sim-
plifying the basin-and-range complexity of the desert landscape through
which its soldiers march into a stylized abstraction. In front of the march-
ers are a few generic desert plants, but the details of the landscape behind them seem to have escaped Remington's notice entirely.[36]

The facts of mechanical reproduction thus made close attention to the
landscape difficult for Remington, but social and psychological factors
actually seem to have been far more restrictive. Clarence Dutton had understood that the Grand Canyon was an "innovation in modern ideas of
scenery." His assessment would have held true for the whole of the
desert. The arid Southwest still appeared to most white Americans to be
nothing more than Pike's "barren wild of poor land," interesting mainly
for the fact that humans were out on it living the strenuous life to its utmost limits. Cowboys and soldiers illustrated in sharp, clean relief sold
magazines. The dramatic light and shadow of jagged mountains did not.

At first, as James K. Ballinger notes, the passing of what Remington
termed "my west" amounted to little more than an "unnoticed erosion" of
his subject matter. The erosion went unnoticed because, in contrast to his
early tendency to take a lackadaisical approach to landscape details (abet-
ted by the exigencies of nineteenth-century magazine printing), Remington's concern with the details of his cowboys and soldiers approached a
fixation. Alex Nemerov writes that "Remington practiced a kind of documentary approach to his western subjects. . . . He collected a staggering
number of western artifacts, including tomahawks, rifles, and still-sharp
swords, to place in the hands of his models and thus ensure the historical
accuracy of his paintings. He wrote to historical societies for information
about prospective subjects."[37] Further, Remington valued his knowledge
of his subject highly. When Frederick MacMonnies received a commission
that Remington had wanted, Remington recorded his immediate concerns
in his diary: "I expect he will want some more information for his Denver
monument but I guess he'll have to go it alone. I haven't accumulated all

Remington's dramatic *On the Southern Plains in 1860* was actually painted from life using models and props he set up in his New Rochelle, New York, studio. (Courtesy of the Metropolitan Museum of Art, Gift of Several Gentlemen, 1911, no. 11.192)

my knowledge of these matters to glorify [a]n artist who knows no more of our West than a Turk."[38] Remington's focus on obtaining (and retaining) a detailed knowledge of the human face of the West seems to have diverted his attention from the ecological realities of the desert.

Remington constructed his West out of props and models in his studio. Even in such pictures such as his *On the Southern Plains in 1860*, Remington posed his models in his yard in New Rochelle.[39] The peculiar realism of his representations of the Southwest and its cowboys became so compelling that his art came to look more "real" than did the West itself. His art was a conceptual field in which "the image of the West becomes the West,"[40] and that very real looking West is a land of cowboys, not landforms. So although by the 1890s the Arizona landscape included fences, railroads, irrigation projects, and cities, Remington seldom if ever took note of them. With its emphasis on men and its elision of landscape, his art implies that the story of the West was a story only of people and that the landscape was a cipher. It could have been anyplace in the world as long as it provided space through which cavalrymen could gallop their horses.

But the desert was not a cipher. In the final analysis, the end of Remington's cowboy West also meant the end of the land that had supported it, and Remington's later work acknowledges this connection to a limited and fairly nostalgic extent. A bison skull, for instance, appears on the ground under the horses' feet in Remington's 1896 bronze *The Wounded Bunkie*. From a modern perspective, the skull looks awkward, a half-hearted attempt to suggest the mass slaughter of the bison and the eventual destruction of the ecosystem. Ballinger dismisses it as "an unnecessary footnote, even in [Remington's] time, to a great work of art."[41] More even than in his paintings and illustrations, the figures are everything in Remington's sculpture, for the simple reason that his early bronzes present their subjects on plain, flat bases. These bronzes have no background, so the bison skull is compositionally distracting; it looks like ground clutter.

On a conceptual level, the bison skull is incongruous. Because in Remington's bronzes the viewer's attention is so effectively arrested by the cowboys in dramatic, even violent motion, the ground is extraneous— hence the plain bases. Remington thought of the bronzes as his ultimate contribution to the chronicle of the American West, because they provided him with the ideal medium through which to express the action emblematic of its best qualities. It was his desire to convey action in his art that moved him to learn sculpture to begin with. "I was impelled to try my hand at sculpture," he once said, "by a natural desire to say something in the round as well as in the flat. . . . Sculpture is the perfect expression of action."[42]

In addition to being the best medium for the expression of western action, his bronzes had the additional advantage (and authority) of permanence. Through their heroic depiction of his new American types, Remington's bronzes would immortalize the Arizona desert, which had affected him profoundly in 1885, and they would immortalize Remington as well. Of his sculpture he wrote, "I propose to do something more, to put the

In his sculpture *The Wounded Bunkie* Remington included, in the skull beneath the horses' hooves, a shorthand reference to the slaughter of the bison. (Courtesy of the Yale University Art Gallery, gift of the artist, 1900)

wild life of our West into something that the burglar won't have, moth eat or time blacken."[43]

There was more to Remington's affection for sculpture than a naive assumption that bronze would stand up to time better than canvas. There was also a conviction that they would somehow stand up better to the decline of American culture that he had come to associate with the end of the frontier. Always a man of his time, he saw his bronzes as an assurance that the most important elements of the former West—the cowboy and his independence—would never be lost. Unfortunately, despite being the apotheosis of American manhood, the cowboy had been all but undone by the advent of barbed wire, a fact that Remington regretted, to say the least. More disturbing to him, however, was his realization that even the idea of the cowboy seemed likely to disappear from the cultural memory. Addressing this frightening possibility, Remington in January of 1895 wrote to his friend Owen Wister with a recipe for greatness—a recipe for the bronze cowboys' greatness and for Frederic Remington's as well:

> I have got a receipt [*sic*] for being great—everyone may not be able to use this receipt but I can. D[amn] your glide-along songs—they die in the ear—your Virginian will be eaten up by time—all paper is pulp now. My oils will get old wasting . . . my watercolors will fade—but I am to endure in bronze—even rust does not touch—I am modeling—I find I do well—I am doing a cowboy on a bucking broncho and I am going to rattle through all the ages, unless some Anarchist invades the old mansion and knocks it off the shelf.[44]

Only the anarchists—who had rioted at Haymarket, had shot Henry Clay Frick, and who generally, as Remington and most of Anglo America saw it, threatened the stability of American society—would ever pose a threat to Remington's bronzes.

By 1905, Remington knew he and his work were in a good position to endure. He also knew that the West had unequivocally failed to endure. His bronzes, always vaguely nostalgic, became strikingly so. As he composed them, Remington began including a good deal more than the odd buffalo skull along with the central figures to denote the passing of the western ideal. Now he introduced imposing backgrounds that threaten his bronze figures. In compositions such as *The Rattlesnake*, not only does the indigenous animal rise up from the surface of the desert to play a part in the narrative of the work but the very surface of the desert itself rises up to grasp the fetlocks of the rearing horse. In *The Horse Thief* the ground billows up to meet the belly of the horse and to surround the rider from behind, and in *The Stampede* the base literally swallows part of the sculpture. As the Southwest of brave white men Remington knew in the mid 1880s receded from his experience, his tendency to conceive its characters in sharply isolated, heroically self-sufficient vignettes lessened and then disappeared.

The landscape literally and figuratively encompasses and supports the central human figure in Remington's *The Stampede*. (Courtesy of the Frederic Remington Art Museum, Ogdensburg, New York)

Significantly, however, the bronze contexts with which Remington begins to surround his sculptures do not include prickly pear cactuses, creosote bushes, or Palo Verde trees. What grows up around horses' hooves and cowboy boots is a highly artificed, almost impressionistic representation of landscape. The land asserts itself as part of the work of art, but it doesn't necessarily resemble the actual land Remington saw in Arizona. The shapes growing under the hooves of *The Outlaw* and the background rising up to encircle *The Horse Thief* are self-conscious expressions of Remington's personal impressions of the desert—expressions of his authority over his subject. Through them Remington lays claim to his West. Coming to terms with the fact that history had done away with the Wild West, Remington had invented his own desert West, a permanent, three-dimensional, bronze West complete with surreal impressionistic formations that replace the old, lost landscape.

In his later paintings, which are often moonlit, human subjects become less and less defined against sky, mountain, or earth, and are more and more likely to be Native American. In overtly sentimental treatments of the "lost west" like *On the Southern Plains in 1860, Ghost Riders,* and *The*

Outlier, coarse brush strokes draw background colors right across the outlines of human figures, causing sky or earth to impinge upon the boundaries between people and their environment, mingling them physically with their surroundings. This sort of violation of the boundaries between the human and nonhuman worlds would have destroyed the effect of an earlier composition like *Cavalryman's Breakfast on the Plains,* which depends for its impact on the stark delineation of the small, brave human communities against the vast desert space.

At times, people drop out of Remington's later compositions altogether. In works like *Untitled (Prairie and Rimrocks)* and *Shoshonie—Prairie, Blue Sky,* he expresses his authority over the desert itself. Far from being merely a space for cowboys, the southwestern desert became the center of Remington's attention in the works that immediately preceded his death, in which he undertook to figure the land itself. Still, devoid of cowboys as the desert became, it was no less clearly defined by Remington's nostalgia for the lost "wild" Southwest.

So interested did Remington become in southwestern form and color that in 1907, two years before his death, he returned to Texas, Arizona, and New Mexico to refresh his memory of the look of the land. Unfortunately, it had rained that winter, and by April the desert was still so green that Remington nearly left. Nature that year failed to comply with his desert aesthetic.

Happily for him, though, he found a suitably parched landscape near the Grand Canyon and was able to find a desert expanse he would use in the unapologetically nostalgic *On the Southern Plains in 1860.* In paintings such as this, detail is suppressed in order to vivify the color and tone of the desert. There is grass on the plains (represented in pronounced brush strokes), there is dust, and there is a carefully inflected desert sky. What would become an aesthetic in and of itself through the work of writers and artists such as John C. Van Dyke, George Wharton James, Mary Austin, Maynard Dixon, Georgia O'Keeffe, and Alfred Stieglitz remained for Remington an object of regret and longing, something that spoke of a glorious past but that said nothing about the future. By placing hazy cowboys in beautifully executed desert settings, Ballinger concludes, Remington "had finally blended the nostalgia of his experience of his subject in the Southwest with the color he had been striving to perfect since the turn of the century."[45]

Blending is the operative function of art like *On the Southern Plains in 1860*, in which Remington expresses his confidence in his ability to render the color of the desert, his obvious pride in his competence, and a vague regret that this desert exists only in his art. The bleaching bison skull over which the cavalrymen are about to ride functions as a symbol of the passing of an untrammeled ecosystem, but it points to Remington's nostalgia more than to the plight of the bison, whose disappearance was, after all, largely a result of the cavalry's campaign to starve the plains Indians.

If he spent a great deal of later life looking backward with longing, Remington also spent a great deal of the same time looking at the present with disgust. In 1907 he claimed: "I have no interest whatever in the industrial West of to-day—no more interest than I have in the agriculture of East Prussia or the coal mines of Wales. My West passed utterly out of existence so long ago as to make it merely a dream. It put on its hat, took up its blankets and marched off the board; the curtain came down and a new act was in progress."[46] Only in its absence, in its irreversible destruction, did the desert Southwest have significance for Remington.

Even though, through the eighties and nineties, he had habitually elided the desert in his work in order to present men more clearly, the desert of 1907 was in fact all too present to Remington. It held a negative significance comparable to the mundane, at best, landscapes of Wales and Prussia. As his nostalgia for the lost mythic Arizona increased, Remington tended to look at the land in a more holistic manner, seemingly prepared at times to address the environmental consequences of American capitalism and its byproduct, industrial civilization.

Still, committed as he was to people and the work they did, and to the idea of the strenuous life and its progressive Darwinian implications, Remington seems never to have fully developed a critical perspective on what had happened to the landscape. As he grew older, more comfortable, and more widely recognized in his role as a painter of heroic western canvases and a sculptor of heroic western bronzes, he seems to have evolved into a sentimentalist.

As Remington's lament implies, his had been an imagined Southwest of actors on a stage, of vitally important human subjects on an incidental background, and the truly regrettable thing about the actors was that the curtain had come down on their fascinating play.

Stephen Crane

Stephen Crane imagined another desert, one that was smaller than Remington's, that tended away from the myth of the Wild West rather than toward it, and that, in the end, took the southwestern ecosystem into account to a greater extent than had Remington's. From the environmental perspective of today, the West Texas that Crane invented in such stories as "The Bride Comes to Yellow Sky" is a more interesting place than Remington's Arizona. Flora and fauna, not just people, live in it.

Unfortunately, although it has become part of the canon of American literature, "The Bride Comes to Yellow Sky" and Crane's other southwestern stories, such as "A Man and Some Others" and "Moonlight on the Snow," did not exercise as much influence on American culture as did, say, Remington's painting *Coming through the Rye*. Crane's desert and Remington's desert arose in the same place—in the popular monthly and weekly magazines of the turn of the century. But when "The Bride" first appeared, its total value, both monetary and cultural, amounted to $200 and the last eight pages of the February 1898 issue of *McClure's* magazine. Crane's choice of venue was dictated by a circumstance Remington never faced: Crane sent it to McClure as repayment for a debt. To Crane's pleasant surprise, McClure "copped" only $71.09 before sending him his payment.[47] Still, Crane's work commanded only a fraction of the popular acclaim, and obviously only a fraction of the price, that Remington's did.

McClure's was not a "high" literary venue, not really comparable to the exemplary monthly magazines of the period like *Harper's* or *Century*, in which Remington regularly published. The magazine sold for only ten cents, making it one of the "cheap class periodicals,"[48] and according to Frank Luther Mott it was notable for four things: its "scientific articles, highlighting new discoveries; its emphasis on locomotives and trains, in stories and features; its articles on wild animals and exploration; and its stress on personalities."[49] Conforming to Mott's profile precisely, the issue in which "The Bride" appeared opened with a piece entitled "The Future of North Polar Exploration" and included "The Last Days of George Washington: From the Manuscript Diary of his Private Secretary, Colonel Tobias Lear," "Some Great Portraits of Lincoln," and a piece of factually presented fiction entitled "Firing a Locomotive." "The Bride Comes to Yellow Sky," in entering literary culture, began much more as a light selection for after-dinner recreational reading than an item in the college syllabi and literature anthologies where it can now be found—much nearer to cactus and six-guns than to its present high place in the estimation of literary critics.

But the piece proved upwardly mobile. In 1979, for example, Frank Bergon noted that in stories like "The Bride," "the increasingly complex world of [Crane's] fiction eluded the conventional orderings of reason and morality that are often reduced in horse operas to simplistic notions of manliness and self-reliance."[50] Now, in the late twentieth century, Crane's story has escaped the genre suggested by its dime-magazine origins, its outlaw, its sheriff, and its saloon, and can justifiably be characterized as actually refiguring "conventional orderings of reason and morality." It represents far more serious art and a far more consequential American landscape than did Remington's narrative paintings and bronzes.

The story's literary stock has risen because it carries cultural capital that has been easy for literary critics to get at—irony. This is not surprising, since Stephen Crane's habitual rhetorical stance was ironic. When he looked to Texas, it was natural for him to imagine an ironic desperado and an ironic sheriff there. And the story's most immediate and most frequently noted effect is that, through ironic treatment of the Wild West, it exposes the fledgling horse-opera tradition as what Jamie Robertson has called "a weak imitation of the vital life that had characterized the West."[51] But that is not all that happens in the story, because while "[e]lements of the Western romance play a . . . prominent role" in "The Bride," according to Michael J. Collins, the world it presents is nevertheless "a world of complex, comic ironies," one that has come to resemble the actual mundane world so much that it "can never offer anything so pure and heroic as a gunfight."[52] By the conclusion of the story, Crane has managed to bring the very possibility of the Wild West, as America had habitually imagined it, into question.

Stephen Crane, like Remington and unlike many other of his contemporaries who wrote about the American deserts, actually saw some of them. In 1895 he traveled from Nebraska to Mexico by train as a correspondent for the Bacheller syndicate, which had just successfully serialized *The Red Badge of Courage* and hoped to continue capitalizing on its popular young writer by having him correspond about the popular young West. And although Crane saw much that was vital in southwest Texas, he also saw much that was mundane. When Crane began setting the vitality of the popular tales he had heard about Texas beside the commonplace things he actually saw there, he exposed the complex ironic interplay of Wild West myth and everyday American life that, for him, defined the Anglo culture of the West Texas desert at the end of the nineteenth century.

One of the most surprisingly mundane things Crane saw as he rode the train through Texas to Mexico was the landscape. Judging from the dispatches he wrote as he traveled in 1895, the land did not always look like it was supposed to, either in the cities or in the countryside. In the town of the "transient monks," San Antonio, Crane had seen "telegraph wires across the face of their sky of hope," and he had been appalled by trolley cars in its Wild West streets.[53] Out in the "wilderness" between San Antonio and the border, which had been one huge cattle ranch for twenty years before Crane ever saw it, the scenery was no more romantic. Crane and Charles Gardner, the Chicago engineer with whom he rode the train from San Antonio to Mexico City, watched southern Texas as

> [t]he brown wilderness of mesquite drifted steadily and for hours past the car-windows. Occasionally a little ranch appeared half-buried in the bushes.
>
> In the dooryards of one, some little calicoed babies were playing and in the door-way itself a woman stood leaning her head against the post of it and regarding the train listlessly. Pale, worn, dejected, in her old and soiled gown, she was of a type to be seen North, East, South, and West.[54]

Disappointed at seeing suffering homesteaders starving on worked-out land instead of cowboys enjoying their freedom, Gardner and Crane, styled respectively by Crane as the "capitalist from Chicago" and the "archaeologist" turned toward the purity of the nonhuman and began to pine for wilderness outside the windows of their train: "[They] wanted mountains. They clamored for mountains. 'How soon, conductor, will we see any mountains?' The conductor indicated a long shadow in the pallor of the afterglow. Faint, delicate, it resembled the light rain-clouds of a faraway shower."[55]

Thus, during his travels in 1895 the desert landscape did not give Crane the material that western stories had promised him it would. Western stories called for wide-open arid plains, but by the time Crane got to them, thickets of "brown mesquite" had replaced the original bunchgrass due to cattle ranching, and huge sections of the landscape were impassable to mounted outlaws, mounted cowboys, cattle, or indeed to any organism larger than a hare because the mesquite in the degraded areas was unnaturally dense.[56] This was not the landscape of free-roaming rangers, and Crane was dismayed. As J. C. Levenson notes, "Crane's West was first of all the Wild West of literary convention, which he had a knack for taking seriously when for others it might seem a question of play."[57] But no one played on this stunted range.

To contemporary readers, Crane's disappointment is not remarkable. We assume that popular expectation is chiefly a product of Hollywood backlots, which are designed by people working from the same dime-western aesthetic that had misled Crane. What is remarkable is that Stephen Crane, sophisticated ironist and social demystifier that he was, ever believed any part of the western myth. By all rights, he should have seen through it. But he did not. In a letter Crane confessed that he "fell in love with the straight out-and-out, sometimes hideous, often-braggart westerners because [he] thought them to be the truer men."[58] In his famous inscription of *George's Mother* for Hamlin Garland, he invokes "the great honest West" and sets it over "the false East."[59]

To Crane experiencing the deserts of Texas initially, Texas-as-Wild-West represented what William Goetzmann concludes it has traditionally represented in Anglo American thought, "a theater in which American patterns of culture could be endlessly mirrored."[60] As Frederick Jackson Turner's hypothesis implies, the stage is the aptest metaphor for the American West in the Anglo American language. Today, more than a hundred years after the frontier became so fragmented that the superintendent of the census abandoned the term, the open landscape of the Southwest, overgrazed as it is, still manages to look for all the world like an empty space in which people can experiment with behaviors that the crowded East would not countenance.

Although Stephen Crane seemed to want to see a wild, wide-open, "great honest West," he was too astute an observer to miss what Texas put before him. He was seldom content with received ideas about any social construct—wide-open landscape included—if the construct looked any less than perfect. Crane thus found himself trapped between the wide desert wilderness he expected and the crowded cities and mesquite-infested range he experienced. And as he saw more discrepancies between the myth of open western spaces and the reality of southwest Texas, he increasingly relied on irony in his writing, which is the strategy of cramped quarters, the strategy of a mind trapped and held by two contradictory impulses.

These two impulses are in large measure a function of the way Americans conceived of the landscape, along the lines of Turner's frontier thesis. Turner, of course, held that "American social development has been continually beginning over on the frontier." Perceiving its geography as dichotomous—Civilization and Frontier, East and West—America became, according to Richard Slotkin, "divided between two realms: the 'Metropolis,' the civilizational center; and the 'Wilderness,' into which the heroic energies of the Metropolis are projected." The urban Metropolis "suffers the defects of its virtues," namely, scarcity, loss of personal freedom, and bitter class competition that "grows fatally violent as resources wane." In its suffering, the Metropolis looks to the "naturally abundant and unappropriated resources" of the Wilderness.[61] One of the resources civilized Americans imagined to exist in the deserts, beyond the imaginary border represented by the frontier, was open space. But the irony of this open space was that, being open and free, it was doomed to be exploited by the very Americans who valued its wildness. As much as Anglo Americans liked stories of wide-open range and carefree cowboys, Crane understood that they liked money better.

Crane works through this irony in a series of short stories, beginning with less well known pieces such as "A Man and Some Others," which appeared in the February 1897 issue of *Century Illustrated* magazine, and culminating in the classic story "The Bride Comes to Yellow Sky," which appeared a year later in *McClure's*. All of Crane's western stories are in some way critical of the myths surrounding the American West. "The Bride Comes to Yellow Sky," however, is the culmination of Crane's critical examination of these myths, and it brings to bear, among other things, an environmental critique of the myth of Wild West Texas.

"A Man and Some Others" is criticism writ large. Bill, the story's eponymous hero, is in the Texas desert because he has run afoul of the "false East." Hunkered down with his flock of sheep, Bill gives the lie to the American doctrine of social Darwinism; he was one of the strongest, chosen to thrive, but he opted out. Violent and physically powerful, Bill began his adult life as a rich man in the West, where he lost his mine by gambling, "killed the foreman of [a] ranch over the inconsequent matter as to which one of them was a liar," left for the East, became a railroad detective, beat up hoboes, struck against the railroad, got a job as a bouncer in a Bowery bar, and finally ran up against three sailors, who hit him so hard with a board that "ultimately . . . it landed him in southwestern Texas, where he became a sheep-herder."[62] In closing his career in southwest Texas, Bill murders two men and in return is murdered by their friends over the right to exploit a piece of desert by ranging sheep on it.

Bill takes part in, and dies in, an absurd version of the process of natural selection played out in the wilderness. In his inability to make reasonable decisions about his relationship to the landscape and to the other people on it—by deciding to stop denuding the desert by running sheep on it, for example, or at least to move to another, uncontested portion of the range in order to avoid armed conflict—Bill places his competitive urge over his ability to think, and he ends up a ludicrous human being. He also ends up dead.

In Crane's "Moonlight on the Snow," another rough articulation of the critique that would later inform "The Bride Comes to Yellow Sky," the same eastern inability to understand landscape in anything but Darwinian terms afflicts the citizens of Warpost. But in Warpost the competition for survival takes an explicitly capitalist turn. Due to its Wild Westernness, Warpost is missing out on the western real estate boom of the 1890s: "Warpost sat with her reputation for bloodshed pressed proudly to her bosom, and saw her mean neighbors leap into being as cities. . . . Warpost saw dollars rolling into the coffers of a lot of contemptible men who couldn't shoot straight." Their problem, the Warposters conclude, is "this here gunfighter business."[63]

Warpost's leading citizen, eastern-educated Tom Larpent, finally comes to understand that "[t]he value of human life has to be established before there can be theatres, water-works, street cars, women, and babies."[64] As a result, the citizens of Crane's nightmarish western town pass a resolution making it a hanging offense to shoot anyone within the city limits. Murder becomes, in addition to a capital crime, a crime against property, because it lessens the value of land. In a nasty irony, Tom Larpent becomes the first citizen to shoot somebody and finds himself standing at the gallows.

The conflict in the story revolves around the ironic fact that, in order to convert the desert ecosystem to gold-backed dollars, its Wild West element must be eliminated. And the conflict is irreducible: it is impossible to have the wilderness, the Wild West, and a real-estate boom all at the same time in the same town. Social Darwinism, in the guise of a real estate market, kills the Wild West. To save his plot, Crane must resort to a meta-solution: Sheriff Potter rides into town from a different story to arrest Larpent on charges pending in another, more civilized city—Yellow Sky.

Yellow Sky is the most civilized town in Crane's western canon. Its residences have nicely watered front lawns, and because they do, Yellow Sky is the setting for Crane's best articulation of the discrepancy between the two American versions of the West he had come to recognize, one imaginary and pretty, one actual and overrun by cattle. In "The Bride Comes to Yellow Sky," Crane expresses grave reservations about this crack in the myth of the wide western landscape. Between his first encounter with the land in 1895 and his imaginative refiguration of it in the story of late 1897, Crane had learned to resist the temptation to swallow western myths whole. If one impulse in "The Bride" is still to see the desert as a wonderland in which "sometimes-hideous" men such as Scratchy and Potter perform their actions, or play their roles, the counterbalance to that impulse is the awareness that the landscape in which they are performing is in large measure a fabrication based on a mistaken conception of the vanishing frontier.

Stephen Crane realized relatively early that Americans, most of whom were suffering in Slotkin's Metropolis, were using the environment of the West, the Earth's actual surface, as a stage on which to play. His realization was triggered by what he observed on the ground in Texas. When Crane came to Laredo in 1895, he wrote that it "appeared like a city veritably built on sand. Little plats of vivid green grass appeared incredible upon this apparent waste. They looked like the grass mats of the theatrical stage."[65] Two years later the same plats appear in Yellow Sky, as plots. Across the street from the Weary Gentleman Saloon "were some vivid green grass-plots, so wonderful in appearance, amid the sands that burned near them in a blazing sun, that they caused a doubt in the mind.

They exactly resembled the grass mats used to represent lawns on the stage."[66] Theatricality has sublimed into the actual fabric of the story, for Scratchy and Sheriff Potter's confrontation is nothing if not theatrical. Those green plots in the real world of Laredo and in the fictional construct of Yellow Sky, are growing in a mesquite desert. They are irrigated, incongruous, Victorian imports from back east, and although Laredo is not Yellow Sky, Laredo's landscape is a leading character in "The Bride Comes to Yellow Sky."

As Sheriff Potter and the bride approach Yellow Sky, they see a romanticized landscape: "To the left, miles down a long purple slope, was a little ribbon of mist where moved the keening Rio Grande. The train was approaching it at an angle, and the apex was Yellow Sky."[67] Similarly, as Stephen Crane approached Laredo on the International and Great Northern Rail Road in 1895, he saw the right-of-way, town, and river laid out in exactly the same way, because Laredo lies in an identical landscape at the bottom of a long slope in a bend of the river. But when Crane stepped off the train at the Laredo depot to change to the Texas-Mexican Railway, he stepped into something of a nightmare, by his lights: an eastern town situated on the edge of the Chihuahuan Desert. He saw streetcars shuttling men in bowlers and women in bustles up and down the streets, which remained dusty and faintly alkaline, tantalizing reminders of the romantic fact that the town sat on the edge of a desert. He was also faced with the central business district of town, which had boomed since the railroad came in 1881 and which boasted the Victorian Italianate-style Orfila House, the Eastlake McKnight House, the Victorian Gothic St. Peter's Church, and the Victorian Garcia House, with its Palladian windows.[68]

Further, Crane saw incongruous green lawns in front of these houses (the Ortiz family residence even sported palmettos in its front yard) and all on less than fifteen inches of rain a year.[69] Ecological anomalies such as these, which caught Crane's attention, had quietly superseded the literary representations of what humans were doing in wide-open West Texas. Crane concluded that Laredo was a "theatrical stage" upon which various human social pretensions were being played out. But more disturbing than his suspicion that Laredo was a stage was the realization that would surface later in "The Bride Comes to Yellow Sky": Laredo was the stage against which the Puritan reformer William Prynne had once railed. It propagated not art but lies. More disturbing still, the stage was identical with the surface of the Earth.

This foundational "theatrical" relationship between human social convention and the landscape informs the irony of "The Bride Comes to Yellow Sky." The climactic irony of the story—social convention, in the person of the bride, defeating the free man of the open spaces, in the person of Scratchy Wilson—begins, literally, on the ground, the irrigated, grass-covered sand of Laredo, Texas, in 1895. The irony is the one Leo Marx sees as implicit in the American "society of the middle landscape," which finds itself subscribing to ideas about the natural world that constitute an "increasingly transparent and jejune expression of the national preference for having it both ways."[70] This is Crane's lesson of Laredo—given a choice, people seem to prefer living in gardens at the same time that they cling, like Scratchy, to spectacular theatrical visions of desert wilderness.[71]

"The Bride Comes to Yellow Sky" is indeed overtly concerned with human undertakings. Wilderness remains implicit; the settings of the story are necessarily associated with human activity. "The Bride" takes place in a Pullman car, a saloon, and a town street, all of which are described with an eye toward human artifacts, not natural facts. The Pullman moves through a landscape simply "to prove that the plains of Texas [are] pouring eastward." From its windows, the countryside appears to be "sweeping into the east, sweeping over the horizon, a precipice."[72] The train's passengers, in fact, have an opportunity to alight only four times in crossing the entire state of Texas, a journey, as Sheriff Potter notes, of over a thousand miles. The overwhelming concern of the narrator is not to describe the landscape but "the dazzling fittings of the coach": "the sea-green figured velvet, the shining brass, silver, and glass, the wood that gleamed as darkly brilliant as the surface of a pool of oil."[73]

Attention to detail is directed similarly in the other settings. By the end of its scene, the Weary Gentleman Saloon is populated by apprehensive whiskey-swilling men seeking refuge from Scratchy's bullets "below the level of the bar," contemplating with gratitude the fact that the bar is equipped with "various zinc and copper fittings that [bear] a resemblance to armor plate." And by the time Scratchy and Sheriff Potter meet in the street, the street exists merely because the confrontation has to occur somewhere, and it provides an accommodating, not to mention traditional, place.

This town is a tiny Metropolis. The citizens of Yellow Sky, as Wild Western as they pretend to be, are not particularly fond of wildness or wilderness on a daily basis. They like their town. The first hint of the dichotomy they have set up between the wild and the civilized arises in the narrator's awareness of something outside the human world of Yellow Sky—the uneasy feeling in the story, congruent with Crane's uneasiness in the 1895 dispatch, that green grass does not belong there and that underneath the lawns and streets and railroad tracks and buildings there was once a desert. By the close of the story, Scratchy is making his way back out into the desert dust, not because of the bride but because that was where he would have gone anyway, since he is still too wild to stay in town when drunk. His defeat by the bride accounts only for his foot-dragging dejection, not his destination.

The original illustrations from the story's 1898 publication in *McClure's,* which present an even more desolate Yellow Sky than Crane described, make explicit the relationship between town and desert in the story. In its magazine incarnation, the story is bounded physically, at the head of the first page and at the foot of the last page, by pictures of a tiny town on a plain. The illustration at the beginning of the story shows Sheriff Potter and the bride leaving a one-story depot that stands in front of three low mud houses behind which the horizon lies perfectly flat and featureless. On the horizon, beyond the people, the buildings, and the pig, train tracks and telegraph wires converge at infinity. A prickly pear and three mesquite trees are the only vegetation visible. At the close of the story, Scratchy stands with his hat in one hand and scratching his head with the other, in the margin between the line of low buildings at the edge of town and a sparse line of bunchgrass that marks the beginning of the desert.[74] The town is a flimsy human construct, seemingly brave, a speck in a vast expanse.

The second example of a confused environmental awareness—the mind of the Metropolis—creeping into the world of the story comes from the Weary Gentleman's bartender as he hides from Scratchy's bullets behind his zinc-plated bar. He tells his customers that the violent Scratchy who periodically emerges drunk from the crusty but lovable Scratchy and

THE BRIDE COME

I.

shoots up the town comes from beyond the limits of civilization, from out in the wild landscape:

"You see," he whispered, "this here Scratchy Wilson is a wonder with a gun—a perfect wonder—and when he goes on the war trail, we hunt our holes—naturally. He's about the last one of the old gang that used to hang out along the river here. He's a terror when he's drunk.

o YELLOW SKY.

Stephen Crane

he Red Badge of Courage," " The Third Violet," etc.

The initial illustration in "The Bride Comes to Yellow Sky" provided Stephen Crane's eastern audiences with a visual understanding of the immensity of the open desert landscape and the inconsequential nature of humans and their constructs within it. (*McClure's* 10 [1898]: 377)

When he's sober he's all right—kind of simple—wouldn't hurt a fly—nicest fellow in town. But when he's drunk—whoo!"[75]

Scratchy retains some natural savage impulses from a precivilized time on the Rio Grande, and when those impulses arise, freed by alcohol from the socialization that holds them in check, the citizenry of Yellow Sky "hunt [their] holes—naturally," in an ironic parody of "natural" animal behavior. And in their bemused nostalgia for what is wild, the citizens quietly enjoy themselves.

Thus, when the bride actually comes to Yellow Sky, the question arises: How much and what kind of wildness could there be in a town with front lawns? When the bride from San Antonio confronts the savage and "simple child of the earlier plains," what exactly does she face? She faces fabricated wilderness. Yellow Sky is remarkably like most other American towns. There is little wild in it except what the people there import from somewhere out on "the river" and somewhere in the past, wildness that is a function of how much Scratchy has drunk (as well as the claims of the bartender, who propagates among the citizenry the myth of Scratchy's savage origins out in the desert). The drunk Scratchy emerges from the extreme eastern margin of the Chihuahuan Desert, evidence of a nearby wilderness that thrills the various characters in the bar. The vestigial wilderness remains, beneath the green lawns and behind the bartender's story, and the more the principal citizens of Yellow Sky, namely Scratchy and Sheriff Potter, insist on imagining themselves as participants in that lost wilderness, the more humorous they become.

But Scratchy, despite the bartender's nostalgic idea that he sprang up out of a sandbar by the river, is simply another ironic construction. Crane leaves no room for doubt on this point; Scratchy is dressed in "a maroon-colored flannel shirt, which had been purchased for purposes of decoration and made, principally, by some Jewish women on the east side of New York. . . . And his boots had red tops with gilded imprints, of the kind beloved in winter by little sledding boys on the hillsides of New England."[76] Scratchy exists first and foremost as the X that marks the spot where eastern preconceptions meet the desert landscape, and he is what the bride defeats. It is not some pure bad man from the chaparral that she runs off, it is Scratchy, who is nothing more than an amalgam of eastern ideas about western freedom and who dissolves before the most evocative (if sexist) symbol of the "false" East that Crane could think of—the woman who would tie a good man down in marriage.

Scratchy's defeat constitutes the climax of the story. Frank Bergon calls it "the unstated premise of . . . the legendary West. The real destroyers in this West are not gunslinging desperadoes or corrupt Eastern capitalists or encroaching railroads." The real destroyer is "the domesticating woman."[77] This is certainly the overt lesson of "The Bride Comes to Yellow Sky." The desperado Scratchy is convincingly routed by the bride, who is as mysterious and powerful to him as a force of nature.

But another premise, a foundational premise, lies behind Bergon's "unstated premise of . . . the legendary West," and "The Bride Comes to Yellow Sky," unlike even the most insightful of the general run of westerns and anti-westerns, gets at it. Behind the irony Crane sees in female domesticity routing the unfettered masculinity of the open country, behind the irony of Scratchy in sledding boots, behind the irony of eastern capitalists experiencing wilderness from a train, and behind all the other ironies in the story is the fact that the wild landscape of the West, for Anglo Americans, was never purely a wild landscape. It was, and is, a potential front lawn. The myth of the West, because it is propagated by Anglo Americans, is always tainted by the spectacle of watered grass in front of West Texas domiciles—watered lawns that literally mean dead desert. From the moment people look out from the false East—the Metropolis— to see a space of desert ground, it becomes a stage, and after they have looked at the stage long enough to compose a story about it, they begin putting props on it in preparation for the play.

This play is set more terrifyingly, more claustrophobically than Samuel Beckett's *Endgame*. The stage of Yellow Sky is final—the sandy ground upon which the green mats are thrown is really the ground, which for all living things on Earth is all there is. If humans have made it into a stage, it is a stage from which there is no exit.

Crane's Yellow Sky Wild West reflects the dilemma that the United States found itself facing at the end of the nineteenth century. There was no longer any escape from human ecological self-determination by lighting out for the territories, which, for Crane, was the irony of the Texas desert. As his stories suggest, most Anglo Americans never stood a chance of seeing those deserts. The landscape, as soon as they got to it, succumbed not to an economic order, not to a domestic order, but to a human ecological order; and in Crane's view, its great conflicts take place not out in wild nature somewhere but within the structure of an environment that has been refigured by human economy and society. As the grass mats in Yellow Sky mutely attest, by the time people see it the desert usually exhibits the profound changes to which they inevitably subject it.

In a fictitious 1897, Sheriff Potter faces down Scratchy in a landscape that exists at what Bill McKibben in 1989 called "the end of nature," the place where "*we have ended the thing that has, at least in modern times, defined nature for us—its separation from human society*" (italics in original).[78] In Crane's story, the theatricality of the traditional Wild West confrontation between the sheriff and the desperado serves as a reminder that the open spaces upon which move "simple child[ren] of the plains" are human ideas, not natural occurrences.

Crane's approach to the eastern Chihuahuan Desert enables him to understand the relationship between Anglo Americans and the land in a way that Remington, with his anthropocentric approach to the Sonoran Desert, could never have done. "The Bride Comes to Yellow Sky" launches a specific examination of human activity in the place where the generalized myth of the wild-and-free West intersects the specific arid ecosystem of the southern Rio Grande Valley. Although Crane's Yellow Sky is a fiction, Crane's imagination never transcends the specifics of the environment in which it is set. He does not imagine people without imagining the place they inhabit, as Remington and others had done, so his desert figures exhibit a sense of place and an environmental awareness that few artists of his time attained.

Chapter **4**

I felt the coming of new empires, the burden of unborn centuries, and grew great with the unspeakable hope and the unspeakable sadness of the wilderness.

—Harriet Monroe[1]

The Desert in the Magazines

In the desert town of Yellow Sky, *wild* becomes a loaded word, and the story itself becomes a cautionary tale about the dangers of repeating naive and contradictory Wild West narratives until they become believable. But the contradictions Stephen Crane's humorous irony uncovers were not peculiar to his fictional Texas town. They arose, in rather less well examined incarnations, throughout the popular literature of the late-nineteenth-century United States.

The venue in which Crane's stories first appeared, the popular New York City literary magazines of the 1890s, bears close examination in a study of the American deserts because these magazines give evidence of a remarkable struggle going on in the minds of educated Americans over the question of how to approach the landscape. Fiction writers like Stephen Crane and Frederic Remington (in his role as a short-story author); nature essayists like John Muir and Mary Austin; scientists and conservationists like Nathaniel Shaler, Gifford Pinchot, and John Wesley Powell; and artists like Maxfield Parrish all participated in the negotiation. A new and short-lived genre even originated during the course of the debate as William E. Smythe, the nation's first "irrigationist," pursued his writing career in the pages of *Century* magazine. The influence of these magazines would be hard to overestimate. Vera Norwood cites *Scribner's* and *Century* as general sources for American women's literature of the Southwest, observing that many frontier women, having been first exposed to desert landscapes in these magazines while they were still in the East, "expected to find 'grand scenery' and 'romantic' vistas in the West."[2]

Walter Prescott Webb, in answering the question of why the West was considered spectacular and romantic, provided an elegant account of the role of the East in building the romance of the West (and hence, the western deserts): "The West appeared romantic to those who were not of it— to the Easterner, who saw the outward aspects of a strange life without understanding its meaning and deeper significance. The East set the standards, wrote the books, made the laws. What it did not comprehend was strange, romantic, spectacular."[3] As a part of this process, everything that was strange, romantic, and spectacular about the West soon became a part of the standards, books, and laws of American culture. When John Wesley Powell began lobbying Congress, for instance, in his campaign to implement his comprehensive plan for developing the arid regions, he saw *Century Illustrated*—one of the most influential magazines of the time—as the obvious medium through which to make the plan public.[4] In the March, April, and May numbers in 1890, Powell published a version of his report to Congress (less technical than the original report but still written for a fairly well educated audience) in order to drum up the popular support he hoped would give him leverage as he presented his plan for the development of the arid West.

The impact of Powell's articles became apparent almost immediately in the "Open Letters" section of the August 1890 *Century*, in which one Abbot Kinney of Los Angeles County, California, took Powell to task over his interpretation of the relationship between forests and watersheds, parts of which Kinney observed that Powell had gotten wrong. Powell argued in "The Non-Irrigable Lands of the Arid Region" that in the desert, "the forests of the upper regions are not advantageous to the people of the valleys" because these forests use up water.[5] Kinney rightly pointed out that the effect of trees on mountain watersheds is, "without known exception, beneficial to irrigators and water users in the valleys below" because they save topsoil and moderate runoff.[6] This is but one example of the way in which the magazine served as a forum that enabled its readers to resolve misconceptions about desert watersheds.

In general, such magazines as *Century,* along with the other influential "qualities"—*Atlantic, Harper's,* and *Scribner's*—and a few cheaper magazines such as *McClure's,* which competed successfully with them, offer insight into the concerns of educated citizens at the turn of the century.[7] These "quality" general monthlies represented what upper-class and especially upper-middle-class Americans thought was best about their culture. They were polite, refined, intellectually rigorous, and exclusive. In many ways they would have served a similar function to a present-day PBS documentary.

The magazines grew up during the second half of the nineteenth century, when educated Americans had begun feeling, in Lawrence Levine's words, that "public life [was becoming] everywhere more fragmented."[8] The magazines' self-consciously intellectual tone was a hedge against the widely perceived decay of American culture. That magazine editors liked to characterize their publications as "quality" implies that they were part of the culture-wide response to this perceived fragmentation, a response in which, according to Levine, "the concept of culture took on hierarchical connotations along the lines of Matthew Arnold's definition of culture—'the best that has been thought and known in the world, . . . the study and pursuit of perfection.'"[9] These magazines were cultural locations at which the "ubiquitous discussion of the meaning and nature of culture, informed by Arnold's views," took place. Throughout this discussion, "adjectives were used liberally. 'High,' 'low,' 'rude,' 'lesser,' 'higher,' 'lower,' 'beautiful,' 'modern,' 'legitimate,' 'vulgar,' 'popular,' 'true,' 'pure,' 'highbrow,' 'lowbrow,' were applied to such nouns as 'arts' or 'culture' almost *ad infinitum.*"[10] One need go no farther than the *The Atlantic Monthly's* subtitle, "A Magazine of Literature, Science, Art and Politics," to form an impression of the self-consciously high subjects addressed in these publications. They were the sorts of subjects generally understood to embrace the "best that has been thought and known in the world."

Fred Robbins has called *Century Illustrated* "a focal point of American culture . . . a bellwether of the entire Gilded Age and a benchmark for the growth of American culture into this century."[11] But the magazine's focus was by no means restricted to conservation issues. Various contemporary concerns were presented together each month as if it were a huge cultural portmanteau. Powell's "The Non-Irrigable Lands of the Arid Regions" was followed immediately by Thomas Wentworth Higginson discussing the cosmopolitan possibility, which had occurred to him at the recent Modern Language Association convention, of a world literature that would include Goethe, Austen, Zola, Omar Khayyám, Quintilian, and Aristotle, among others. Conservation, literature, art, politics, and toward the end of the 1890s, war, were all of interest to the eclectic readers of *Century Illustrated*.

The other magazines were equally invested in defining, refining, and redeeming American culture. *Scribner's* editor Edward Burlingame focused his magazine on "the great working life and practical achievements of the country."[12] The self-consciously refined *Atlantic* magazine stood, according to a contemporary *Dial* critic, "more distinctly for culture than any other American magazine,"[13] and at the turn of the century *Harper's* may have been the most vital literary organ in the country, publishing in its fiftieth anniversary issue of May 1900 pieces by Stephen Crane, Frederick Remington, Owen Wister, Mark Twain, Howard Pyle, Mary E. Wilkins Freeman, Theodore Dreiser, William Dean Howells, Victor Hugo, Rudyard Kipling, and Thomas Hardy. Still, *Harper's* cultural focus was not limited to literature; its editorial policy "emphasized 'timely interest,' and articles on popular science, exploration, and sociology were dominant."[14]

Thus, when the desert was discussed in these monthly magazines, it was in the context of the pressing issues of the time. One such issue was the notion that the deserts were still wild, still resisting human institutions, and therefore still natural. Educated Americans, both fascinated and horrified by the social and environmental fallout of the industrial revolution, clearly suffered at least one of the "antinomies of bourgeois culture," described by Georg Lukács in his *History and Class Consciousness*, the antinomy in which nature "acquires the meaning of what has grown organically, what was not created by man, in contrast to the artificial structures of human civilisation."[15] Like the British Romantics before them—who, as Raymond Williams has shown in *The Country and the City*, learned to love the once-abhorrent "natural" landscape of the Alps as nature became more and more scarce in their home countries—educated Americans exhibited an increasing interest in their deserts at the turn of the twentieth century.

The American deserts thus began to develop attractive features. For one, as Remington's art implies, they provided Anglo Americans with the image of a wild nature capable of standing up to artificial human civilization, and Americans responded to that image in a variety of ways. Ultimately, these responses came to characterize the edge of the desert as the boundary between civilization and wilderness.

This move toward a culture-wide understanding of the significance of the nation's arid regions was commonly conducted in huge, vaguely organized ruminations on the desert, such as Harriet Monroe's *Atlantic* article "Arizona," which she concluded by suggesting that the wilderness of the North American deserts provided citizens of the United States with "deep vision[s] that would enable them to build their future." Inspired by the desert, she asks: "Does not [man] need a deep vision of things unachieved in order that he may face the threatening future in the spirit of an epic hero, eager to search and conquer, to found the new happier order, to build the new capital of the world, and adorn it with beauty surpassing the beauty of the experimental and divided past?"[16] The general monthlies, published in New York City and Boston, were perhaps the only cultural organs providing sufficient scope and context in which to undertake this project, in which to discuss the future of the country, the future of its landscape, and the future of mankind simultaneously.

Almost always the future of humankind was at stake, specifically the sort of progressive, American, continent-taming humankind of which most magazine readers counted themselves a part. If, as noted earlier, the superintendent of the census had declared that the frontier could not "any longer have a place in the census reports," and if, as Frederick Jackson Turner had proposed, "the advance of American settlement westward explain[ed] American development," then Americans had good reason to fear a decline in the national character.[17]

Part of the *fin de siècle* mood of the nineties, Roderick Nash notes, involved "the belief . . . that the United States, if not the entire Western World, had seen its greatest moments and was in an incipient state of decline."[18] Tom Lutz includes "the 'closing' of the continental frontier and the beginnings of an overseas empire" as one of the "social and cultural change[s]" between 1890 and 1910 that contributed to the common turn-of-the-century condition he calls American Nervousness.[19] Further, Nash finds that "[a]s a result of this discontent with civilization, which was no less uncomfortable because of its vagueness, *fin-de-siècle* America was ripe for the widespread appeal of the uncivilized."[20] A romantic affection for things natural pervaded the culture, finding practical manifestation in the founding of such institutions as the Sierra Club in 1892 and the United States Forest Service in 1905.

Popular "quality" monthly magazines, in addition to carrying isolated articles regarding wilderness, nature, or the desert, provided a forum in which such civilizational/environmental anxieties could be discussed. As in the example of Powell and his critic Abbot Kinney, open letters to the editor often provided direct and fairly immediate critical commentary on magazine articles that led to clearer conceptions of the desert ecosystems. At times, more extended discussions of environmental topics occurred, editorially mediated conversations consisting of a series of articles addressing specific environmental topics from different perspectives. These conversations were seldom clearly focused, and it is impossible to say precisely what the editorial impulse behind them was, but simply to observe the course of a representative series is often enlightening.

One such interaction sheds light on the nation's ambivalent attitude toward its deserts, though more because of what it omitted than what it included. In February 1895, demonstrating his admirable environmental awareness, Richard Watson Gilder, the editor of *Century*, published "A Plan to Save the Forests" (from mechanized foresters), by Charles Sargent. Gilder included written responses to Sargent's plan by, among others, Frederick Law Olmsted, Theodore Roosevelt, Gifford Pinchot, Nathaniel Shaler, and John Muir, devoting a total of nine pages to the question. Most of the responses came across as strongly in favor of conservation. Muir, like many of the respondents, agreed that "one soldier in the woods, armed with authority and a gun," would be the most effective way of protecting trees.[21] A hard line on conservation, at least when it came to forest land, was common among contributors to *Century Illustrated*. But three months later the magazine published William Smythe's "The Conquest of Arid America," a sunny account of America's progress in destroying its desert ecosystems for agricultural purposes. As this small cultural transaction implies, impulses toward the American deserts were by no means consistent even in a fairly small cultural space—three months in the history of one magazine. When it came to protecting western forests, many of which existed directly up mountain slopes from various deserts as elevated "island" ecosystems, America's leading thinkers professed to be ready to turn the military upon trespassers, while in the case of the desert ecosystems themselves, the idea of preservation was completely lost in the call for irrigation and "reclamation."[22] As of 1895, the Southwest, although valuable as a scenic backdrop for Remington's canvases, was not yet understood as a complex of ecosystems that was unequivocally valuable in and of itself.

Treatments of the desert that were more explicitly capitalistic than even the tracts on irrigation appeared as well. Around 1905, after selected locations in the desert had been domesticated into tourist attractions, magazines approached the desert in another way: it was a hot commodity for western railroads, which bought a good deal of advertising space. In 1905 an article by William Allen White entitled "On Bright Angel Trail" appeared in *McClure's,* an article that the magazine's table of contents did not fail to note was "illustrated in color." In fact, it was illustrated in unnaturally lavish color. It was also somewhat overwrought, beginning with a once-upon-a-time vignette about an artist "who loved the wilderness [and who] brought his bride to the head of the Bright Angel Trail." This artist leads his bride out of the El Tovar Hotel, blindfolds her, and leads her down the sidewalk to the wilderness, which he loves. At the edge of the Grand Canyon he takes the bride's blindfold off, and when she sees the Canyon she turns and "crie[s] vehemently to her artist husband: 'If you ever try to paint that, I'll leave you,'" thus applying one of the earliest layers of the patina of kitsch that now scumbles the Grand Canyon.[23]

The next layer follows immediately, for in the back of the issue is a full-page Santa Fe Railway advertisement featuring a quarter-page picture of the El Tovar hotel above the admonition:

You should read William Allen White's notable article about the *Grand Canyon of Arizona* in this number of McClure's.

Then arrange to visit the world's greatest scenic wonder on your next trip to Pacific Coast.[24]

Clearly, once Anglo Americans got the hang of the desert, they could make it fit into cultural interactions at nearly every level of their society.

Writers also projected several late Victorian anxieties into imaginatively rendered versions of Arizona, New Mexico, Texas, Utah, and southern California. One such group of anxieties—the series of cultural and literary concerns we now gather under the umbrella of "American literary naturalism"—found various expression in representations of the desert. Stephen Crane's early poetry, fittingly enough, exhibits one such expression. Crane makes the desert a natural metaphor for the human condition in a post–social Darwinian world.[25] Crane's desert is a figure for the sort of wasteland that the human condition had become in the wake of the mechanistic, progressive, evolutionary machine of Darwinian nature.

The "nature" of American literary naturalism was not, in the 1890s, the nature of the Romantics, not Wordsworth's "rocks and stones and trees"; it is determinism, natural selection, and social Darwinism. This version of nature worked fairly well in a country whose frontier had recently passed away and whose reserve of wild, nonhuman living things had largely disappeared. It is a monistic nature, incorporating humans into the same mechanism that drives the rest of the universe. In the most rigorous construction of this naturalism, as William James put it, there can be no human subjects making choices about objectified nature. Human choices are determined by natural laws, and those who posit any sort of free will operating in nature are only "soft determinists," not true determinists at all.[26] True determinists were at the top of Anglo American society, the same society that not coincidentally produced and consumed "quality" monthly magazines. Teddy Roosevelt, whose articles appeared regularly in *Century Illustrated*, imagined the machine that was nature to have been whizzing along since "the shadowy dawn of . . . history," when it first set the Germanic peoples on their way to conquer America.[27] According to Andrew Carnegie (another extremely successful American to whom natural selection had been kind), although the natural law of Darwin and Spencer "may be sometimes hard for the individual, it is best for the race, because it insures the survival of the fittest in every department."[28] At the end of the nineteenth century, it was helpful for Americans such as Roosevelt and Carnegie to think of a nature that moved inexorably along from primitive past to glorious future, yet another megamachine resembling the ones in the factories, only bigger, enriching the strong and culling the weak while it conveniently provided a "natural" justification for the social system over which they presided.

Three desert conceptions in particular moved from the writers' studies, editors' offices, and reading parlors of the East onto the wide-open spaces of the desert. First, deserts challenged the country to fulfill its obligation to spread Anglo-Saxon industrial civilization. The nation wouldn't have placed its continental house in order until the deserts were "reclaimed." Second, the deserts, because they were some of the harshest landscapes on the continent, became the ultimate place in which to pursue the "strenuous life," to work against the perceived moral and racial decay that Americans such as Roosevelt had begun to feel followed directly on the heels of civilization. Third, the desert, strange and different-looking as it was, did not lend itself to immediate aesthetic appreciation. It became a challenge not only to the strength, practicality, and grit of the white Americans who came to it; it also challenged their higher sensibilities. In the end, this third impulse took on a "deep ecological" cast and became part of an argument for appreciating nature for its own sake, for seeing the attributes of nature as valuable in themselves, apart from practical or economic concerns such as the advancement of civilization or the advancement of the railroads.

Desert Progressivism

As of 1890 there was still a zone along the edge of the desert in which the citizens of the United States might attempt conquest, and that is exactly the way in which William E. Smythe conceived the arid regions in his May 1895 *Century Illustrated* article entitled "The Conquest of Arid America." "The material progress of the United States in its first century under the Constitution is a supreme record of achievement in the history of nations," he asserted, attributing to the economic progress of the young country rather a high world-historical importance. Smythe goes on to echo Turner's frontier thesis, perhaps even from a less ecologically aware perspective than Turner's own. In contemplating the conquest of arid America, Smythe does not fail to note admiringly that it was the conquest of humid America that got the country successfully through its first hundred years. "The material greatness of the United States," he posits, "is the fruit of a policy of peaceful conquest over the resources of a virgin continent"—certainly an uncritical application of the terms *conquest* and *virgin*. Further, in looking ambitiously toward the future, Smythe notes that "the conquest is only half accomplished."[29] With the best of intentions, Smythe perceived the desert regions as offering a wonderful opportunity to pursue the new science of irrigation. In the tradition of Josiah Gregg, John Wesley Powell, and especially Horace Greeley, he also saw in the desert a grand opportunity to exercise practical ingenuity.

But Smythe, like most of his contemporaries, was not simply interested in exploiting the land west of the hundredth meridian for the challenge of it. Nor was he interested in exploiting it in the same way that the land to the east had been exploited. Given the aridity of much of the West, such an endeavor looked difficult on its face, and as experiments with dry farming and with cattle and sheep ranching have subsequently shown, it was nearly impossible. In Smythe's eyes, however, the impossibility of approaching arid landscapes using traditional strategies was fortunate. Like Irving in the 1830s and Smythe's contemporaries Remington and Wister in the 1890s, all of whom saw the Southwest as a kind of grand proving ground for the young civilization of the United States, Smythe saw "the conquest of arid America" as a way for the country to demonstrate that it was in fact "a civilization new, distinctive, and more luminous and potential [sic] than any which preceded it in the world's long history."[30] He called the United States' future incarnation "The Republic of Irrigation."[31]

Contemplating the desert thus provoked a kind of domestic patriotism. There was plenty of work to be done right here in our desert backyard, work that would keep the country from going soft. In addition, the arid West provided a focal point for specific racial, often racist, anxieties about the future of Anglo-Saxon civilization, which looked to many Americans as if it were stagnating. In arguing for a concerted national initiative to irrigate the desert, Smythe formulated the problem thus: "The great engine of material progress stands idle in its tracks. The nation halts and falters upon a mysterious boundary line which marks the ending of familiar conditions and the beginning of problems strange and new to Anglo-Saxon men."[32] This argument was simply an extension of the conception of American civilization that Teddy Roosevelt, Owen Wister, Frederick Remington, and Frederick Jackson Turner had been developing since the beginning of the decade. Roosevelt's *Winning of the West,* from which the "shadowy dawn of history" theory of Anglo-Saxon progress came, provided the paradigm for this conquest model of America's history in the West. Roosevelt's version of the West, according to Alex Nemerov, "embodied the era's social Darwinism. In the Darwinian view of history the conquest of the frontier could be explained as only the latest in a centuries-old pattern of Anglo-Saxon victories."[33] This was a pattern that men like Smythe and Roosevelt meant to extend into Arizona and southern California.

If there is any doubt that textual versions of the desert became literal ones at the turn of the twentieth century, Roosevelt's first address to Congress on December 3, 1901, and the Reclamation Act, which Congress soon passed, should put it to rest. In his address, Roosevelt, demonstrating his sympathy with Smythe's approach to arid land, told Congress that the "reclamation and settlement of the arid lands will enrich every portion of our country, just as the settlement of the Ohio and Mississippi valleys brought prosperity to the Atlantic States." In the same address he advised Congress that the "western half of the United States would sustain a population greater than that of our whole country today if the waters that now run to waste were saved and used for irrigation."[34] By 1904, Roosevelt was able to tell Congress that during "the two and a half years that have elapsed since the passage of the Reclamation Act rapid progress has been made. . . . Construction has already begun on the largest and most important of the irrigation works."[35]

Aside from such straightforwardly progressive concerns about reclamation and manifest destiny, there is a distinct fixation with race and specifically with the evolution of the "Anglo-Saxon race" in turn-of-the-century discussions of the American desert. Smythe, Remington, Wister, Mary Austin, Ray Stannard Baker, Harriet Monroe, and other writers tended to confuse biological evolution with cultural evolution when they looked West. Austin seems to have avoided the chauvinism of her time to a great extent, although some of her references to race nevertheless grate a bit on the modern ear, as when, like Smythe, she referred to "the Amerind savage and the unlettered American pioneer" attempting to make the landscape fructify. To her credit, Austin articulated her racial theories with a fair amount of grace, noting that "both of these married the land because they loved it, and afterward made it bear. If more lines of natural development converged here, between the bracketing rivers, more streams of human energy came to rest than anywhere else within what is now the United States, it was because men felt here the nameless content of the creative spirit in the presence of its proper instrument."[36] Smythe was less tactful. It need not be particularly disturbing that the words "material progress" and "national greatness" appear in nearly every paragraph of Smythe's irrigation texts. But other words appear with equal frequency in such parabolic passages as this:

> The best crop ever grown on the trans-Mississippi plains sprung from wheat which perished ungathered in the parching winds of a rainless summer; and the most valuable grist ever ground in that locality came from a mill projected, but never built. To explain this paradox is to record the most dramatic incident of an evolutionary process which revealed the extraordinary possibilities of an apparently worthless region, and established industrial forms, unique in Anglo-Saxon experience, as the foundation of economic life in half a continent.[37]

The desert is the upcoming race-reforming challenge in the "Anglo-Saxon experience."

As anxieties over the future of the country became increasingly conflated with anxieties over the future of the white race, the desert became a field in which cultural elitism transmogrified into white supremacism, all under the sign of "the strenuous life" that could be pursued there. By 1902 the desert itself, due to its apparent hostility to most forms of living creatures, had begun to give people what Ray Stannard Baker described as "the impression of a strong man beset by a terrible weakness, but who is going forward with set jaws and straining muscles to conquer in spite of it."[38] The desert had somehow become a figure for an entire anxiety-ridden nation, a heroic male figure with a chiseled jaw.

In Baker's view, the desert helped Anglo Americans to realize the most noble possibilities of their race, which becomes painfully evident as he catalogs and ranks the human residents of the desert. At the low end of the hierarchy of desert humans, he placed "the aboriginal Indians, in every state of civilization and savagery." After them came "the Mexicans in great numbers, and in all mixtures of blood from the nearly pure Indian peon upward." Alongside these Mexicans were "African Negroes in considerable numbers, emigrants from the Southern States, and every town has its Chinese and usually its Japanese contingent, the overflow from California." Finally, "above all these, and in greatly superior numbers," he reported, apparently relying on faulty demographic figures, "rises the white man, usually American by birth, and yet generously mixed with many of European nationalities."[39] If Baker had left any doubt that his intention was to project across the Southwest a Rooseveltian version of history as a function of Anglo-Saxon conquest, he removed it in the following paragraphs. The men who took on the challenge of the Southwest (meaning the prospector, the cowboy, and the hunter) were "a healthy, rugged lot, virtually all pure Americans. The Rough Riders sprang from this element."[40]

This Rough Rider–breeding Southwest, then, alleviated the anxieties aroused by the closing of the frontier. The deserts provided a place to develop first-class Americans, and they did more than that. In the best Darwinian form, they culled out the Americans who were not first-class, for, as of May 1902, Baker said,

> there had been little immigration of Italians, Russians or the lower class of Irish, most of whom are by preference city-dwellers. The menial labor usually performed by these classes here falls largely to Mexicans, Chinese, and Indians. The Jew, as usual, has set up his trading-places here, and, as everywhere else, he thrives.
>
> It will be seen therefore, that the Southwest is peopled with the very best Americans, segregated by the eternal law of evolutionary selection, with almost no substratum of the low-caste European foreigner to lower the level of civilization. Of course there is no danger from the Indians, Negroes, Mexican, or Chinese, because there is rarely any mixing with them by marriage, as formerly. With such a start, and such a commingling of Americans from all parts of the Union, the man from Boston rubbing elbows with the Atlanta man, and Kansas working side by side with Mississippi, it would seem that the region may one day produce the standard American type.[41]

The desert—empty stage, virgin land, new beginning that it was—provided an opportunity for America to start over.

Admittedly, Baker—despite his progressive stance on "the color line," despite his earning W.E.B. DuBois' and Booker T. Washington's admiration, and despite his honorary induction into the NAACP in 1915—seems to have been afflicted by a particularly nasty racist streak. It would be inaccurate to infer that his entire audience of *Century* readers sympathized with him in the particulars of his racial paranoia, but many of his readers did agree with him on general principles. Harriet Monroe looked at the Painted Desert of Arizona and "felt the coming of new empires."[42]

Teddy Roosevelt looked at West Texas and saw empire and domination as well—white empire and domination. In his notorious response to Stephen Crane's "A Man and Some Others," Roosevelt advised Crane to write "another story of the frontiersman and the Mexican Greaser in which the frontiersman shall come out on top; it is more normal that way!"[43] William Smythe, the nation's leading proponent of irrigation in the West, could not exorcise the words "Anglo-Saxon conquest" from his vocabulary. According to Smythe, non-Anglos—that is, "Indian and Mexican irrigators"—were notable only for "their ignorance and laziness."[44] Ultimately Smythe, like Baker, saw white men in the desert as the vanguard of American civilization, the "pilgrim fathers of the new West."[45] Just as, during the seventeenth century, the pilgrim fathers had conquered a tangled green wilderness and shaped it into a civilization, then in the nineteenth century their Anglo-Saxon heirs, conveniently forgetting their Spanish precursors in the region, seemed to stand in a position to do the same for the western deserts, and given the rhetoric which surrounded the conquest, it promised to be just as racist and just as violent as any North American conquest of nature that had come before it.

Desert Play

The pragmatic impulse toward the desert that ran through the work of traders like Gregg and boosters like Smythe and Baker crested in the surprisingly chauvinistic irrigation empire rhetoric of the early twentieth century. But the playful impulse toward the desert that had arisen in Twain's *Roughing It* and lived on in dime westerns, desert adventure stories, and art like Frederic Remington's, reached a high point as well. Again, as the progress of Crane's western writing and Remington's western art implies, play in the deserts ultimately became much less fun as civilization moved into the region. This is not particularly surprising. It should be expected that civilizing institutions such as streetcars, women, babies, waterworks, and the bride who came to Yellow Sky might take the wildness out of the wilderness. But what is surprising is how desperately Americans insisted on clinging to stories of play in the desert and how long they insisted on playing there after it became apparent that the things that went on in the turn-of-the-century desert were deadly serious, as in the case of the white supremacists.

Remington produced most of his magazine fiction during the mid 1890s, when his artistic project to put cowboys and soldiers into heroic motion across the deadly wastes of Arizona was well underway. And if his Apollonian sculpture, in its understated depiction of heroic American virtue, left open at least the possibility that he had in mind an America in which all its citizens might better themselves, his magazine fiction exploded any such notion. All the social tension and racial anxiety that Baker, Smythe, and the other irrigation boosters managed to project into the world of desert work Remington, Wister, and other writers of magazine fiction managed to project into the world of desert play.

That world of play has the obligatory soldiers, cowpunchers, and horses in it, and for the most part none of them are remarkably different from the ones traditionally encountered in western American literature. Owen Wister supplied one such cowboy in the pages of *Harper's*. In a story called "Where Fancy Was Bred," he stands in a western street, antagonizing an old man standing in his front flower garden. The prototype Virginian feels compelled to stop and ask the man, "Picking nosegays?" because the old fellow's flower growing doesn't seem appropriate to this sparse and barren "country for men."[46]

Thomas A. Janvier, another representative magazine author, contributed another typical westerner, one Bill Hurt, to *Harper's*. Bill is a man who resembles nothing more than a non-ironic, broadly characterized Scratchy Wilson. Bill is a typical Wild Westerner who, in his misogyny, feels threatened by feminine domesticity: "When Bill Hurt, who was a good fellow and kept the principal store in Palomitas, got word his Aunt in Vermont was coming out to pay him a visit—it being too late to stop her, and he knowing he'd have to worry the thing through somehow till he could start her back East again—he was the worst broke-up man you ever saw."[47]

Remington also wrote and illustrated standard western fare, contributing to *Harper's* such pieces such as "The Essentials at Fort Adobe"—a dissertation on "horse-gymnastics," which he claimed was one of the chief elements of Indian-fighting. Remington and Wister collaborated in stories like "La Tinaja Bonita," which Wister wrote and Remington illustrated. "La Tinaja Bonita" tells in sentimental, paternalistic tones of a doomed Anglo-Mexican romance in which the Anglo man has to leave and the Mexican woman has to stay behind and suffer.

These desert narratives, taken in their monthly-magazine contexts, are enlightening. Although they are fictional, their central concerns differ little from the language of contemporary nonfiction magazine articles on the desert, which invariably discussed irrigation and land development. Like the nonfiction treatments, the desert fiction is concerned with empire building, civilization boosting, and the betterment of the "Anglo-Saxon race."

A stock character of such stories is the white man from back east who is equal to every situation—a typical western type. But in the Southwest, more than in other places, this white man is engaged in the project of ensuring the continuity of Anglo American civilization, the same project his engineer counterparts were pursuing as they "reclaim" the desert through irrigation.

Remington provided an early formulation of this white American destiny in an 1889 *Century* article, "Horses of the Plains." When he wrote it, the means by which the Anglo-Saxon conquest of the arid Southwest would be secured were as yet unclear in Remington's mind, so he displaced what he and Wister would later see in cowboys onto their horses even though, as Remington was quick to point out, there was a real contradiction between the good of horses and the good of people. As Remington put it in 1889, "the golden age of the bronco was ended some twenty years ago when the great tidal wave of Saxonism reached his grassy plains"—that is, when the Anglo-Saxon pushed the mustang out of its adopted ecosystem.[48] Nevertheless, Remington used the history of the horse as an allegory through which to project the future of the United States. Having recently been in Arizona, he reported firsthand the attributes of the bronco that had evolved in the deserts and high plains.

Remington found the horse to be a remarkable physical specimen. "I am not noted for any of the physical characteristics which distinguish a fairy," Remington is careful to state for the record, and when he rode the broncos "the thermometer stood as high as you please in the shade." Still, he continues,

> at the end of the journey I was confirmed in the suspicion that he was a most magnificent piece of horse-flesh for a ride like that, and I never expect to see another horse which can make the trip and take it so lightly to heart. He stood there like a rock, and was as good as at

starting. . . . Some of the best specimens of the horse and rider which I have ever had occasion to admire were Mexican *vaqueros,* and I have often thought the horses were more worthy than the men.[49]

The final illustration Remington made for his article, a perfectly poised, perfectly balanced man in a bowler hat riding his gaited (the man is posting in his English saddle), crop-tailed bronco through Central Park resonates with all the growing anxieties of the coming decade. Would that every man in New York City, the picture implies, spend some time in Arizona with a horse and bring back with him the grace and balance he had learned in the desert.

But a season in the desert was not an option for most New Yorkers, a problem which became harder and harder to ignore among those who propagated the myth of the chaparral-riding cowboy. Owen Wister's "Evolution of the Cowpuncher," published in 1895, represented a dead end, if not an ending, for play on the range, although Wister had trouble acknowledging this particular implication of his article. The piece began, fittingly enough, as a project entitled "The Course of Empire." In 1893, having given up law in favor of a writing career, Wister began an ambitious historical study that was probably modeled on Roosevelt's *The Winning of the West.*[50]

It developed that Wister had undertaken an overly ambitious project, or at least one that was too ambitious for his prospective editors. According to Ben Vorpahl, Henry Mills Alden, Wister's editor at *Harper's Monthly,* told Wister he "would have to wait until he had produced 'a series of pure adventure' in order to attract to himself and his subject matter the popular attention felt to be necessary for success in a large national magazine."[51] So Wister dutifully turned out the cowboy-and-Indian series *Red Men and White* to pave the way for his larger project.

But by 1894 Remington had talked Wister into engaging in the historical project of chronicling the rise of the cowboy. The article came out in September 1895 complete with illustrations by Remington. As Richard Etulain tactfully puts it, the article "summarizes Wister's ideas about race, reveals his view of the cowboy, and indicates his misgivings about the passing of the frontier and the coming of a new West."[52] "The Evolution of the Cowpuncher" is a disturbing, if representative, racist vision of Anglo-Saxon conquest in the empty spaces of the turn-of-the-century desert. Further, as Ben Vorpahl has argued in *My Dear Wister: The Frederic Remington–Owen Wister Letters,* the article is not so much about the evolution of the cowboy as it is about the reincarnation of the Anglo-Saxon in the cowboy, the Anglo-Saxon who overcomes the nastiness of urban civilization and the nastiness of the people who make up that civilization by remaking himself in the clean air of the Southwest. Wister's cowboy is the classic example of what Walter Prescott Webb presented as the "plainsman, as represented by the Indian fighter, the cowboy, the peace officer, and the bad man, [who] led a life that was full of novelty, spiced with danger, and flavored with adventure. At all times he was dependent on his own resources, which had to be many and varied."[53]

In his article Wister maintains that if one should set down in Texas an effete English nobleman who has been spoiled by the soft life of Europe, "[d]irectly . . . the slumbering untamed Saxon [awakes] in him" a "perfect athlete" who fits in beautifully with the other cowboys galloping through the bunchgrass.[54] This perfect Saxon athlete, in the purifying air of the desert, transcends even the filth of modern American civilization, and his is a vitally important transcendence in light of the fact that, when it comes to "our continent," "No rood of modern ground is more debased and mongrel with its hordes of encroaching alien vermin, that turn our cities to Babels and our citizenship to a hybrid farce, who degrade our commonwealth from a nation into something half pawn-shop, half broker's office."[55] Besides a pronounced, if typical, racial anxiety, Wister demonstrates here a remarkable capacity to live in blissful ignorance of the millions of dollars some cattle ranchers had made by converting the ecosystems of western Texas and eastern New Mexico into cash during the twenty years preceding the publication of his article.

Given his almost willful ignorance of what cattle ranching actually implied for the Southwest, Wister's reference to the pawnshop and broker's office was obviously not an indictment of venture capitalism; he thought ranching was a fine idea. As his article develops, it becomes apparent in Wister's treatment of the open country of Texas that his pawnshop comments are indeed the anti-Semitic slurs they appear to be: "to survive in the clean cattle country requires spirit of adventure, courage, and self-sufficiency; you will not find many Poles or Huns or Russian Jews in that district; it stands as yet untainted by the benevolence of Baron Hirsch."[56]

Immediately following this passage, Wister's fixation with desert wilderness becomes hysterical—and frightening even after a hundred years. "Cattle country"—the desert—provides something like a final solution to America's urban malaise. "Even in the cattle country," Wister exults,

> the respectable Swedes settle chiefly to farming, and are seldom horsemen. The community of which the aristocrat appropriately made one speaks English. [This "aristocrat" is the aforementioned Englishman whose "slumbering untamed Saxon" awoke when he moved to Texas.] The Frenchman to-day is seen at his best inside a house; he can paint and he can play comedy, but he seldom climbs a new mountain. The Italian has forgotten Columbus, and sells fruit. Among the Spaniards and the Portuguese no Cortez or Magellan is found to-day. Except in Prussia, the Teuton is too often a tame, slippered animal, with his pedantic mind swaddled in a dressing-gown. But the Anglo-Saxon is forever homesick for out-of-doors.
>
> Throughout his career it has been his love to push further into the wilderness, and his fate thereby to serve larger causes than his own.[57]

As a result, according to Wister, the Anglo-Saxon carried an especially difficult white man's burden in his treks across the desert wilderness, without the help even of the Teuton, who was dressed inappropriately.

At some point, then, the inadequacy of the figurative representations of the Southwest that Remington, Wister, and others contributed to the popular monthly magazines seems bound to have become apparent because of their *prima facie* ethnocentrism and bigotry. Still, what looks like racism from the perspective of today merely looked like pride in the superiority of Anglo-Saxons in 1895. Thus it was not the ethnocentrism of Wister's project that initially perjured his version of the Southwest. It was instead a historical fact that was fairly obvious even to Wister's audience: This transcendent, civilization-carrying Anglo cowpuncher had evolved right out existence by 1895. By that year there were enough fences and railheads, financed and built almost exclusively by white Anglo-Saxon Protestants, to have put thousands of Wister's cowboys out of work. The barbed-wire fence, and with it the closing of the open range, began as early as the late 1870s.[58] But neither Wister nor his audience was quite willing to come to terms with this historical fact. E. S. Martin praised Wister's article in an August 11, 1895, *Harper's Weekly* column. He noted that Wister's West was twenty years dead but still referred to it as if it existed and as if Wister had just returned to New York from a visit there:

> Mr. Wister's West is nearly twenty years older than Mr. Harte's, and is a country of cowboys instead of miners. Moreover, it is not the West of the Pacific, which the hand of man has already tamed, but the mid-West of the great plains, which is still sparsely settled and rudely populated. Mr. Wister has not merely been there, but has lived there, persistently and conscientiously, with his eyes and ears open, and his intellectual faculties alert. What he has brought back is valuable matter, and he sets it forth for all it is worth.[59]

Although this Southwest had not existed for at least twenty years, Martin writes about it in the present tense, which is how Wister struggled to think of it all through his article. But in the end even Wister had to admit that this world was gone. Progress had not selected the cowboy for survival, so the Anglo-Saxon of the desert wilderness "went to town for a job; he got a position on the railroad; he set up a saloon; he married, and fenced in a little farm; and he turned 'rustler,' and stole the cattle from the men for whom he had once worked."[60] He failed due to three circumstances that Wister concluded were beyond the cowboy's control: "the exhausting of the virgin pastures, the coming of the wire fence, and Mr. Armour of Chicago, who set the price of beef to suit himself."[61] And so "the cow-puncher, the American descendant of Saxon ancestors, who for thirty years flourished upon our part of the earth, . . . because he was not compatible with Progress, is now departed, never to return." Although Wister's "our part of the earth" would seem to indicate Arizona, New Mexico, and West Texas, it also seems likely that New York City mourned the extinct cowboy more than any other place in the nation.

In the closing sentence of his "Evolution of the Cowpuncher," Wister demonstrates how little the article really differed from its original incarnation as "The Course of Empire." He puts a cheerful, if exceedingly bizarre, face on the departure of the last civilizational and racial hope of the Anglo-Saxon in the person of the cowboy, managing somehow to conclude the piece with the Fourth of July:

[B]ecause Progress has just now given us the Populist and silver in exchange for [the cowpuncher], is no ground for lament. He has never made a good citizen, but only a good soldier, from his tournament days down. And if our nation in its growth have no worse distemper than the Populist to weather through, there is hope for us, even though present signs disincline us to make much noise upon the Fourth of July.[62]

In this passage Wister reveals that he really had been imagining Saxon knights in ten-gallon hats and boots with underslung heels jousting on the plains of New Mexico all along, even if he does talk the cowboy down in order to explain his early departure from the stage of history. Finally, even though by the end of his article Wister does seem less confident in staking the future of his civilization on some hoodlums stealing cattle in Texas, Arizona, and New Mexico, he and his sympathetic critic, Martin, reveal that the passing of the desert frontier, which for a time seemed to have survived the superintendent of the census's report, was a matter of grave concern for educated Anglo Americans. The manly Tournament in the Southwest had ended.

By the close of the century, two popular but paradoxical approaches to the desert had collapsed upon themselves. First, it had become apparent that Americans could not have their desert both ways. Anglos could not irrigate the wilderness and have it too, because irrigation consumed wilderness, transforming it into mundane cropland. Any one civilization can only "tame" the wilderness once (as the Anasazi, for instance, had done with this landscape in prehistory). Second, Americans couldn't play cowboy in the wilderness either. In eating their Kansas City steaks, supplied by Mr. Armour, they had consumed the original wilderness. Anglo Americans needed a third way into the desert, a way to conquer it without consuming it. Thus, as the last remnants of wilderness threatened to disappear, the irrigated desert and the wild desert became less and less viable as concepts. Another, less destructive way of conceiving of arid land arose, one that continues to inform much thinking about the desert today.

Desert Literature

If cowboys and irrigation ditches were thus inadequate to the purposes of a nation that was becoming enamored of desert wilderness, by the late

1890s other conceptions of the deserts that did not involve their immediate consumption began to appear. Just as Wordsworth, Emerson, and Thoreau before them had learned to attribute value to the wildest versions of nature precisely because this nature was innocent of human concerns, writers such as Harriet Monroe began to think of the desert as valuable in its extreme wildness. The parts of the deserts that had not been irrigated or denuded by sheep or cattle began to appear attractive to Anglo American eyes; desert became something like an aesthetic commodity. During the 1890s, as Crane's travel dispatches ironically attest, convenient, safe railroad travel was making the wilderness more accessible to large numbers of Americans (although the term *wilderness* must be used advisedly to describe any landscape with a railroad running through it). Late Victorian wealth put leisure travel within the reach of rich and upper-middle-class people in the United States—the people who became Thorstein Veblen's "leisure class," conspicuously engaged in nearly every sort of vigorous activity except work.

This wealth, one of the material benefits American society had generated by exploiting the natural resources of the continent, was also one of the leading causes of the uneasiness that manifested itself at the turn of the century in such cultural institutions as the pursuit of the "strenuous life" and in the Boy Scouts, the Sierra Club, and the general social and racial anxiety of the time. Americans who became increasingly invested in the idea of abstention from hard work as a mark of respectability were left with fewer and fewer constructive activities to pursue.[63] While William Smythe was assuaging this uneasiness by inventing new conceptual conquests to undertake in irrigating the West, and while Remington and Wister were grimly hanging on to their cowboys, other writers took what came to be considered a higher approach.

In 1898, Nathaniel Shaler—the dean of the Lawrence Scientific School, a former student of Louis Agassiz at Harvard, and a "voluminous contributor to magazines and scientific journals" such as *Century, Scribner's,* and *Harper's*[64]—suggested a direction humans might take in their effort to lift up their civilization, a direction that would not produce the sorts of problems inherent in environmental exploitation. He suggested that Americans learn to see their continent as an aesthetic resource rather than an economic resource.

Shaler had long been a critic of the massive exploitation undertaken by the United States after the Civil War, and he added an aesthetic dimension to this critique in his 1898 *Atlantic* article "The Landscape as a Means of Culture." The idea that nature is simply "the world around [us]" and that people could profit from learning to appreciate its beauty instead of ceaselessly endeavoring to consume its resources is one of the central tenets of his argument. "The habits of civilized life," he begins, "tend to separate men from the charm of the world around them." He then describes industrial capitalist civilization more directly: "The insistent activities which are the price of success, in the effort to win the harvests of an immediately profitable kind, fix the attention on certain limited fields of the environment, and necessarily exclude all recognition of the larger features of nature."[65] And in a remarkable reconstruction of the social Darwinist, evolutionary-progress rhetoric (as well as the profit-and-loss rhetoric) of his time, Shaler makes an argument for nature. He warns that the tendency to ignore nature shown by civilized people in 1898 represents

> no new state of man; indeed, by the demands of economic life, the primitive savage and the barbarian have ordinarily followed in the path of the prehuman species whence they came, giving no more heed to the scenes about them than their needs called for. Now and then, in moments of poetic exaltation, the beauty of the natural realm has forced itself on their attention, but only the rarer spirits see that there is here a great field to be won for the profit of man. The art of appropriating the landscape is not a lost art, but one which is yet to be invented and applied to the profit of our kind.[66]

Here in the pages of the *Atlantic Monthly* Shaler in one stroke turns the self-congratulatory progressive rhetoric of Roosevelt, Smythe, Remington, Carnegie, and in fact all of venture capital America back on itself and points out that the one thing Anglo Americans have never learned to do is to appreciate nature in and of itself, apart from its economic potential. Shaler makes this shortcoming a problem soluble only by civilizational advancement, shrewdly mobilizing the national anxiety over the malaise of American civilization in support of his cause.

As Joseph Porter relates, the paradigm of society in America during Shaler's time held that human culture moved along a rising curve,

progressing from the "primitive" societies of indigenous peoples to Western industrial civilization, and thus that "the Euroamerican culture represented the highest level of social evolution."[67] Shaler's is an anthropocentric argument that only accidentally benefits rocks, trees, the green
wilderness, and the desert wilderness, and he does not try to present it as
an altruistic plea for the pure good of nature. That sort of biocentric argument would not become truly current in mainstream American culture
until after such events as Aldo Leopold's founding of the Wilderness Society in 1924. Shaler is interested in facilitating the process of "social
evolution."

Thus to Shaler the natural landscape is important because of its association with people. The landscape provides an answer to one of the
pressing questions of Shaler's day: How can humans, having stopped
natural selection in its tracks through the process of civilization, make
the next move up the evolutionary ladder? As Porter explains in his biography of the nineteenth-century ethnologist John Gregory Bourke, pre-
vailing contemporary theories of social development, articulated most
influentially by the American Lewis Henry Morgan, held that "social development [was] a continuing process with societies progressing from
savagery to civilization."[68] Nineteenth-century ethnologists such as Bourke
and John Wesley Powell followed the lead of eighteenth-century Scottish
Enlightenment philosophers such as David Hume, whose school of thought
held that, according to Joseph Porter, "all human society represented
'progress' from 'rudeness' or 'savagery' to 'civilization.' "[69]

Shaler's concept of "landscape as a means of culture" has an investment in this ethnological paradigm of cultural development. His position
is that people should continue to move away from rudeness and towards
civilization by refining themselves into deep, aesthetic appreciators of
nature in the same way they have "evolved" into appreciators of music
or drama. "[T]he pleasure which we have from music or from the drama,"
he explains, "is of the same primitive nature as that which the earth's
prospects afford. Yet these arts have been subjected to a process of culture, to the vast advantage of men."[70] On a more basic level, by conceiving of the aesthetic enjoyment of nature to be similar to the aesthetic enjoyment of art, Shaler shows that, just as "[e]ven more purely instinctive
actions, such as the movements of the limbs," may be "removed from the
animal plane" by "training in dancing or fencing," the natural responses

to natural stimuli may be trained into a *"second nature* stage of the culture" which "again makes [man] free with a perfected freedom."[71] Learning to understand the nonhuman world on an aesthetic level rather than
an instinctive or practical one was to be one of the next steps in human
evolution, one which might move American society past the instrumental
relationship to landscapes implicit, for instance, in desert irrigation projects, which are necessary things but not, in Shaler's view, transcendent
ones.

Shaler's article was part of a general impulse in the quality magazines
to help bootstrap American culture to a higher plane, an impulse that
Fletcher Harper, first managing editor of *Harper's,* expressed as a wish that
his magazine fill the role of educator to the popular culture of the time[72]
and that it would "place within reach of the great mass of the American
people the unbounded treasures of the Periodical Literature of the present day." The "great mass"—the restless population of urban Americans
whom periodical authors imagined they were reaching through the magazines—stood to benefit from the disbursement of "unbounded treasure"
that, in Harper's view, only something as culturally rich as "Periodical
Literature," capitalized, could offer.

Nature, approached not as potential farmland and lumber but as an
aesthetic subject, was one such treasure. Shaler gave one of the most coherent articulations of the connection between aesthetic nature appreciation and the progress of American cultures, but he was by no means the
only writer engaged on the topic. Four years before Shaler's "Landscape
as a Means of Culture" appeared in the *Atlantic,* an anonymous piece
entitled "Man and Men in Nature" had appeared in the same magazine.
The writer had observed a new, contemplative, noninstrumental thinking
about nature, which he described in breathless prose. He concluded that
"[t]here is something dramatic in the present attitude of thinking men towards the great question of man's relation to the Cosmos." "Of old," he
writes, "this problem was one for mild speculation." Now, however, the
"greater host" of humans wait for the answers to questions about nature
"in terms of hope and duty," feeling compelled by discoveries about nature
"to go forth on the great march towards a promised but unknown land."[73]

This intellectual questing, for which the peregrinations of medieval
knights-errant become the author's metaphor, takes place in a desert:
"All great wanderings of folk are tragedies," he intones, "whether they be

over the desert of reality or the ideal wastes of belief."[74] These are the same ideal wastes of belief in which Crane sets his desert poems—the bare and rocky ground on which the post-Darwinian intellectual often found himself stranded. But one is never stranded in these deserts; they are actually a desirable place to wander. In their innocence of anything human, they provide an opportunity to contemplate and to learn. As did Shaler, the author of this article promises an inchoate intellectual prize at the end of his nature quest through the wastes.

The implication of the author of "Man and Nature" that the desert would be the most likely setting in which to quest after a new relationship with nature was a fortuitous one. The desert would provide the setting for many attempts to work out a new aesthetically defined relationship at the turn of the century. These attempts are the culmination of the project Clarence Dutton had undertaken in the "Point Sublime" passage of his *Tertiary History* in 1882. A fair portion of "quality" magazine readers were members of a growing tourist class—privileged members, because train travel to the West was not cheap. Descriptions of the western landscapes undertaken in elevated language appealed to these readers. Magazine contributors, supplying such descriptions, created for themselves the "special culture" of viewers that Dutton had predicted would be necessary if Anglo Americans were ever to appreciate the scenery of arid regions. Also, as attested by the relationship between "On Bright Angel Trail" and the advertisements that follow it in *McClure's*, railroad companies were interested in buying advertising space in the issues in which such descriptions appeared. There was, ironically, a potential for making money from the aesthetic desert.

Apart from their developing economic potential, deserts inspired magazine contributors to resort to high and broad abstractions. Arid nature provoked ruminations on Good, Power, Force, and God. In articles about the deserts there arises the firm conviction that being able to understand the sublime beauty of the desert (even when such understanding was mediated through the pages of a magazine) could put one in touch with the Truth. In as mystical a piece of nature writing as ever appeared in the *Atlantic*, Verner Z. Reed posits that

[d]eserts are equal to the sea in the ideas they give of extent, solitude, and infinity, and equal to the mountains in beauty and weirdness. . . .

[T]here is silent communion with the powers and laws of nature, with the Power or Force or God that somewhere back of its visible and invisible mysteries looks so carefully after the things that exist. . . . They are the places where Truth wears no disguises, and whose face may be studied even by a fool.[75]

These deserts, Reed continued, "have a physical beauty" that "varies with each one as much as do the individual beauties and peculiar attractions of different ranges of mountains." The different beauties lead people to a state "away from all the mistakes and cares that burden life in the inhabited places"—a Truth that is all the more attractive because it is found outside civilization. The deserts provide a "counter-irritant" to the evils of American civilization, for

[w]hen the Juggernaut car of Civilization presses unduly and unusually hard, when things are most out of joint, when the disease of progress is at such an acute and critical stage that a powerful counter-irritant is needed, then the beauties of the hottest and most barren desert are unfolded, and are appreciated, as is strong drink after exposure to severe cold.[76]

Here Reed explicitly sets the beauty of the desert over and against the ills of civilization and looks to the desert for salvation. Concluding his article, Reed anthropomorphizes the desert and puts cautionary words in its mouth. "'Come to me,'" the desert calls,

for I am solitude, and in solitude is wisdom. Come to me, for I am silence, and in silence is communion with God. Come to me, for I am beauty, and beauty is a thing beyond the creation of Cæsar or of Midas. But come not to me at all unless you come in humility and right thinking, for in exacting those things I am as one with God, and with me a king is no greater than a beggar.[77]

The beauty of the desert becomes a corrective for the ills of nineteenth-century American civilization.

Such desert ecstasies as these recorded in magazines like the *Atlantic Monthly* often provided not only a spiritual transcendence but also a social transcendence. As it developed in the monthly magazines, people who could appreciate the difficult, strange, and weird landscapes of the desert could do so because they were more "civilized" than other people, as Shaler had suggested they might be in "Landscape as a Means of Culture." To understand the mysteries of the desert was to possess advanced sensibilities—remarkably advanced American sensibilities—which sometimes eclipsed even Continental sensibilities. Ten years before she became, through her magazine *Poetry,* one of the chief arbiters of literary taste in America, Harriet Monroe visited Arizona. As she experienced its landscape, she was moved to express regret at having "wander[ed] in history-haunted Europe" and wasted her time in Italy, all the while living in ignorance of the Earth's "sublimest secrets," which were to be found in Arizona. Monroe claims to have been mistaken in her original fixation with Italian art, because

> [i]ts beauty is self-contained and measurable; one rests in it with profound content, analyzes and imitates it without taking a step forward. Have not the Italians themselves become the slaves of their own past, so that for centuries they have been incapable of anything but banalities in art? In Arizona, on the contrary, man has done nothing, and even Nature has done no little things. There Nature is not conciliatory and charming; she is terrible and magnificent. With one stroke of her mighty arm she lays bare the foundations of the earth, with one hot breath she strips the soil; and we venture into those ultimate primitive ages—the beginning and the end of things—upon whose fundamental immensity and antiquity our boasted civilization blooms like the flower of a day. It is not strange, perhaps, that we should quail from this unfamiliar and incomprehensible beauty.[78]

But unlike Dutton's projected observer twenty years earlier, who was not a member of the "special culture" capable of appreciating this "incomprehensible" beauty, Monroe assumes that her reader can participate in her appreciation of the overwhelming landscape, and given the twenty-five or so articles about deserts published in the quality monthlies within five years of hers, it appears that her assumption was correct.

The unfamiliar desert scenery takes Monroe out of her accustomed world and moves her into one of pure possibility. The "magic of the scene" of Arizona inspires her to see "the strangest transformations."[79] She describes truly sublime, transformative chromatic visual experiences in the desert, as when the sun sets and through a wide crevice in the nearer purple hills, range after range of distant mountains shaded off through the whole rich scale of violet to a scarlet horizon, from which the sky paled upward through yellow and green to a vivid blue at the zenith. Only a swift five minutes was given for this vision, before we rounded the hills, which spared us the tragedy of its failing, and then gradually the darkness fell and the stars came out—Arizona stars, which love the earth better than those we know in the North.[80]

The remarkable desert vegetation, the saguaros with their "white flowers at the tip of the obelisk, flowers springing white and wonderful out of this dead, gaunt, prickly thing" she regards as "Nature's consummate miracle, a symbol of resurrection more profound than the lily of the fields" and more profound than the "utter solemn words" of the Sphinx.[81] Monroe here engages the desert in terms so enthusiastic that her description would have been incomprehensible to Josiah Gregg or Susan Shelby Magoffin and would probably have proven challenging even for Clarence Dutton.

Other writers followed in her path. William Allen White saw an opportunity for transcendence at the rim of the Grand Canyon, on Bright Angel Trail, where "[o]ne may hold communion with . . . Nature, as God made it." And he cautioned that "[t]he pilgrim to the Cañon must not go as one who visits a peep-show or a freak of Nature, but approach it as Moses came to the burning bush."[82] Even Ray Stannard Baker, after he had excoriated the Jews and Native Americans who were abroad in the arid regions, noted that "[y]ou feel your smallness here, your utter helplessness in the face of the great, impassive, elemental things of nature; but it calms you like music. Crowded cities and the fever of men seem unreal, far-distant, improbable to you; you feel God, and you never forget."[83]

Mary Austin, in an article from an *Atlantic Monthly* series that would later become part of her classic desert book *The Land of Little Rain*, presents one of the few constructive "strenuous life" allegories in American literature, one gleaned from observations of the desert Amaranthus. Her figure has none of the obligatory jingoism that informs traditional "strenuous life" constructions: "It is recorded in the report of the Death Valley expedition," she recalls, "that after a year of abundant rains, on the Colorado desert was found a specimen of Amaranthus ten feet high. A year later the same species in the same place matured in the drought at four inches. One hopes the land may breed like qualities in her human off-spring, not tritely to 'try,' but to do."[84] Despite an occasional slip into the sort of broad abstraction that clouded the writing of her contemporaries, as when she describes desert mountains as "forsaken of most things but beauty and madness and death and God,"[85] Austin characteristically ben-efited from observing the small, specific interactions between desert dwellers and their arid environment. The challenge of Austin's Amaran-thus is to survive the desert, not to conquer it.[86]

It seems, then, that by the early years of the century, many well-read Americans from outside the region had been given the opportunity to learn how to appreciate the desert without destroying it, to enjoy it with-out consuming it, and to love it without killing it. Simply to see the des-ert, to learn to appreciate its visual music in the same way people had learned through the centuries of their rising civilization to appreciate ac-tual auditory music, had become a sufficient means of interaction in the minds of many Americans. And simply looking at an ecosystem does not destroy it.

Does not destroy it, that is, unless people have learned to look at ecosystems with the self-contradictory gaze with which Anglo Americans had begun to look at the desert. The truly remarkable aspect, to modern readers, of Harriet Monroe's description of sunset over desert mountains is not the chromatic detail she manages to express in the description, re-markable as her expression is. The truly remarkable thing is that she was viewing the sunset through a veil of locomotive smoke. She experienced her wilderness from a train. William Allen White and his bride experi-enced theirs within a mile or two of the porch of the El Tovar Hotel. T. Mitchell Prudden, recording "Glimpses of the Great Plateau" for *Harper's* in 1901, inserted a plug both for the Rio Grande Railroad and the booming town of Mancos: "Perhaps the best place, accessible by rail, from which to get a first glimpse of the plateau country and its ruins is the little town of Mancos, in southwestern Colorado, on the Denver and Rio Grande railroad."[87] By 1903, railroads seem to have become, in the eyes of some *Scribner's* editors and readers, natural parts of the desert scene. To judge by articles such as Benjamin Brooks's "The Southwest from a Locomotive," the train ride itself had become one of the challenges of the landscape, a change in desert travel conditions indicating that American sensibilities had developed quite a bit of conceptual flexibility where arid wilderness was involved. Instead of brave Latino men who left the bones of their horses beside the trail somewhere on the Jornada del Muerto in New Mexico, the challenging landscape now exhibited eastern travelers boasting, like Brooks, that they "had come West a truly interminable distance" on the train before they could look out the windows and say, "Yes, this [is] surely the West."[88]

And when train travelers looked out their windows, it was indeed a recognizable desert West they saw. It was the Yellow Sky West, although Brooks perceived Arizona with none of the irony with which Stephen Crane had perceived Texas. At times Brooks is strikingly cognizant of the symbolic role this landscape played in dividing the wilderness from civilization, seeing the foothills of the Rockies as "a line of dim hills, the buttresses of the mountain forts that guard a still mysterious land against 'the course of empire.'"[89] But along with his fascination with the mountains goes a contradictory, and very uncritical, tendency to thrill at seeing "Remington's cow-boy, broad-hatted and long-spurred, leaning nonchalantly down from Remington's lean, unkempt horse" as the horse tries to buck the cowboy off in front of the depot.[90] And in a remarkable conflation of aestheticism, ecological awareness, railroad boosting, and real-estate promotion, Brooks, in the space of one page, "learn[s] that all those things the artists drew—the cow-boys, the Indians, the long-horned cattle, the savage little horses—really did exist." In fact, it does seem possible, given the mutually beneficial effects of railroad tourism and showy cowboy culture on one another, that he may have seen a cowboy or two near the train station. Brooks reacts with enthusiasm to their color—literally. He breathlessly assures his readers that the "impossible colors" in which cowboys, Indians, and longhorns are usually represented in magazines are "true." Further, he shows a dawning sense of the ecological distinctiveness and integrity of this desert:

One bunch of yellow "cowgrass," one green-gray sage-brush, one bit of red earth (for all Eastern Arizona is red)—how would they look, I wonder, transplanted together in some every-day Eastern place? Like nothing at all, I presume; yet here each homely thing seemed radiant with a something of its own. The fabled rose-colored spectacles could not accomplish greater transformations; for where the yellow grass stretched away it was yellower than any color in the most impressionable impressionist's color box, and where the bare red earth was visible, it was red as blood.[91]

Two paragraphs later he makes certain to add that, in Tucson, "the poorest man may still have sun on all sides of his house and plenty of ground," because the city is "so new it has never yet occurred to the streets to go and get paved."[92]

Here is Shaler's "landscape as a means of culture" in its most constructive form, followed by a very practical observation pertaining to real-estate speculation. With its careful attention to ecological detail, Brooks's description might have represented a satisfactory perspective from which to begin the next century in the desert—had he not recorded it from atop a 130-ton Pegasus locomotive, which, to his delight, rested on "eight great drivers nearly seven feet in diameter" and had he refrained from imagining Remington's cow-boys everywhere he looked and noting that corner lots were still available at low prices in Tucson.[93]

But Brooks, along with other contributors to the monthly magazines of the late nineteenth century, did not refrain from conflating aestheticism and boosterism. Indeed, it would be unreasonable to expect him, or any of his contemporaries, to have done so. Although the idea of a purely aesthetic appreciation of the desert divorced from more prosaic concerns such as economic exploitation might be overwhelmingly attractive, it is the case that such a "pure" appreciation, given the symbiotic relationship between arid landscapes and literary culture at the turn of the century, would probably have been impossible. In their genesis, in their propagation through American culture, in their economic ramifications, and in the practical technological developments they embrace (developments that ranged from transcontinental railroads to mass circulation magazines to cheap color reproduction techniques), the three different deserts—the desert of the progressives, the desert of the playboys, and the desert of the writers—which on the surface appear to be radically different from one another, are interrelated.

From its early articulation in magazines, the idea of "landscape as a means of culture," as Shaler put it, or of "man's relation to the Cosmos," as the anonymous *Atlantic* contributor put it, had to do with progress—the evolutionary, civilizationwide progress mandated by the tenets of social Darwinism and industrial capitalism. The natural progression of the world's affairs, people believed, was for things, especially human civilization, to get bigger and better. Thus the conception of progress that led Shaler to suggest that Anglo Americans would better themselves by learning to appreciate the beauty of nature is the same conception of progress that led William Smythe to hope that Anglo-Saxons would better themselves by conquering the desert, and they are both integrally related to the conception of progress that led Ray Stannard Baker to hope that Anglo-Saxons would rise above the mud-people of the cities by moving out onto the harsh fastnesses of the western deserts.

The impulse to profit from the desert's beauty shares its provenance with the impulse to conquer the desert and profit from its resources, and in the work of magazine contributors ranging from Baker to Wister to Austin the two approaches remained Siamese twins. In the last paragraph of the article in which she presents her humble Amaranthus allegory, for instance, Austin unself-consciously refers to her "sense of mastery as the stars move in the wide clear heavens" above the desert,[94] a sense of mastery that in the next twenty years would evolve into what she called "that sense of mastery over the environment which is the first awakening of man to the presence of God within himself."[95]

Further, because these various deserts grew up together—with one functioning as an aesthetically pleasing natural wilderness and the other two functioning as the next proving grounds for the Anglo-Saxon race, they are difficult to separate. As the epigraph to this chapter shows, it is possible to find literary treatments of the desert at the turn of the century that make unself-conscious appeals both to the idea of "the coming of new empires" and to "the unspeakable hope and unspeakable sadness of the wilderness" in the same sentence, as if empire and wilderness were in no way contradictory. Because of the portmanteau aspect of the quality magazines in which the puzzle of the desert was worked out—as in *The Atlantic Monthly: A Magazine of Literature, Science, Art and Politics*—all that was "high," or "quality," or "refined," or "polite" tended to be grouped together and sold in two-hundred-page lots. Thus, Mary Hallock Foote's mauzy piazza scene looked perfectly at home in William Smythe's irrigation propaganda piece "Ways and Means in Arid America" because both pieces seemed to be related to a "better life" theme.

In addition, by the time the twentieth century was well under way, it was possible to sell the untouched desert wilderness as an aesthetic

Mary Hallock Foote's dreamy illustration for William Smythe's article "Ways and Means in Arid America" implies not only that arid America was suitable for irrigation but also that an irrigated desert would become a domesticated, pastoral, even Edenic landscape. (*Century* 51 [1896]: 753)

commodity. As Ann Ronald has shown in discussing Nevada nature writers, "aesthetics may be a cash crop, too."[96] Thus the chromatic wonder of far-off mountains and wildflower-drowned desert valleys behaved like copper mines or railroad rights-of-way or irrigable land. The wonder returned money, and in so doing it gave an unintended dimension to Shaler's "profit of our kind." In addition to being a place where people could learn to appreciate the value of a place completely outside of their previous experience, the desert also became a place to which the Santa Fe Railway, the Harvey House Company, and the magazines that ran their ads could sell excursions. Aside from the fact that the vague, race-uplifting sort of profit gained from learning a new aesthetic often became confused with the more definite profit involved in exploiting the natural resources of the desert, the aesthetic profit itself became commodified as a tourist attraction when it could be easily transformed into tourist dollars.

Finally, this seemingly benign, aesthetically conceived desert involved an always-already-lost element. That most people who saw the desert did so by train, and that the trains ran on tracks that had been surveyed for purposes such as bringing borax back to industrial civilization from the Mojave Desert meant that the wilderness, the harsh aesthetic wonderland of the deserts, was doomed as soon as large numbers of people were capable of seeing it. The very same rails that brought refined tourists in to look at desert mountains also brought salt, copper ore, and gypsum back out. Baker proudly watched a locomotive, probably in the Salton Basin, "breathing sonorously in the palpitating air" as it waited "to carry a load of salt to people of distant cities." Fortunately for men and for the desert, to Baker's way of thinking, a pioneer "came here and learned that this spot was the bottom of an ancient sea, and that this was the salt of the waves which once dashed on these silent beaches, here precipitated; and he came in with men and plows to make the desert fruitful."[97] This is a practical paradox that Americans have yet to work out. The very devices that make the desert wilderness accessible to our aesthetic sensibilities also make it accessible to industrial capitalism and recreational tourism. The Americans of 1902 were not delusional fools; they had a large part of the nation to "tame," and their way of looking at its deserts was a function of the task in which they were engaged. Neither are Americans of the present delusional fools. If our continent has indeed been tamed, we should learn a lesson from its tamers: Seeking aesthetic escape the way our culture currently does—through ecotourism, for instance—is a human endeavor that works no differently in the desert than it does elsewhere. Aesthetic escapes are experiences that people enjoy immensely and for which an ecosystem must pay dearly.

Chapter **5**

But not even the spot deserted by reptiles shall escape the industry or the avarice (as you please) of man. —John C. Van Dyke[1]

A Desert Paradox

The nascent aesthetic desert, though it was in general vaguely conceptualized, nevertheless exhibited one unequivocal characteristic: In the eyes of late-Victorian Americans, it was wild. Because industrial civilization tended to destroy what contemporary taste held to be natural beauty, deserts were beautiful precisely to the extent that they were wild. Unfortunately for those who like neat distinctions, however, interpretive approaches to wilderness during the time ranged along a continuum. Hands-on empire building—taming the wilderness—represented one extreme, while awe-struck observation of its beauty from a safe distance represented the other. But more often than not—as in the case of Ray Stannard Baker's "The Great Southwest," for example—writers conflated the entire range of approaches into one amorphous, vaguely conceived desert sensibility. With very few exceptions (Mary Austin may have been one, and John Muir was perhaps another) late-nineteenth-century magazine contributors were unable either to see or to avoid the contradiction of applauding arid beauty while at the same time applauding Anglo America's desert conquests. As long as the aesthetic desert remained a product of cultural venues such as the "quality" magazines and on a larger scale a function of the progressive culture that produced and consumed such cultural commodities, it remained trapped in a series of forced marriages to the irrigated desert, the Anglo-Saxon desert, and the railroad tourism desert.

In 1901, at the height of the debate over arid land and how it might fit into U.S. culture, John C. Van Dyke—professor of art history at Rutgers College, librarian of the Gardner A. Sage Library of New Brunswick Theological Seminary, and a widely known art critic whose articles appeared regularly in *Century Illustrated* magazine—published a small book entitled *The Desert*. He persuaded his audience that he had written it during a three-year solo trek across the Mojave, Colorado, and Sonoran Deserts.[2] Van Dyke's was the first purely aesthetic book-length treatment of the American deserts in English, and it has provided a model for literary treatments of the region to this day. Lawrence Clark Powell, in fact, holds that "All Southwestern book trails lead to *The Desert* by John C. Van Dyke."[3]

If Powell has overestimated the book's importance, it is not by much. Years after *The Desert* was published, Edward Everett Ayer, who had first traveled through the Southwest in 1862 as part of Major Harvey Fergusson's California Column, remarked in a journal entry for June 9, 1918, "I had been on the desert 30 years before I really had any idea of its grandeur or its beauty."[4] Ayer had written Van Dyke a letter two years before, advising him that *The Desert* had profoundly affected not only him but also his friend Benjamin Winchell, the vice-president and traffic manager of the Union Pacific Railroad. Winchell had "sat up until two o'clock reading it and was anxious to go on the Desert again. He had often recognized the feeling that [Van Dyke] expressed, but never had known himself how to express it or put it together."[5] It seems to have taken Van Dyke's book to enable them to comprehend their feelings for the place.

The Desert seems to have affected tens of thousands of Americans in a similar way. It was reprinted fourteen times by its original publisher between 1901 and 1930 and again in 1976 by the Arizona Historical Society, and in 1980 Peregrine Smith included the book in its Literary Naturalists series, in which form it remains in print, selling about a thousand copies a year.

The book's influence during its first series of imprints was quite remarkable. It was reviewed not only in the United States in such magazines as *Critic* and *The Dial* (which reviewed both the original 1901 edition and the photographically illustrated 1918 edition) but also in England in the *Athenaeum*. The *Dial* treatments exemplify the sort of reception the book received. In the review of the 1901 edition, entitled "In the Western Wastes," *The Dial's* reviewer enthusiastically reports, in language he or she copied from the book's preface-dedication, that "[i]n Professor John C. Van Dyke we have at last a pathfinder through these wastes who does not pin Nature to a board and chart her beauties with square and compass, but portrays her glory, her grandeur, and her mystery with an artist's appreciation of color and form and with a Nature-lover's enthusiasm for this somewhat novel and unusual part of the out-of-door world."[6] Seventeen years later, when the book came out with photographic illustrations by J. Smeaton Chase, *The Dial* was no less enthusiastic. In its illustrated form, the reviewer said, the book "re-creates the great arid stretches of the Southwest pictorially, poetically, and scientifically—such a satisfying and altogether delightful blend as one seldom meets in an authoritative work. The fact that, after seventeen years in print, the subject matter is still fresh is evidence of something more than the changeless quality of the desert."[7]

Critics have thus accorded the book an influential place in the canon of desert literature. Peter Wild holds that *The Desert* "did what few books do. . . . As the first work to praise the desert for its beauty, it led the way in a major shift of the culture's outlook on the arid portion of its natural heritage."[8] Franklin Walker sees in it the first extensively developed "major break in the traditional attitude toward the desert," the nation's general distrust, that is, of the barrenness of the landscape.[9] So pervasive has the influence of *The Desert* been that it is generally acknowledged to be a "predecessor of most desert writing since its publication, from works by Mary Austin, Joseph Wood Krutch, Edwin Corle, and on down to those by Edward Abbey and Ann Zwinger."[10]

Part of the reason for this success in re-creating the American deserts is that Van Dyke had been accustomed to creating, mediating, and revising Anglo American tastes long before he traveled to the Southwest. Not only was he an author of popular books of art history, but by the late 1890s when he left New Jersey for the desert, he had also firmly established himself as an art critic. His articles appeared regularly in *Century Illustrated* in the three years before his desert trip, and they continued to do so after he returned home to the campus of Rutgers College. He was a renowned Rembrandt scholar. At his death in 1932, the New York news-papers remembered him almost solely for the controversy he had raised by challenging the attribution of nearly a thousand reputed Rembrandts around the world. They gave no hint that he had ever been to the desert.[11]

But Van Dyke's range of talent extended far beyond the merely schol-arly. His reputation as a well-versed New York aesthete notwithstanding, Van Dyke also gave the appearance of being a Rooseveltian outdoorsman. According to his own account, for years he had wandered alone and with very little provision across some of the continent's harshest arid ecosys-tems and had survived where many before him had died. Readers of *The Desert* have until very recently assumed that its author possessed the mind of a scholar and the soul of a mountain man—an intriguing combi-nation that has done nothing but increase both the book's popularity and its influence.

Nevertheless, the fact is that Van Dyke's contact with wild nature in the desert was much less direct than he liked to claim, as Peter Wild and Neil Carmony point out. They describe a pattern of errors, misrepresenta-tions, and outright impossibilities in Van Dyke's work that seem to dis-count his solo desert experience. One does not survive for years alone in the desert while suffering, as he apparently did, under the delusions that rattlesnakes are in fact sluggish and that Gila monsters are harmless.[12] In the Southwest, Van Dyke most likely sat on the front porch of his broth-er's ranch house and rode the train to locations around the countryside.[13] In 1901 he sent the corrected tearsheets for his book *Old English Masters, Engraved by Timothy Cole* back to the Century company not from a desert water hole but from the Hotel Almada, in Guaymas, Mexico, which its stationery proclaimed to be a "Hotel Moderno de Primera Clase."[14]

Nonetheless, the strong probability that Van Dyke faked the trip out of which *The Desert* arose does not diminish the book. If anything, it makes his narrative more compelling, for the deception he perpetrated in 1901 has colored American perceptions of the desert for the past ninety years. Because, as David Lowenthal suggests, people tend to see the nature that surrounds them through "preferred and accustomed glasses," and be-cause Van Dyke reground modern America's "preferred glasses" for des-ert applications, he and his book provide an opportunity to understand better the process by which our culture learned to appreciate arid land-scapes.[15] If Van Dyke departs from the facts of his sojourn when he recounts it, then those departures must be addressed, because they are part of that process.

Significantly, the provenance of *The Desert* lies as much in Van Dyke's experience as an art historian in New Jersey as in his experience of southern California or Arizona. In his position as the first professor of art history at Rutgers College and in his published art criticism, Van Dyke had developed his own fairly complex art aesthetic before he visited the desert, and it became the nature aesthetic that informs *The Desert*.

Like John Ruskin, who influenced him greatly, Van Dyke believed that in nature lay the highest beauty and that beautiful representations of nature should be the ideal of art.[16] But he departed from Ruskin's aesthetic at important points, for Ruskin's ideal of art often comprised a high degree—often an almost photographic degree—of fidelity to the natural subject.[17] Van Dyke instead subscribed to what might be called, after Harold Bloom's theory of the strong poet,[18] a theory of a strong seer, a person whose particular vision imposes itself on the natural phenomena he or she represents.

Van Dyke did not mind seeing traces of the artist in works of art that portrayed natural subjects; in fact, he demanded to see such traces.[19] According to Van Dyke, only average people expected art to be strictly representational. He was especially impatient, for instance, with the sort of paintings that required "titular explanation" for their effect, or pictures that conveyed narratives in order to please the average person.[20] Average people—unlike Van Dyke and, he hoped, the audience for his books—were incapable of the conceptual leap involved in seeing that beautiful art could be an end in itself.

Sophisticated lovers of art, on the contrary, did understand that artistic representation could be its own end, and if they followed Van Dyke that far, they understood more: "[C]anvases are pieces of color, light, air, painted brilliantly sympathetically, artistically."[21] In Van Dyke's writings, this ability to appreciate an artist's sympathy and brilliance rather than merely the fidelity of his or her representations of nature sets aesthetes such as himself above the merely average. Thus, his aestheticism became elitism.

Van Dyke's art aesthetic finds parallels in his nature aesthetic. To Van Dyke's mind, nature was a beautiful thing—the most important beautiful thing—whose beauty could and should be approached using the same aesthetic discipline with which one approaches paintings. The parallel-ism evident in the titles of his two companion volumes on beauty illus-trates the connection: In 1893 Van Dyke published *Art for Art's Sake,* and in 1898 he published *Nature for Its Own Sake;* the thesis of which is that nature itself provides the supreme aesthetic experience for people who know how to appreciate it.[22] The two books share more than a titular affinity. Both provide extended technical discussions of the interactions of light, line, and color which constitute beauty. Both books are technical studies in perception written by an art expert.

According to Peter Wild, Van Dyke's art-for-art's-sake aesthetic, when translated into nature-for-its-own sake, held that "the appreciation of beauty is life's highest good, and in nature herself we find the greatest beauty."[23] *The Desert,* the second volume, after *Nature for Its Own Sake,* in the Natural Appearances series, is indeed a celebration of nature's beauty for its own sake. The book begins and ends by insisting on the primacy of the unartified allure of the desert. "[M]y book is only an excuse for talk-ing about the beautiful things in this desert world," Van Dyke humbly tells his reader in the preface-dedication,[24] and he concludes *The Desert* by reiterating that the barren spaces of the Southwest "are beautiful in themselves."[25] The book—which includes chapters with such titles as "Light, Air, and Color," "Desert Sky and Clouds," and "Illusions"—was a visual education for refined Americans who had never seen the desert, and inscribed in its nature-for-its-own-sake aesthetic is the hubris of Van Dyke's art-for-art's-sake aesthetic.

This is not to say that *The Desert* is not compelling. It is extremely compelling. In it Van Dyke directs the capable gaze of which he is so proud at the desert landscapes he encounters, and his book well deserves to be thought of as one of the main sources of the nation's collective af-fection for its deserts. Such natural phenomena as a sunrise often pro-voke genuinely affecting rhapsodies:

That beam of light! Was there ever anything so beautiful! How it flashes its color through shadow, how it gilds the tops of the moun-tains and gleams white on the dunes of the desert! In any land what is there more glorious than sunlight! Even here in the desert, where it falls fierce and hot as a rain of meteors, it is the one supreme beauty to which all things pay allegiance.[26]

In addition, Van Dyke often employed esoteric literary devices, as in his kenning description of a gray wolf: "[N]ow that the sun is up you can see a long sun-burned slant-of-hair trotting up yonder divide and casting an apprehensive head from side to side as he moves off."[27] He presents the harsh landscape with a grace few writers before him had possessed.

As modern readers of *The Desert* are quick to note, Van Dyke makes several bold pronouncements in the book that address concerns far outside the aesthetics of light, line, and color. As well as being one of the first Anglo Americans successfully to capture the beauty of the desert in words, Van Dyke was also one of the first to say that capturing it in words was exactly as far as the human conquest ought to go. Van Dyke saw that the beauty of the desert depended on keeping human civilization out of it. His endeavor to instill a sense of the wild desert's value in his audience also had the effect of encouraging them to approach it in a materially nondestructive, nonexploitative way. Simply looking at a wild place does not destroy it, and not destroying a wild place makes it much nicer simply to look at.

Thus Van Dyke, as he developed his desert aesthetic, exhibited a compulsion to denounce the economic exploitation of the desert. His book presents an early aesthetic critique of industrial capitalism: "The aesthetic sense . . . is just as important a factor in the scheme of human happiness as the corporeal sense of eating and drinking; but there has never been a time when the world would admit it. . . . The main affair of life is to get the dollar, and if there is any money in cutting the throat of Beauty, why, by all means, cut her throat."[28] Van Dyke eulogized huge sections of the continent that had been brutalized by "practical men" who left behind them "[w]eeds, wire fences, oil-derricks, board shanties, and board towns—things that not even a 'practical man' can do less than curse at."[29] In what must be his most famous pronouncement on the desert, Van Dyke anticipates the ecologically absolute tone of a member of Earth First! by proclaiming, "The deserts should never be reclaimed. They are the breathing-spaces of the west and should be preserved forever."[30] Looking back as we do from the age of Las Vegas and the Imperial Valley, Van Dyke's pronouncement seems remarkably prescient.

Removed from American civilization out in the fastnesses of the Southwest, Van Dyke mounted a sophisticated critique of his own society's heedless material exploitation of nature. Starting at the very heart of the matter, he suggested that the doctrine of social Darwinism implicit in his culture was misconceived. By seeing Anglo America's conquest of nature as merely another instance of the survival of the fittest, Americans had illicitly applied Darwinism to human society in order to justify the rise of fortune-making industrial capitalism.

But in what he calls the Colorado desert (essentially what we now call the Colorado Plateau), Van Dyke saw natural selection firsthand. He saw fierce and unfamiliar manifestations of the competition for survival, "a war of elements and a struggle for existence . . . that for ferocity is unparalleled elsewhere in nature."[31] It was possible to lose much more than a fortune in the desert, as Frank Norris had famously demonstrated in his classic of Naturalism *McTeague* (1899). It was possible to lose one's life there in the bitter struggle for survival.[32] Van Dyke perceived the desert as "a show of teeth in bush and beast and reptile. At every turn one feels the presence of the barb and thorn, the jaw and paw, the beak and talon, the sting and poison thereof."[33] He paid a great deal of attention to the competition for survival among the plants and animals of the desert.

Like most late Victorians, Van Dyke was fascinated by the idea of the survival of the fittest. But in the midst of this fierce natural struggle for existence, he seems to have begun doubting that the sort of competition that went on for water among desert organisms was the same sort of competition that went on between, say, the Missouri Pacific and Southern Pacific Railroads, or between U.S. Steel and the Amalgamated Association of Iron and Steel Workers.

Upon encountering the remains of an ancient desert civilization, his first reaction was to note that, in human affairs, "[w]ith what contempt Nature sometimes plans the survival of the least fit, and breaks the conqueror on his shield,"[34] a sentiment not calculated to strike a chord with Frederic Remington or Teddy Roosevelt, or most Anglo American men of the time. He goes on differentiating human social evolution from natural selection, going so far as to doubt, as he considers the ruins of an ancient southwestern civilization (he is conveniently vague about its location), whether human society had actually evolved as neatly as it was generally supposed. In a passage as remarkable for its condemnation of the American doctrine of progress as for its prescience, Van Dyke makes a prediction about the future of social Darwinism as an intellectual construct. He notes, after considering the Stone Age civilization he encountered, that "[t]he man of the Stone Age exists to-day contemporary with civilized man. Possibly he always did. And it may be that some day Science will conclude that historic periods do not invariably happen, that there is not always a sequential evolution, and that the white race does not necessarily require a flat-headed mass of stupidity for an ancestor."[35] The contemporary ethnological paradigm of society held exactly the opposite: that the white race did require a flat-headed mass of stupidity for an ancestor, that, as in the example of Shaler and his "Landscape as a Means of Culture," "all human society represented 'progress' from 'rudeness' or 'savagery' to 'civilization,'" and further that "the Euroamerican culture represented the highest level of social evolution."[36] Here, once again, Van Dyke stands in the desert proclaiming against the assumptions of his culture.

Van Dyke goes on to argue for a different definition of "useful" from the one most Americans had recently begun to apply indiscriminately to themselves and to plants and animals alike. Generally, since people were at the top of the evolutionary ladder, what benefited them seemed to benefit all of nature. But as he observed the desert, it occurred to Van Dyke to challenge this culture-wide complacency. He asks about desert plants: "[A]re they useful, these desert growths?" "Certainly they are," he answers, "just as useful as the pine tree or the potato plant. To be sure, man cannot saw them into boards or cook them in a pot; but then Nature has other animals besides man to look after, other uses for her products than supporting human life. She toils and spins for all alike and man is not her special care. The desert vegetation answers her purposes and who shall say her purposes have ever been other than wise?"[37] In asserting that human species is not guaranteed nature's favor, Van Dyke shoots the heart out of any evolutionary argument for the *a priori* primacy of human needs over the well-being of nature at large.

Van Dyke claimed to find himself slipping the bonds of industrial civilization in the desert, losing his taste for privileged society and its cultural assumptions, forgetting the lecture halls of Rutgers and repudiating his ties to humanity. In the desert, he feels, "there is a reversion to the savage. Civilization, the race, history, philosophy, art—how very far away and how very useless, even contemptible, they seem. What have they to do with the air and the sunlight and the vastness of the plateau!"[38] He withdraws from civilization to the extent that he equates people in nature with the serpent in Eden and asks "What monstrous folly, think you, ever led Nature to create her one great enemy—man!"[39]

The persona Van Dyke projects in *The Desert* is an amalgam of John Ruskin and John the Baptist, crying out in the beauty of the wilderness, proclaiming against the destructive, selfish ecological decisions his capitalist society seemed intent upon making. And that persona dedicated *The Desert* to "A.M.C."—Andrew Michael Carnegie.[40] At one stroke, Van Dyke's nature-for-its-own sake aesthetic, which can sound very right-minded when he applies it in the Southwest, becomes somehow linked to the highly problematic world of big eastern industry. *The Desert* is dedicated to one of the nation's most notorious robber barons. Suddenly it seems not to have been intended for the general run of aspiring desert lovers who have naively taken it to be theirs. As is his art criticism, Van Dyke's desert writing is predicated on an elitism, a disdain for "the average unobservant traveller" who cannot appreciate the desert air and so does not know to value it. In the book, Van Dyke betrays a suspicion of public opinion, which makes the deserts "seem remarkable for only a few commonplace things."[41] Regarding his audience, Van Dyke commented to his editor that *The Desert* was "a whole lot better than the swash which today is being turned out as literature, and it will sell, too, but not up in the hundreds of thousands. It is not so bad as that. My audience is only a few thousand, thank God."[42]

Andrew Carnegie was, as *The Desert*'s dedication implies, the most important of these few thousand elect readers. Carnegie's role as dedicatee of the book presents a problem to those who would read *The Desert* either as an aesthetic or as an ecological treatise. Indeed, as Zita Ingham and Peter Wild have suggested, Carnegie's "belching steel mills blighting America's landscapes surely would disqualify him from the ranks of people dear to high-minded, nature loving aestheticians."[43] And from a late-twentieth-century perspective, those steel mills surely do disqualify Carnegie. But the fact is that, in 1901, it was unlikely that many Americans outside of the Van Dykes and Carnegies would be capable of appreciating a desert wilderness. The rest of America, not having personal fortunes, was intent upon earning a living, not expanding its aesthetic horizons. Van Dyke's innovative approach to the desert, as wonderful as it seems to more ecologically aware readers in the 1990s, was, at the time he espoused it, necessarily "an exclusive view, for only he and a small band of men and women possessed the sensibilities for proper appreciation." That small band "meant his own coterie of friends and those like them, people often well-off, if not wealthy, and supposedly higher-minded than the mass of mankind."[44]

Appeals to high-mindedness always bear examination, because to judge some part of society "high" necessarily involves judging some other part "low." Just as Van Dyke's art-for-art's-sake philosophy is predicated on a low class of "uncritical lovers of art" who appreciate a low class of pictures—pictures that tell stories—so his nature-for-its-own-sake philosophy is predicated on a worthless class of landscape—namely, any part of nature that is not beautiful to John C. Van Dyke.

Homestead, Pennsylvania, the site of Andrew Carnegie's steel mills, was a part of nature that during the 1890s was decidedly not beautiful. As described by historian Roger Butterfield, the Monongahela's "banks were lined with cinders and other refuse, metal scrap, and sickly ground upon which little grew but scattered weeds and dry, scrubby bushes," and whose water was "saturated with chemicals (notably sulphuric acid) used in making metals and coke."[45] Homestead was "the gem of the world's steel plants."[46] At Homestead, after having destroyed the local environment, and after having, in partnership with John D. Rockefeller, bought the hematite-rich Mesabi Range in northern Minnesota to provide ore for the Pennsylvania plant, Andrew Carnegie proceeded to devastate his workers in the most "savage [and] significant chapter . . . [i]n the history of American labor."[47] Although Butterfield's estimate of Carnegie is harsher than some, it is nevertheless rather uncomfortable to think that one of America's favorite nature writers dedicated his most popular book to a union buster who also killed a river and put an entire mineral range through his smelters. But Van Dyke did just that, and it does not seem to have troubled him.

Herein lies a valuable part of Van Dyke's contribution to the Anglo American nature aesthetic if only it can be recovered. Van Dyke not only organized art—and his audiences—hierarchically, he did the same for ecosystems. There was beautiful nature and there was preterite nature, and Van Dyke wasted few words on what was already lost.

As was the case with many of his contemporaries, a hidden premise of Van Dyke's nature-for-its-own-sake aesthetic was what Richard Slotkin calls the bifurcated geography of America.[48] Because such a geography posits a Metropolis in which people have their way with nature and a Wilderness in which nature remains pure, this structure not only bifurcated the nation's geography, it also bifurcated the nation's conception of nature. Carnegie, of course, had a huge stake in the Metropolis and its industrial capitalism. But Van Dyke's investment in the Metropolis was fairly large as well. He moved in the circles of Henry Clay Frick, Frank Thomson, and Andrew Carnegie.[49] These were not only three of the most preeminent industrialists of the time, they were also three of its most preeminent art collectors, men who lent credibility to, and had a great deal of money to contribute to, art history professors and their endeavors. It was Van Dyke, in fact, according to his own account, who guided Carnegie's first investment of six thousand dollars in American art and who had "carte blanche" to acquire art for Carnegie "during his later life."[50]

Thus, for Van Dyke the distinction between the Wilderness and the Metropolis would have been an important one. Wilderness, like that in the southwestern deserts, existed as a sort of holding pen for beautiful nature. The deserts represented a pristine place in the West to imagine that wild nature, the fit subject of beautiful art, was thriving, while in the East, the U.S. Steel plants of his friend Carnegie converted nature into rails and dollars.

The distinction becomes complicated, however, when Van Dyke actually brings U.S. Steel with him to the desert. Somehow, at La Noria Verde in northern Mexico, the place from which Van Dyke dedicated *The Desert*, he ran into "an English-speaking man, who proved to be American,"[51] and who proved to be one John McLuckie, a former mayor of Homestead, Pennsylvania, and a former employee of Andrew Carnegie. The managers of U.S. Steel had ruined McLuckie in retaliation for his support for the steelworkers in the Homestead strike. After the strike, "Honest John McLuckie" was refused the amnesty offered other U.S. Steel employees, and he was sent out, according to Arthur Burgoyne, "into new and untried fields" to live out his life "under the handicap of a lost cause and the diversion of energy from the familiar pursuits of a lifetime."[52] After McLuckie had been, in Van Dyke's words, "indicted for murder, riot, treason, and I know not what other offenses," and had been "compelled to flee from the State . . . wounded, starved, pursued by the officers of the law, and obliged to go into hiding," and after "his wife died and his home was broken up,"[53] Van Dyke miraculously found him in the middle of the desert in northern Mexico. Somehow, during this suspiciously coincidental meeting, Van Dyke neglected to tell McLuckie that he "had been with [Carnegie] at [Castle] Cluny in Scotland shortly after the Homestead strike"—that is, shortly after McLuckie had been destroyed by Carnegie's steel corporation.[54] Nevertheless, Van Dyke relates, McLuckie was remarkably forthcoming during their conversation, speaking kind words about Carnegie, saying "several times that if 'Andy' had been there the trouble would never have arisen." McLuckie took the occasion of this chance meeting in Mexico to place all the blame for the labor dispute on Carnegie's manager, Henry Clay Frick.[55]

Upon hearing by mail of Van Dyke's fortuitous discovery of McLuckie in the desert of northern Mexico, Van Dyke recalled, "Carnegie answered at once, and on the margin of the letter wrote in lead pencil: 'Give McLuckie all the money he wants, but don't mention my name.'" McLuckie, displaying a "right-enough American spirit," refused the money, and Van Dyke had to content himself with securing McLuckie a job on the Sonora Railway. In a later meeting with McLuckie, Van Dyke revealed that Carnegie had been the source of the generous offer of money, thus eliciting the famous words, "Well, that was damned white of Andy, wasn't it?" Carnegie, with Van Dyke's editorial help, subsequently managed in his *Autobiography* to work McLuckie's apocryphal comment into an absolution of all guilt regarding his treatment of labor during the entire course of his career.[56]

Important elements of Van Dyke's and Carnegie's story are fabricated. In a scrapbook at the Gardner A. Sage Library compiled by Van Dyke there is a letter dated June 29, 1898. It is the letter Van Dyke describes above and dates as having been written in 1900, for across the top margin of it Van Dyke himself wrote in pencil: "This is the letter in which A.C. wrote in pencil to give McLuckie all the money he wanted and to 'rub this out' see autobiography p. 237."[57] The letter has an erasure, of which only the words "rub this out" are legible, written in pencil in Carnegie's hand. Why "rub this out," and why is the letter dated before Van Dyke left New Jersey for the desert if, as Van Dyke claims, he did not come across McLuckie until 1900? The answer seems to be that Van Dyke went to the desert to deliver money to McLuckie on Carnegie's behalf. The date of the letter implies that one of the most pervasively influential works in the

Anglo American canon of desert literature began as a delivery of conscience money for the nation's most egregious exploiter of nature. It seems that Van Dyke used the emptiness of the Sonoran Desert of northern Mexico to his advantage by setting mysterious, unprovable meetings there that were intended, Van Dyke later wrote, to "vindicate Mr. Carnegie."[58]

In his desert book and in its preface-dedication, Van Dyke betrays no suspicion that his behavior toward Carnegie, McLuckie, and the desert is conflicted. Van Dyke seems to be sincere in his insistence that the deserts should be protected at all costs from human despoilers, an insistence that is unequivocally correct from an ecological standpoint and which becomes more compelling daily. How, then, could Van Dyke tour the Southwest by train, undertake work for Carnegie while he was there, secure employment for McLuckie on the Sonora Railway (whose tracks destroyed thousands of acres of desert), and in the end lie about what he had done?

The answer is simply that Van Dyke, like many privileged late Victorians, seems to have worked with a series of unfortunately rigid distinctions that tended to separate the entire world into two categories: the worthwhile and the rest. Apparently the categories upon which Van Dyke predicated his nature aesthetic must have conditioned this response to the desert. Heavily weighted in favor of the "high," they set the aesthete above the "average person," Carnegie above McLuckie, the beautiful above the practical, the ·desert wilderness above the Monongahela Valley, and open land above railroad rights-of-way. These foundational categories seem to have been so essential to his perceptions of the natural world that such paradoxes as steel rails laid over his beloved desert, or Carnegie's money riding those rails over that beloved desert, are not acknowledged in his book. Van Dyke figures the wild, beautiful landscape as part of an aesthetic hierarchy that set the Mojave and Sonoran Deserts above the Mesabi Range and the Monongahela Valley, and if the deserts were not perfect in all their particulars, he was capable of ignoring unpleasant particulars so that the desert might occupy the apex of his hierarchy of natural appearances.[59]

The debt our culture unequivocally owes to *The Desert* for its aesthetic reworking of a landscape Anglo Americans had previously found unattractive and uninteresting it owes also to the classism and wealth of late-Victorian American society. Van Dyke was part of this society; he understood and shared its fascination with the strenuous life that, after the advent of railroads, could conveniently be pursued out west, and he indulged that fascination. Furthermore, precisely because he was privileged, his education and experience provided him with the aesthetic vocabulary necessary to make the visual phenomena of the desert accessible to his audience. Finally, he subscribed to his society's ideas of hierarchy to the extent that he could, in effortless prose, privilege "unspoiled" wilderness over other parts of nature.

The Desert should not be dismissed as a nature fake or as mendacious. Certainly, Van Dyke was less than honest in presenting the book's circumstances to his audience. Nevertheless, *The Desert* and the aesthetic and environmental tenets it espouses, are now deeply engrained in our culture. Thus the book forces a realization: The process of representing wild nature to Americans is more complex than it appears. Behind what seems to be Van Dyke's straightforward description of a remarkable landscape lies a difficult series of social and cultural negotiations with which readers must come to terms. Somewhere within the mechanism that produced *The Desert* lies the squalor of Homestead, Pennsylvania.

There now exists a much richer if more difficult context in which to read *The Desert*. Van Dyke's admonition, "The deserts should never be reclaimed" was unequivocally the proper thing for him to say, but readers must see in it the landscapes it ignores—the Mesabi Range, the Monongahela Valley, large parts of the desert itself—as well as the landscape it would protect.

There is one noteworthy parallel between the positions of Van Dyke and his readers at the turn of the century, who were deciding how to behave in the face of a declining natural world, and present-day Americans, who are deciding how to behave now that that world is almost entirely gone. The two temporally separated groups tend to say similar things about the deserts. When it spoke to Verner Reed, the arid West promised that "[I]f you will know me, and study me, and love me, I will give you peace, and a great content, and a knowledge that is beyond what you may gain from men, or from events, or from books."[60] Yet, despite the admirable sentiments about the desert articulated regularly and in accessible cultural venues by Americans such as Reed since the turn of the century, the country has nevertheless proceeded to destroy its deserts almost completely. And despite the continued popularity of Edward Abbey's *Desert Solitaire* and the plethora of Discovery Channel treatments of the "fragile desert," the United States' fastest growing cities lie in its deserts.

Thus it is important to recognize and come to terms with the paradoxes writers such as Van Dyke and artists such as Remington have propagated through their culture. In Van Dyke's case, the paradoxes are even more compelling because they are so very contemporary. Even if the approaches taken by Twain, Remington, Wister, and the various magazine writers like Harriet Monroe who have disappeared from our culture may be written off as the quaint products of a long-gone worldview we have now outgrown, the fact remains that Anglo American culture has not outgrown Van Dyke; he is with us still, in bookstores and in literary journals across the country and at roadside gift shops across the West.

And Van Dyke's dilemma is still with us. His relationship to the desert was a conflicted one involving Pullman cars and first-class hotels. It was conflicted in the way all American wilderness relationships are now, when we ride on paved loops through our favorite wild preserves, and when we must drive in our cars and Winnebagos and minivans and park them on the melting asphalt at the Arizona-Sonora Desert Museum to see a wild desert because the "real" wild deserts have become cottonfields, dustbowls, shopping malls, and parking lots. Our deserts are fast becoming, if they are not already, versions of what Umberto Eco has called hyperreality, in which the "'completely real' becomes identified with the 'completely fake,'" and "[a]bsolute unreality is offered as real presence."[61] This is, as Eco warns, especially the case with wild entities such as deserts, for "the theme of hyperrealistic reproduction involves not only Art, and History, but also Nature."[62]

Van Dyke's desert experience resembles the exemplary modern desert wilderness experience in nearly every sense of the word, because it involved a genuine nostalgia for wilderness along with an affinity for high-speed luxury transportation. Such experiences become more compelling as the modernity of the twentieth century becomes increasingly environmentally untenable. To understand fully Van Dyke's relationship to the desert, it is necessary to admit that, despite his many contradictions, Van Dyke's approach to it generally makes sense for those of us who live in modern American society. Like it or not, we are much like Van Dyke and his turn-of-the-century peers in our treatment of the natural world, and we either implicitly or explicitly share many of his conclusions.

There is no escaping the fact that Van Dyke was a brilliant observer and that most of his Anglo American readers needed him to describe the desert before they could understand it, someone to contain its striking appearance in refined American English. And there is no escaping the fact that wilderness appreciation is still, in this country, predicated on the sort of class privilege that enabled Van Dyke to appreciate it in the first place: Very few people hike into Organ Pipe Cactus National Monument or Canyonlands National Park. Those of us who visit them ride there in vehicles that are as often as not air-conditioned.

Van Dyke's prediction that "low" capitalist entrepreneurs would consume the southwestern ecosystem has proven correct. Golf courses dot the arid landscape, and our culture's endeavors to protect desert wilderness from such development in national monuments and national parks, inadequate as they have been, have arisen from Van Dyke's and others' sense of the aesthetic worth of deserts and from his conviction that some deserts needed to be protected from progress. His most notable desert pronouncement, still trenchant today, adorns the wall of the Saguaro National Park West ranger station and daily greets visitors: "The deserts should never be reclaimed. They are the breathing-spaces of the west and should be preserved forever."

But the implicit assumption that beauty is somehow a detachable attribute of desert land, that it exists apart from the degradations visited on the desert ecosystem by humans, has developed, for instance, into the boom of Tucson, Arizona, the population of which swells daily with those who enjoy watching the desert sun play on the Santa Catalina Mountains while they enjoy the convenience of a convenience store on every other corner. Tucson and Saguaro National Park share a common border. Tucson bisects the park, and in several places the boundary of the park is also the edge of Tucson's urban sprawl.

This physical boundary, and the conceptual boundary it represents, merit consideration. Artificial separation is one of the lessons of the southwestern deserts, the uncomfortable and uncertain line of demarcation between wilderness and civilization that few Anglo American desert writers have noticed, much less addressed, in their work. As in Van Dyke's desert treatment, the boundary tends to remain an unexamined assumption, a dividing line between the pure desert wilderness and the foul Monongahela (or Colorado, or Gila) River so obvious that it need not be discussed.

The idea of fixed boundaries does not work, however, in literature or in ecology. It is a mistake to think that entities such as books or landforms are constituted by essential properties contained within rigid forms. The sharp delineations U.S. citizens have insisted upon applying to the arid landscape have moved Jean Baudrillard to call it a country without hope, where, as its inhabitants strive to deny the realities of the natural world in which they live, they have evolved an unnatural culture in which "its garbage is clean, its trade lubricated, its traffic pacified."[63]

In practical terms, Tucson, Saguaro National Park West, and Saguaro National Park East make this obvious. There are lines on the map separating them, but there is no way to keep wind, water, or animals (including people) on one side of a line. The lesson of the desert, as taught by the progression of representations of it that have arisen in Anglo American literature, is that the idea that a wilderness and a civilization can coexist with just a boundary line between them is not tenable. Wilderness and civilization share too many things. Most notably, they share American citizens, who, civilized animals that we are, constantly violate the boundaries we draw.

Chapter **6**

The sound of rushing water echoes down the valleys. It will leave the earth well-moistened. After that, various seeds will sprout. All over the land, greet one another, my relatives. Call one another by your relationship. —From "Rain Goes Away," a Tohono O'odham story[1]

Early Voices

In the early to mid nineteenth century, as English-speaking people began seriously to explore the deserts of the American West, they encountered numerous Indian cultures that described the natural world in narratives that were much different from traditional English-language narratives concerning landscape.[2] Understandably, the landscape descriptions of these Native Americans hardly resembled those Europeans developed regarding the desert Southwest, and for the most part, their existence has been ignored until fairly recently.[3] This absence of indigenous imagination silently cuts through the written record of American activity on the desert from beginning to end.[4] It is in many ways an ironic silence, for in the deserts, where the land exhibits much of what Europeans would term scarcity and little of what they would call abundance, the Pueblo and other southwestern Indian cultures evolved and sustained themselves for thousands of years.[5]

The origin myth of most southwestern Native cultures is the emergence story, which tells of the journey of insect-like proto-humans through an underworld and onto the surface of the earth, where they become fully realized human beings. Unfortunately for modern-day readers, as Paul Zolbrod has observed concerning the Navajo creation story, these myths are part of an oral tradition, and their effects are diminished considerably when they are transcribed and translated into English.[6]

Nevertheless, they provide an enlightening contrast to the origin myth of the European culture that aspired to supplant Native Americans in the desert. The book of Genesis details how humans fell from perfect, transcendent Grace into a chaotic natural world; Navajo and Pueblo creation stories tell of humans' rise from chaos into a harmonious natural world. In the indigenous tradition, a secure place among the processes of the natural world is something to which people aspire. In European traditions, nature is generally something people disdain as being associated with failure—original sin, a disorderly and frightening force to be conquered or subdued, either outwardly or inwardly.

In Ruth Benedict's transcription of the Zuñi emergence story, people began their existence "living in the fourth world. It was dark. They could not see one another. They stepped on one another, they urinated upon one another, they threw refuse on one another. They could not breathe."[7] Because the father of these creatures, the Sun, "took pity on them" and thought, "'My people shall come to the daylight world,'" their ascent began.[8] By planting first pine, then spruce, then silver spruce, and then aspen trees to use as ladders, two sons of the "father Sun" brought the unfinished humans progressively closer to the surface of the Earth, where they would reside as fully realized human beings "in the middle of the world."[9] This narrative makes the Zuñi beholden to rather mundane natural objects, such as trees, for their emergence into the world. But more important, inscribed in the Zuñi myth is the idea that all human life on earth begins with the sun and the natural order it imparts to life on the earth. The Zuñis' rose from a human chaos below to a natural order above.

The Navajo emergence story, as transcribed by Paul Zolbrod, exhibits a structure similar to the Zuñi myth but describes more fully the process by which people developed their final shape and found their niche on the land. The proto-humans of the anarchic, chaotic first, second, and third worlds of the Navajos were imperfect. They "fought among themselves" and "committed adultery, one with another."[10] These people also offended the world around them, for when they assembled in the second world, the four directions of the second world were so appalled by the behavior of the early people that they asked them to leave, to climb to the third world. Because the early people were fundamentally incapable of respecting either each

other or their surrounding environment, they were thus expelled from
three succeeding worlds and so came out onto the surface of the fourth
and final world, the Earth. Because they wanted to remain in this last and
best world, the humans held a council meeting, "and they resolved to
mend their ways and to do nothing unintelligent that would create disor-
der. This was a good world, and the wandering insect people meant
to stay here, it is said."[11] Nevertheless, as well-intentioned as the first
Navajo people were in their insect form, they were unacceptable to the
Holy People of the fourth world, the Earth. The Black God of this world,
observing the way the insect people lived, told them that the Holy People
wanted only "intelligent people, created in their likeness, not yours" on
the Earth. The imperfect people were further informed, "you have the
teeth of beasts! You have the mouths of beasts! You have the feet of
beasts! You have the claws of beasts! The new creatures are to have
hands like ours. They are to have feet like ours. They are to have mouths
like ours and teeth like ours. They must learn to think ahead, as we do."[12]
In order to bring forth such perfect people, the Gods performed a ceremony with a white ear of corn and a yellow ear of corn. After the ceremony, the Navajos say, the "white ear of corn had been transformed into
our most ancient male ancestor. And the yellow ear of corn had been
transformed into our most ancient female ancestor."[13] Thus the Navajos
conceive of themselves as people who arose from one of the things in the
natural world on which their existence most depended—corn. Their emergence story enables the members of their culture to see that they indeed
spring from the arid land around them, and so, "[b]ecause of their origin
as ears of corn they remain as basic as germinating seeds."[14]

The Hopis, emerging similarly from a disordered world "[d]own below,
where the rain does not fall, the springs do not flow, the corn dries up in
the fields, and there are numerous persons who do not respect the virtues
of life," tell of a similarly delicate relationship to the arid physical world
around them. Upon their emergence into the Upper World, where there is
land and water,[15] the new people, under the direction of the Spider Grand-
mother (who wove the intricate web of the world), fashioned a sun and a
moon and put them in motion in the sky for light and warmth.[16]

Also at this time—after all the new people had been differentiated by
a mockingbird into the Hopis and other Pueblo people, the Navajos, the
Sioux, the Supais, the Comanches, the Utes, and the Apaches—the tribes

had to make "the selection of the corn." Laying out seven different strains of corn and grain, the mockingbird instructed each group of people to choose one and warned that "each of these ears brings with it a way of life. The one who chooses the yellow ear will have a life full of enjoyment and prosperity, but his span of life will be small. The short ear with the blue kernels will bring a life full of work and hardship, but the years will be many."[17] The mockingbird went on to illustrate the correspondence between particular means of subsistence and particular ways of life. The correspondences reflected the cultural patterns of the peoples involved (the Apaches, who in Hopi eyes are not particularly agricultural but instead are seen as nomads and raiders, chose not corn, for instance, but a kind of wild grass). The Hopis went away from this gathering with "the smallest ear of all," saying, "We shall have a life of hardship, but it will be a long-lasting life. Other tribes may perish, but we, the Hopis, will survive all adversities." Thus the Hopis became the people of the short blue corn.[18] The Hopi origin myth makes explicit what the European origin myth, Genesis, does not, that a people's culture must be a function of their relationship to the environment in which they live.

Inscribed in the southwestern origin myth in all its variations is the assumption that people ought to move toward a balance with the natural world they inhabit. Thus, an awareness of the balance of the nonhuman desert world itself—its arroyos, its sunlight, its corn, its order—informs the Native stories. And although to read Native American emergence narratives as cautionary tales about balance and relational thinking is a fairly standard thing for Anglo literary critics to do, such a reading is helpful.[19] As Patricia Clark Smith and Paula Gunn Allen have argued, "[l]ong before *context* became an academic buzz word, it was a Spider Woman word. It speaks of things woven together, and of understanding the meaning of a thread in terms of the whole piece of goods. For southwestern American Indians, that whole is the land in its largest sense. . . . The land is Spider Woman's creation; it is the whole cosmos."[20] These stories are, as countless critics have observed, narratives about human coexistence with their physical environment.

North American deserts thus exercised a profound influence on the human imagination long before Europeans ever saw it, and one of the most compelling imaginative responses is one of the oldest: The Tohono O'odham people of Arizona address the fact of their homeland's aridity in their myths, which express insightful and highly imaginative representations of conditions in the desert. These desert myths often culminate in what might be called (to apply anachronistically a relatively modern term from literary criticism) moments of aesthetic transcendence.

The climactic rhetorical moment of the Tohono O'odham story "Rain Goes Away" is, not surprisingly, the Call for Rain, delivered by a medicine man who is inebriated, having performed "the ceremonial number of performances" with *nawait,* the sacramental drink prepared to "cause Wind to forget the words they [had] used to drive him away," because driving away Wind had precipitated the drought through which the Tohono O'odham are suffering in the story.[21] The medicine man's call for rain seems intended to be more evocative than effective—more descriptive than prescriptive. It is a compelling oral representation (now transcribed and translated by Anglo scholars) of a monumental event for desert dwellers, a storm gathering and breaking. The storm is a "beautifully shining ancient house," which "stands there in the east, wrapped in white clouds." The caller asks the cloud,

> Start there and be kind to us, mixed within, speaking softly within, lightning moving very zigzag, roaring beautifully, pattering rain and moving along. Although the earth is wide, the clouds are braced across it and will come, though far away. They are hung on the heads of the mountains standing there, and will come. They will leave the earth soaked everywhere, even the highest hills. The water will gently flood the little washes, wherever they are. The driftwood is stopped crossways where the trees are standing. The sound of rushing water echoes down the valleys. It will leave the earth well moistened. After that, various kinds of seed will sprout. All over the land, greet one another, my relatives. Call one another by your relationship.[22]

In addition to providing a striking specimen of natural description, both in the balance and rhythm of its language (as far as it is possible to tell from its English translation) and in the careful particularity of its description, the Call for Rain also presents a distinct articulation of the Tohono O'odham approach to the nonhuman world. As Peter Wild notes, the Tohono O'odham "know that, whatever the efficacy of their exuberant party to please the rain spirits, their survival will entail a good deal of care, conservation, and hard field labor. . . . Their myths . . . set them free to develop a practical and lasting rather than short-term modus operandi with the earth."[23]

The Tohono O'odham myth here implies a relationship between people and the arid land: The event of a rainstorm is a call for humans to greet relatives "all over the land," to "call one another by your relationship"—to acknowledge and endeavor to understand the fragile relationships between living things in a place that is always alive but never abundant, even when rain comes.

My reading of narratives about ecological relationships is not meant to imply that it would be possible, or even desirable, to initiate a culture-wide retreat to the Stone Age. The Tohono O'odham story is from another time and another culture. Wishing its circumstances back would involve the most severely unreconstructed sort of nostalgia.[24] But recovering carefully considered parts of it and attempting to integrate those parts into our thinking about the natural world would certainly be desirable. It would be especially helpful to recover the relational element of Tohono O'odham thinking about the world.

The first Europeans coming to the American desert, of course, were Spanish speakers, who exerted different imaginative pressures on the landscape from those of the Pueblo, Tohono O'odham, or Navajo peoples. Not equipped with narratives in which people understood even the European landscape on its own terms, much less the sparse desert landscape, a long line of explorers, missionaries, traders, and settlers rarely thought of balance when they saw the southwestern deserts.[25] Not only did Hispanic[26] groups such as Coronado's explorers, when they met the Zuñi people, find that "nothing in either group's previous experience had prepared them to comprehend one another,"[27] but in fact the two groups, as demonstrated by their misunderstandings about the golden cities of Cibola, seldom saw themselves as inhabiting the same Earth. David Weber maintains that Native Americans "lived in a world of myth and legend while Europeans inhabited a world of rationality and well-grounded religious faith. In truth, each world contained elements of the mythic and rational, but these worlds did not harmonize well with one another."[28] Coronado did not experience a perfectly unmediated, transparently "real" version of the new lands; his "view of reality had been shaped by literature and lore."[29] His perceptions of the landscape were partly a function of the narratives he had read and heard before he set foot in the arid Southwest.[30]

Fray Marcos de Niza casting about the arid plains for a glimpse of the golden cities, seems at first to have been largely unable to understand the landscape and the people he encountered except as facilitators of his treasure hunt. But de Niza, having committed himself to living on the land, did learn about it. In the desert, for instance, he noted that the Natives traveling with him "gave me of the food they had, though it was little because they said they had three years without rain."[31] Upon hearing their explanation, de Niza observed that it was also likely that the Natives were poor "because the Indians of that region think more of hiding themselves than of planting crops, through fear of the Christians of the *villa* of San Miguel, who until then had been accustomed to go there to make war and slaves."[32] De Niza was a perceptive man, so at times, despite his unfamiliarity with the exigencies of agriculture in the desert, he began to perceive the difficulties that people faced in living there.

But at other times, the power of the narrative he imagined himself to be living, the narrative of wealth and fame in the New World, shaped his vision. Initially unused to looking at the desert landscape, and committed to seeing golden cities in it, de Niza famously managed to delude himself into thinking he had seen Cibola in the desert before his expedition concluded. As he recounted,

> I saw only, from the mouth of the gorge, seven settlements of fair size, at some distance a valley farther below very green and of very good land, from which arose many smokes; I was informed that in it is much gold, and that the natives of it trade in vessels and jewels for the ears. . . . Here I placed two crosses and took possession of all the gorge and valley after the manner and ritual of the possessions above.[33]

Rather than seeing a desert riverbottom in which a few indigenous people were pursuing a meager subsistence, de Niza saw the seven richest cities in history and claimed them for the Crown.

This delusion, this tendency to see the landscape in the terms in which he wanted to see it, when finally brought to light by Coronado, cost de Niza his career. But Coronado, too, managed to live and travel for years in what Castañeda called "wilderness where nothing grew, except some very small plants about a span high," where "instead of settlements great deserts were found,"[34] because in the deserts and plains of the Southwest he persisted in using his imagination to picture himself as a rich man in Spain (an image he had gotten from books) as well as using it to filter what he saw in the landscape before him.

But in general the early Spanish explorers maintained a less directly destructive outlook on arid lands than the Europeans who would follow them, because, in the end, wealth proved not to be the sole attraction for them in the Southwest.[35] Spanish missionaries saw the land as a field on which to spread their religious culture. In large measure this meant winning greater glory for their God by carrying out the religious conquest of the indigenous inhabitants, whom they often regarded as "pliable, childlike innocents, uncorrupted by Europeans."[36] Spanish missionaries abroad in the deserts regularly undertook such endeavors as Father Eusebio Francisco Kino's "great expedition to the sea of California, in which [were] discovered and reduced more than four thousand new Pima Indians, who [gave him] four hundred and thirty-five infants to baptize."[37] Given received notions of the behavior of conquering priests in the desert, it is hardly surprising to find described in Kino's journal "[a]nother great entry," introduced as a passage "in which are discovered more than eighty leagues of lands and new peoples; from the Río Grande to the Río Azul is sighted; detailed information is secured in regard to the very populous and very large Rio Colorado near-by; and the new Yuma nation is reduced."[38]

But despite their primary concern with reducing (that is, saving) human souls, Jesuit missionaries did pay attention to the landscape, because Christian civilization required a steady local food supply, something arid land does not provide easily. Kino's associate, Juan María Salvatierra, often advised him of exceptionally promising stretches of desert land. In one message he wrote: "It has rained much here all this winter, and this whole land is as fragrant as a sweet-smelling garden; and if there had been lands prepared, much seed could have been sown, and all would have brought forth fruit; but one can not do everything."[39] Upon his first entry into the California region, Kino's expedition found, by turning north, "another good post, with plenty of domicile and domesticated people."[40] Unlike Coronado and other wealth seekers, his main concerns lay "in spiritual and temporal matters" such as "Christian teaching, beginnings of baptisms, buildings, planting of crops, etc."[41]

A significant few early Spanish explorers thus managed, when they found it necessary and when given no choice, to live in a kind of harmony with the land.[42] Alvar Núñez Cabeza de Vaca, cast away after the disastrous failure of Pánfilo de Narváez's exploratory expedition through Florida, was to learn much about American landscapes after he made landfall near Galveston Island in southern Texas. Near the edge of the southwestern deserts, Cabeza de Vaca at first expressed a self-righteous disgust with the subsistence life the indigenous Yguaze people led on the sparse land, noting that

> Their principal food is roots of two or three kinds. . . . The roots are very bad and cause people who eat them to swell up. . . . [M]any of them are very bitter. On top of this, they are very difficult to dig. Those people are so hungry that they can not do without them, and go two or three leagues looking for them. Sometimes they kill some deer, and sometimes they catch fish. But this is so little and their hunger so great that they eat spiders, and eggs, worms, lizards, salamanders, snakes and poisonous vipers. They eat dirt and wood and whatever they can get, as well as deer excrement and other things I will not talk about.[43]

This was in August of 1530. By September of 1534, Cabeza de Vaca, in even less hospitable country south of present-day San Antonio, had become expert at surviving on prickly-pear juice. He even spoke of it in the voice of a connoisseur, noting that the juice "is sweet and has the color of syrup. . . . There are many kinds of prickly pear, some of them very good, although they all seemed good to me, since my hunger never allowed me the luxury of being selective or thinking about which were better."[44]

Later that year, after winter had set in, Cabeza de Vaca covered part of central Texas, walking barefoot and alone and carrying firewood and "firebrands" in order to stay warm, without even cactus fruit to eat until he could rendezvous with others from his shipwrecked party, from whom he had become separated, on the bank of the Colorado River of Texas. There they found prickly pear enough to satisfy their "great hunger."[45] Eventually, having learned to live off the desert land, Cabeza de Vaca crossed the Sonoran Desert all the way to the Gulf of California, where he uneasily assumed the customs of his countrymen, having become something of a renaissance desert rat.

But the experience of Cabeza de Vaca, as he was forcefully stripped of his Old World perspective by the land's scarcity and learned how to survive in the desert, presents a striking contrast to the experiences of many Europeans who would follow. It indicates that, no matter how much evidence there may be to the contrary, people of even the most imperialistic backgrounds and self-righteous attitudes have the potential, when necessary, to develop viable means of existing in the desert.

Chapter **7**

Dypaloh. There was a house made of dawn. It was made of pollen and of rain, and the land was very old and everlasting. There were many colors on the hills, and the plain was bright with different-colored clays and sands. Red and blue and spotted horses grazed in the plain, and there was a dark wilderness on the mountains beyond. The land was still and strong. It was beautiful all around.

—N. Scott Momaday[1]

In Beauty It Is Finished

It is under the hopeful signs of the Tohono O'odham stories and the story of Cabeza de Vaca that I turn to the present by way of a second hopeful voice from the past: Mary Austin. A contemporary of John C. Van Dyke, Austin was one of the first writers in the United States to see exactly how its citizens would have to adjust their conceptions of boundaries—all kinds of boundaries, not just geographical ones—in order to thrive in the desert. For Austin, the "land of little rain" and the "land of journey's ending" provided places from which to mount a critique of her culture, a critique informed, as Lois Rudnick has observed, by a concern not only with environmental responsibility but also with social equity, the latter of which sets her in direct opposition to Americans like Van Dyke. In Austin's eyes, as John O'Grady suggests, the desert lands of the Southwest were "a New World whose terrain, climate, and indigenous peoples offered a model of ecological, spiritual, and artistic integration to an alienated and decadent Western civilization."[2] Austin believed that the "New World" of the desert "destroys those who are not prepared to change the way they live their lives, but it always offers the possibility of self-transformation."[3] According to John P. O'Grady, "[t]he dissolution of borders" in Austin's desert spaces "is a sort of mobile anti-structure, anti-hierarchy, as Deleuze and Guattari phrase it. . . . Here, the self is made anew."[4]

Unlike many of her peers, Austin saw in the deserts the possibility not only of an aesthetic rapprochement with arid land but also a cultural rapprochement among the people who lived on the land. She thus stands apart from Van Dyke, Harriet Monroe, Remington, and other artists who rested content to consider only their own intellectual traditions. According to O'Grady, "Although Austin does perceive the 'beauty' in the wild, she never denies its polarity"—that, for most people, as a place to live the desert is both beautiful and difficult. O'Grady observes that Austin's "most engaging books are those about the land—specifically, *The Land of Little Rain* (1903) and *Lost Borders* (1909)—but a close look at these works reveals their subject is actually the land's effect upon the human individual and community."[5]

Notably, Austin looks upon the social adaptations of certain indigenous desert peoples as a guide for her own culture. In mounting a gender critique in her chapter "The Basket Maker" in *The Land of Little Rain*, Austin devotes her attention to Seyavi, a Paiute woman actively engaged in revising gender definitions as a result of her people's tribulations in the harsh California desert. Struggling to survive in her desert culture, Seyavi learns self-sufficiency, a self-sufficiency with implications outside her own culture, as Austin implies. Seyavi comes to value the universal "sufficiency of mother wit, and how much more easily one can do without a man than might at first be supposed."[6]

For Austin, the possibility not only of gender reconciliations but also of certain cultural reconciliations arises in this "mobile anti-structure" of the desert. Because she assumes that human beings are essentially defined by their environments, that "Man is not himself only, not solely a variant of his racial type in the pattern of his immediate experience. . . . He is the land, the lift of its mountain lines, the reach of its valleys; his is the rhythm of its seasonal processions, the involution and variation of its vegetal patterns."[7] Because she perceives the exigencies of arid landscapes, in the way they hinder traditional Anglo civilization in its more chauvinistic aspects, to be inherently life- and culture-enhancing, Austin concludes that "in New Mexico and Arizona, we approach nearest, in the New World, to the cultural beginnings which produced the glory that was Greece, the energetic blond engrafture on a dark, earth-nurtured race, in a land whose beauty takes the breath like pain."[8] In her view, the desert will provide a new and better beginning for the civilization of the United States, for, as Austin holds, "new races are not made new out of the dust as the first man was. They are made out of old races by reactions to new environment."[9]

Austin's hope is that the new environment of the desert, in its resistance to unsatisfactory and unexamined Anglo culture-ways, will inspire a new civilization that is more conscious of gender, culture, and the environment. She hopefully, if somewhat patronizingly, points toward such a tradition in stories like "The Little Town of the Grape Vines" in *The Land of Little Rain*. "At Las Uvas," she relates in an endorsement of the hybrid desert culture there, "they keep up all the good customs brought out of Old Mexico or bred in a lotus-eating land; drink, and are merry and look out for something to eat afterwards; have children, nine or ten to a family, have cock-fights, keep the siesta, smoke cigarettes and wait for the sun to go down."[10]

Austin's cross-cultural curiosity arises from genuine interest in other desert cultures as well as dissatisfaction with her own society's attempts to develop a desert culture of its own. If her vision proved ultimately to be less than compelling to her contemporaries, it was not because it lacked force. Rather, it was because she failed, as Rudnick maintains, "to see that much of what [she] hoped to teach the Anglo world was too rooted in Native American and Hispanic cultures to be 'borrowed' by an increasingly urban, industrial civilization that shared little of the ethos of either group."[11] Nevertheless, Austin's vision of a sustainable, equitable, and not least a very aesthetically pleasing culture in the desert remains one of her enduring legacies.

The challenge that Austin saw desert land as posing to traditional Anglo American habits informs much contemporary thinking about the region. Her belief that the desert provides a fertile ground for the re-evaluation of mainstream American culture accounts for a great deal of what Edward Abbey, in *Desert Solitaire,* said he valued in southern Utah. Utah's red desert was far from Anglo American civilization, and because its deserts are inimical to this civilization, they encouraged a perceptual sensitivity that most citizens of the United States (including Abbey, by his own admission) often lacked. Contemplating Delicate Arch, Abbey realized that in the desert, "there is a different world, older and greater and deeper by far than ours, a world which surrounds and sustains the little world of men as sea and sky surround and sustain a ship. The shock of the real. For a little while, we are again able to see, as the child does, a world of marvels."[12] The beauty and emptiness of the desert thus disable many cultural narratives. Most notably, as Abbey argues, desert lands cast doubt on narratives of technological civilizational progress with "the weight of all modern history behind" them. According to Abbey, time spent abroad contemplating spectacularly eroded and sun- and moon-lit arid land proves that such narratives are "quite insane,"[13] a thesis that photographer Peter Goin has amply proven in the chapter on the Nevada Test Site in his book-length photo essay *Nuclear Landscapes*.[14]

But Abbey's polemic and his arguments are also problematic. Once he helpfully debunks the boosterism of progressive industrial civilization, his solutions become paradoxical and often untenable for those looking to have a conversation with the natural world. At bottom, Abbey values desert wilderness because his "basic assumption [is] that wilderness is a necessary part of civilization"[15] so, as many readers have come to realize, he did not escape the binary trap of the wilderness-civilization opposition that constrained his turn-of-the-century forebears. In Abbey's formulation, wilderness exists *for* people, not *with* them.[16]

Nevertheless, Abbey locates new and important literary ground when he recognizes the desert's ability to subvert, both practically and aesthetically, the United States' mainstream progressive cultural ideology, which in Abbey's eyes leads only to landscapes like that of the industrialized East from which he was fleeing. The nation's deserts will not admit the strictures with which Western civilization would ordinarily bind the natural world. Instead, they provide a geographical and ecological zone of human possibility. Thus Abbey locates a space in which authors who followed have constructed dynamic paradigms for the interaction between people and the natural world, a space where the traditional American progressive, consumption-oriented aesthetic fails to suffice.

Since the Vietnam War, contemporary writers have provided more and more sophisticated explorations of the interaction between people and the desert, supplying insight that Abbey, central figure that he was, often did not, or could not supply. Often these insights arise in cultural traditions outside the mainstream. In an essay entitled "A First American Views His Land," N. Scott Momaday draws on his Kiowa heritage to suggest that "the American Indian has a unique investment in the American landscape. It is an investment that represents perhaps thirty thousand years of habitation." This unique investment is predicated on "the recognition of beauty, the realization that the physical world *is* beautiful."[17] The investment in the landscape of which he speaks is an aesthetic one.

Momaday recounts a childhood experience in planting two cornfields at the Jemez Pueblo: "I have not forgotten that day," he writes, "nor shall I forget it. I remember the warm earth of the fields, the smooth texture of seeds in my hands, and the brown water moving slowly and irresistibly among the rows. Above all I remember the spirit in which the procession was made, the work was done, and the feasting was enjoyed. It was a spirit of communion, of the life of each man in relation to the life of the planet."[18] Momaday's claim is that the "process of investment and appropriation is . . . preeminently a function of the imagination. . . . The Native American is someone who thinks of himself, imagines himself in a particular way. By virtue of his experience his idea of himself comprehends his relationship to the land."[19] For Momaday, the practical implication of such an imaginative act is that "As an Indian I think: 'You say that I *use* the land, and I reply, yes, it is true; but it is not the first truth. The first truth is that I *love* the land; I see that it is beautiful; I delight in it; I am alive in it.'"[20] In Momaday's conception of the arid West, beauty, which he strives to comprehend in his language, is what ultimately draws people to the land. This is a conclusion implied but seldom articulated by many of the desert aestheticians of the past.

Momaday's aesthetic is similar to what Gary Nabhan in *The Desert Smells Like Rain* has identified among the Tohono O'odham of southern Arizona as a kind of perceptual filter, a device that enables the people to coexist with their arid environment. He observes two Tohono O'odham farmers, Julian and Remedio, "growing food in a desert too harsh for most kinds of agriculture—using cues that few of us would ever notice. Their sense of how the desert works comes from decades of day-to-day observations. These perceptions have been filtered through a cultural tradition that has been refined, honed, and handed down over centuries of living in arid places."[21] This practical approach to the desert is shaped by a history of perceptions, as is Momaday's.

Leslie Marmon Silko carries Momaday's aesthetic reconciliation of use and beauty further. In her essay "Interior and Exterior Landscapes: The Pueblo Migration Stories" Silko describes the aesthetic tradition from which she works, using the squash blossom on a Pueblo pot as an emblem for the Pueblo aesthetic. "The squash blossom," she relates,

> is *one thing:* itself. So the ancient Pueblo potter abstracted what she saw to be the key elements of the squash blossom—the four symmetrical petals, with four symmetrical stamens in the center. These key elements, while suggesting the squash flower, also link it with the four cardinal directions. By representing only its intrinsic form, the squash flower is released from a limited meaning or restricted identity. Even in the most sophisticated abstract form, a squash flower or a cloud or a lightning bolt became intricately connected with a complex system of relationships which the ancient Pueblo people maintained with each other, and with the populous natural world they lived within.[22]

Thus, in writing of their aesthetic connection to the desert, these two authors go beyond oppositions such as beautiful versus useful, or wild versus human. Silko, in her description of the Pueblo imagination, for instance, shows that the "beautiful land" versus "useful land" distinctions that Van Dyke, Abbey, and others have made are not that simple—indigenous people use beautiful abstractions for practical purposes that enable them to live better and to know the landscape itself better. Momaday writes of how naturally beautiful desert farming can be. But more important, Silko and Momaday demonstrate that thinking in aesthetic terms, even if they are abstractions, does not necessarily entail removing beautiful things from one's everyday surroundings, as Harriet Monroe or John C. Van Dyke might have done. The practical environmental ethic that writers such as Silko and Momaday espouse is one and the same with the environmental aesthetic they espouse. Silko's and Momaday's art is not predicated on the transcendence of everyday culture—on the contrary, it is an organic part of that culture.

Leslie Marmon Silko's application of the concept of natural beauty causes her version of epiphany in the natural world to be much different from that of the desert writers who have come before her. In her novel *Ceremony,* Silko's protagonist, Tayo, completes his quest to cure the sickness he has felt since watching his cousin die in World War II by finding "something great and inclusive of everything."[23] But Tayo's everything will prove much different from Van Dyke's, Verner Z. Reed's, or Monroe's. At the entrance to a desert mine in New Mexico where the uranium for nuclear weapons had been extracted, Tayo sees a vision. Having arrived at the place where people had taken the resources of the Earth in order to engage in the single most environmentally destructive act in their history, he had also

> arrived at the point of convergence where the fate of all living things, and even the earth, had been laid. . . . [T]he lines of cultures and worlds were drawn in flat dark lines on fine light sand, converging in the middle of witchery's final ceremonial sand painting.
>
> . . . [T]he pattern of the ceremony was completed there. He knelt and found an ore rock. The gray stone was streaked with powdery yellow uranium, bright and alive as pollen; veins of sooty black formed lines with the yellow, making mountain ranges and rivers across the stone. But they had taken these beautiful rocks from deep within earth and they had laid them in a monstrous design, realizing destruction on a scale only *they* could have imagined.
>
> He cried the relief he felt at finally seeing the pattern, the way all the stories fit together—the old stories, the new stories—to become the story that was still being told.[24]

Tayo's epiphany is not a transcendence, not beauty lifting him out of his present circumstances, but rather beauty locking him down to the desert world and the things people have done in it.

In this epiphany, Silko unwrites nearly two hundred years of America's divided mind toward its deserts. The idea that the effects of the arid land's beauty, light, and color are somehow a talisman against the abuses of industrial civilization, and the idea that beauty and the transcendent, epiphanic moments it inspires, are somehow separate from the practical facts of history no longer hold. Uranium ore, extracted from and tested in the deserts of the Southwest and then utilized in weapons of mass destruction, becomes a talisman of the entire endangered world. When Tayo sees the exquisite pattern of the world, there are dead Lagunas and dead Japanese in it.

Momaday's stylistics in *House Made of Dawn* are similarly inclusive. As S. K. Aithal has observed, "Momaday returns again and again in the novel to the history of the Indian land and people. . . . The novel is full of descriptions of nature and points out the close kinship of the Indians with land and nature."[25] In *House Made of Dawn,* Abel's is a much more highly aestheticized, much less objectively structured relationship to the world around him than is Tayo's, yet Abel's epiphanic moments are similar to Tayo's. Abel does not look for escape from the degraded natural world, does not seek transcendence. In the foul world of humans—in Los Angeles—he goes out of his way to antagonize other people into breaking his hands. In the natural world, he confronts pain similarly. The final scene of *House Made of Dawn* finds Abel running through blinding pain across a frozen desert landscape, embracing both the pain and the beauty of his experience. Abel is no Clarence Dutton, Frederick Remington, or John C. Van Dyke—the pain and the beauty of existence on the desert are simultaneously parts of his experience of the land. As Silk and Momaday rework the traditional nature-inspired epiphany so that it becomes an inclusive experience, they differentiate themselves from their predecessors by proposing a new nature aesthetic—by tying the artist to the landscapes he or she represents in ways other American writers have not done.

Certain cultural critics long considered novels like Momaday's and Silko's to be ideal templates for democratic societies. Richard Rorty, á la Mikhail Bakhtin, has gone so far as to hint that the United States ought to be structured like a novel, because novels level people on the plane of language, diffuse inequities of power, and give every citizen a chance to speak to other citizens about concerns such as the environment and so offer opportunities for political change.[26]

Silko's *Almanac of the Dead* represents just such a novel-as-template, provides just such a leveling landscape. Because the desert on which much of the novel is set so consistently breaks down oppressive, monolithic narratives of progressive Anglo dominance, the book represents a world in transition, a state struggling to become ideal, democratic. It represents nearly a hundred voices struggling to be heard by one another rather than one voice speaking out above the rest. Like Richard Rorty and Mikhail Bakhtin, many of the characters of *Almanac of the Dead* know that to find voices for the dispossessed is to foment revolution: to find a place in the discourses of the world is to find a place in the world.

In *Almanac of the Dead*, because the land will allow no single story to dominate, narratives compete. In one narrative thread of the novel, the "official" U.S. version of Geronimo as one person, as a criminal, competes with the native story of Geronimo as four people, all heroic in varying degrees.[27] In another, conceptually related narrative thread, Zeta and her nephew Ferro, smuggling guns and cocaine across the U.S.-Mexico border, are criminals in one story, the one told by white Americans. But in Zeta's version, gun running and drug smuggling are revolutionary acts that weaken the powers that be and prepare the way for indigenous people to retake their land and live a sustainable existence upon it.[28]

The clash between voices often ends in violence, as it does when the rhetoric of the Marxist Bartolomeo threatens to occlude the tribal history of Angelita, La Escapia, and she kills him.[29] Such violent conclusions to the book's dialogues are common, and they are the type of human interaction the cultural theorists Rorty and Bakhtin certainly would not allow in the novelistic world, but they nevertheless exemplify the power that Silko attributes to discourse as it functions upon the earth's landscapes, and they exemplify the extremities of distress into which arid landscapes often reduce human beings.

Silko's faith in the revolutionary potential of discourse is in itself nothing new. She shares it with Eliot, Tolstoy, Mann, Pynchon, and countless others. Silko, however, foregrounds the ecological potential of novelistic discourse by giving distinct cultural groups distinct things to say about the role of human beings in the natural world. Her characters, in addition to being characters, often represent entire aesthetic systems, or even entire lifeways. Thus Silko utilizes novelistic discourse in a way few novelists before her have done.

The prime mover in the discursive universe of *Almanac of the Dead* is the voice of the natural world. This is not to say that Silko is a naïf who would anthropomorphize nature, nor would she, as Andrew Ross has put it, "mystify organic village life" in order justify her environmental critique of technological society.[30] In her novel, nature speaks in the only way a voiceless entity can, by inflecting human voices. But while it has been customary for desert writers to assume that human voices are inflected by little but human desires,[31] Silko makes the issue of reclaiming the Southwest and Mexico from the abstracted, industrialized culture that would "own" them the motive force of the book. Every voice raised in this dialogical world speaks to the balance that is possible between people and nature because, in the indigenous storytelling tradition of the desert lands that I've sketched above, the most important topic of conversation between humans and nature is whether people will admit to this balance or not.

Gloria Anzaldúa's *Borderlands/La Frontera* focuses and intensifies the conversation Silko explores by staging it in the multiple voices of one person. The book sophisticates Silko's many dialogues in certain ways, but at the same time it subtly reins them in, utilizing the normative effect achieved by filtering experience through one central consciousness.

Anzaldúa represents one of what Raymond Paredes has identified as a "new generation of Chicano writers, [who have] not only reaffirmed their ties to the cultures of contemporary Mexico and Latin America but also rediscovered, as Mexican artists had earlier in the century, their aboriginal heritage."[32] Anzaldúa's text explores the possibilities for cultural regeneration growing out of the place where Hispanic and indigenous cultures intersect.

The history Anzaldúa supplies of the Borderlands/La Frontera region highlights the environmentally tenuous position the land has historically occupied in Anglo American culture. After drought hits southwest Texas in the 1920s and 1930s, enabling what Anzaldúa identifies as "Anglo agribusiness corporations" to cheat "the Chicano landowners of their land," she chronicles the process by which the desert is made suitable for large-scale agriculture: "[T]he corporations hired gangs of *mexicanos* to pull out the brush, chaparral and cactus and to irrigate the desert" until twenty years later, in the 1950s she "saw the land, cut up into thousands of neat rectangles and squares, constantly being irrigated. In the 340-day growth season, the seeds of any kind of fruit or vegetable had only to be stuck in the ground in order to grow. More big land corporations came in and bought up the remaining land."[33] This sets up a culture that is uneasy with itself because rich Anglo landowners exploited the most recent inhabitants of the landscape, whom they had recently displaced, as well as exploiting the landscape itself.

Within this uneasy swirl of border voices, Anzaldúa places herself and her ability to speak in many voices—she who is a "*tejana* lesbian-feminist poet and fiction writer." She is a "rebel" who carries within her persona a

"Shadow-Beast" that refuses authority.[34] This Shadow-Beast refuses the authority of the culture that would dominate the borderlands of southwest Texas both physically through its agribusiness and culturally through its refusal to allow Anzaldúa's voice and voices like hers to be heard. Anzaldúa, as a speaker of many languages, occupies many cultural positions. She unequivocally threatens the monolithic Anglo society that would deny the border or *frontera* aspects of her homeland. And the threat she poses is a real one to any culture that would aspire to homogeneity. Speaking directly to the Anglo power elite in a section entitled "Linguistic Terrorism," Anzaldúa announces: *"Deslenguadas. Somos los del español deficiente.* We are your linguistic nightmare, your linguistic aberration, your linguistic *mestisaje,* the subject of your *burla."*[35] This is because she speaks "Chicano Spanish," "a border tongue which developed," as she claims, "naturally": "Change, *evolución, enriquecimiento de palabras nuevas por invención o adopción* have created variants of Chicano Spanish, *un nuevo lenguaje. Un lenguaje que corresponde a un modo de vivir.* Chicano Spanish is not incorrect, it is a living language"[36] and therefore it is culturally subversive.

In Anzaldúa's world, this cultural subversion is not the anarchy toward which Bakhtin's (and perhaps Silko's) linguistic carnivals tend. Anzaldúa's poetry of revolution "works out the clash of cultures. It makes us crazy constantly, but if the center holds, we've made some kind of evolutionary step forward. *Nuestra alma el trabajo,* the opus, the great alchemical work; spiritual mestizaje, a 'morphogenesis,' an inevitable unfolding."[37] And there is always a center to this kind of revolution—the culture-monolith-destabilizing center of Abbey's screeds, the antihegemonic revolutionary center of Silko's political and narrative carnival, the "natural" heart of Anzaldúa's evolving languages. It is the desert landscape, the arid country that Western European culture has never quite understood, the Borderlands, *la Frontera,* a land that has, as Anzaldúa reminds us, survived possession and ill use by five countries: Spain, Mexico, the Republic of Texas, the United States, the Confederacy, and the United States again. It has survived Anglo-Mexican blood feuds, lynchings, burnings, rapes, and pillages. Anzaldúa enlists this remarkable land itself as an ally in her fight for cultural and environmental justice.

It is a fragile landscape with which Anzaldúa aligns herself, a region where one's culture and the voices heard in it must be almost preternaturally sensitive to the exigencies of arid landscape, where a culture's conversations must be constantly about the land in which one lives, and must be sensitive to the implications of life on that land. Such conversation—as Anzaldúa, Silko, and Abbey all insist—will inevitably wreak havoc on monolithic, homogeneous cultural narratives, for the desert demands, as Anzaldúa concludes, a "constant changing of forms, *renacimientos de la tierra madre*," a changing of forms of which the dominant culture is not readily capable.[38]

The deserts thus continue to be proving grounds for the imaginative figures U.S. citizens use to figure the natural world. They continue to challenge the accustomed ways of seeing the nonhuman, and this challenge is reflected throughout the contemporary literature of the region.

As do Silko, Momaday, and Anzaldúa, Terry Tempest Williams, of Utah Mormon heritage, acknowledges the transformative power of the landscape on both personal and cultural levels, as she stands in the flats of the Great Salt Lake, struggling to come to terms with the human and environmental cost of nuclear testing in the Utah desert, relating to her readers that "[t]he understanding that I could die on the salt flats is no great epiphany. I could die anywhere. It's just that in the forsaken corners of Great Salt Lake there is no illusion of being safe. You stand alone in the throbbing silence of the Great Basin, exposed and alone. . . . Only the land's mercy and a calm mind can save my soul. And it is here I find grace."[39]

This is also one of Peter Goin's "landscapes of fear."[40] The desert in this case simultaneously separates these two artists from their civilized culture, reminds them of it, and redeems them, in a greater or lesser way, aesthetically—as it seems to do for authors and readers across cultures and from diverse heritages.

It is still fortunate that the desert encourages innovation on the part the people who would live in it, and fortunate that no single tradition, no single language, no single literature, and no single voice has yet comprehended the significance that desert lands hold for the people who inhabit them. In their intransigent allure, desert landscapes both entice Americans toward change and insist upon it.

Notes

Chapter 1. Introduction

1. Muir 23.

2. As William Goetzmann ("The Mountain Man" 415), Patricia Nelson Limerick (*Desert Passages* 6–7), and David Emmons ("The Influence of Ideology" 126), among others, have argued, this period saw a marked rise in American enthusiasm for desert scenery. Peter Wild, for instance, in "A Western Sun Sets in the East," concludes that "a major shift of the culture's outlook on the arid portion of its natural heritage" (217) occurred in 1901 with the publication of John C. Van Dyke's *The Desert*. In the larger scheme of history, Limerick's three-phase conception of the nation's relationship to its deserts is quite helpful, and it informs my study. Limerick posits that from about 1820 to about 1860 the desert presented merely a threat to physical existence that had to be endured by those who crossed it. From about 1860 (with the opening of the Nevada silver mines and the rise of irrigated agriculture) to the turn of the century, the deserts were seen as valuable if not attractive places. Starting around 1900, the deserts became beautiful and suitable for appreciation in the eyes of "cultured" Americans.

3. One such cultural reassessment, I argue, was in fact the newfound appreciation for desert landscapes that Americans began to exhibit during this period.

4. Commager 41.

5. Limerick, *Desert Passages* 3.

6. Warkentin 155–57.

7. Zimmer 51.

8. Wild, *Desert Reader* 2. As D. W. Meinig has noted in attempting a definition of the desert Southwest, it "is a distinctive place to the American mind but a somewhat blurred place on American maps" (*Southwest* 3).

9. Austin, *The Land of Little Rain* 3.

10. Limerick, *Desert Passages* 5.

11. Wigglesworth 83.

12. As Charles Bowden writes in *Killing the Hidden Waters,* the "arid lands are a merciless place for . . . societal experiments. They are full of dead people and cultures because the weather fluctuates a great deal," (21–22), and the history of the United States shows that societal experiments intended to dominate arid nature have consistently failed. As desert writers Alice Corbin Henderson, Mabel Dodge Luhan, and Mary Austin saw nearly a hundred years ago, the "fragile ecology of the Southwest, and the ways in which its indigenous populations had adjusted to it, provided important lessons in setting limits on human greed and will" (Rudnick 12).

13. Aridity is, of course, the central objective criterion that underlies this conceptual definition. To follow Peter Wild, a "good rule of thumb is that a desert is any place receiving ten or fewer inches of precipitation per year." As I note, Americans have been willing to call any landscape that did not easily support their lifeways a desert, but over the past two hundred years or so, arid landscapes have earned the epithet most consistently.

14. Patricia Nelson Limerick's *Legacy of Conquest,* Donald Worster's *Rivers of Empire,* Marc Reisner's *Cadillac Desert,* and Mike Davis's *City of Quartz* all provide compelling treatments of various ill-advised and ill-fated experiments modern Americans have undertaken in the desert.

15. Tuan 64. Aschmann in his ethnogeography of the Baja Peninsula, *The Central Desert of Baja California: Demography and Ecology* (1959), has demonstrated the scholarly potential of the study of this phenomenon by examining the accounts of the first Spaniards to encounter the region and by using such accounts to explain subsequent human behavior in this arid landscape.

16. English and Mayfield 7. As D. W. Meinig has so elegantly put it in the introduction to his *Interpretation of Ordinary Landscapes,* "Environment sustains us as creatures; landscape displays us as cultures" (3).

17. Meeker 3–4.

18. Tuan 1.

19. Evernden 3–17.

20. Buell 2, 3.

21. Kolodny, *The Lay of the Land* ix.

22. Kolodny, *The Land before Her* xii.

23. Austin, *The Land of Journey's Ending* 72.

24. It is impossible in this introduction to do justice to the blossoming study of the relationship of literature and art to the environment, a field sometimes called ecocriticism. For an important early articulation of the aims of this movement, see Love's

"Revaluing Nature: Toward an Ecological Criticism." A more recent treatment of the topic is Branch's "Ecocriticism: The Nature of Nature in Literary Theory and Practice." For a broader variety of perspectives, see Cheryll Glotfelty's introduction to the volume she and Harold Fromm edited, entitled *Ecocriticism*. For a remarkably innovative take on the issue, see Andrew Ross's *The Chicago Gangster Theory of Life*. Those pursuing the subject in depth will find the *Association for the Study of Literature and Environment Bibliography*, edited by Zita Ingham, to be essential.

25. Limerick 9.

26. Kolodny, *The Land before Her* xiii–xv.

27. Buell 4.

28. For the classic description of this episode in American history, see Turner, "The Significance of the Frontier in American History" 1.

29. For a detailed discussion of the economic and technological factors underlying this conceptual shift, see Donald Worster's *Rivers of Empire* 65–74.

30. Austin, *The Land of Journey's Ending* 440.

Chapter 2. A Barren Wild

1. Pike 302.

2. Austin, *The Land of Journey's Ending* xxviii.

3. Henry Nash Smith 204.

4. Thacker 2.

5. Novak, *American Painting of the Nineteenth Century* 63.

6. Quoted in Novak, *American Painting* 80.

7. Bjelajac 40.

8. Bjelajac 52.

9. Fryd 211.

10. Potter 78–90.

11. Berger 8.

12. Nelson 4.

13. Nelson 6.

14. Emmons 125–26.

15. Kinsey 2.

16. Rosenberg 13.

17. Horkheimer and Adorno 3.

18. Pike 302.

19. Feltskog 82.

20. Feltskog 83.

21. Frémont 599.

22. Raymond, "Desert/Paradise" 12.

23. Raymond, "Geographic Purgatory" 187.

24. Henry Nash Smith 201.

25. Lamar ix.

26. Lamar's opinion is that "in all likelihood she was the first American white woman ever to go over the rude trail of the Santa Fe traders" (ix).

27. Magoffin 2.

28. Magoffin 39.

29. Magoffin 195–96.

30. Manly's experience of the desert gave rise to the popular literary tradition of desert space as poisonous watering holes separated by interminable bone-littered stretches of plain, a tradition that finds its apotheosis in the final scene of Frank Norris's *McTeague,* as the eponymous dentist finds himself afoot, lost, without water, and handcuffed to a man he has killed in the "vast, interminable . . . measureless leagues of Death Valley" (442).

31. Manly 130–31.

32. Manly 254.

33. Irving, *The Rocky Mountains* 238.

34. Irving, *A Tour on the Prairies* 68.

35. Limerick also notes this phenomenon in discussing Mark Twain's written account of the Nevada deserts in *Roughing It* (*Desert Passages* 168).

36. Foster 7–9.

37. Gregg 25.

38. Gregg 110.

39. Gregg 45–46.

40. Gregg 64.

41. Gregg 46–52.

42. Gregg 118.

43. Gregg 135.

44. Gregg 118.

45. Kant 99.

46. Kant 99.

47. Powell published *Exploration of the Colorado* in 1875; Dutton published *Tertiary History* in 1882.

48. Kant 99.

49. McKinsey 31.

50. Greeley 230.

51. Greeley 231.

52. Greeley 236.

53. Schuyler, in his "The Sanctified Landscape," argues that the concern of the Hudson River School painters was for a domesticated landscape, one far removed from the wildness of the desert.

54. Greeley 233–34.

55. Stegner 149.

56. Stegner 62.

57. Quoted in Stegner 62.

58. J. W. Powell, *The Exploration of the Colorado River* 83.

59. J. W. Powell, *The Exploration of the Colorado River* 100.

60. J. W. Powell, *The Exploration of the Colorado River* 89.

61. J. W. Powell, "The Cañons of the Colorado" (1875) 304, 305.

62. J. W. Powell, "The Cañons of the Colorado" 525.

63. J. W. Powell, "The Cañons of the Colorado" 394–95.

64. J. W. Powell, "The Cañons of the Colorado" 395.

65. J. W. Powell, "The Cañons of the Colorado" 396.

66. Novak, *Nature and Culture* 7.

67. Childs 8.

68. Childs 7, 12.

69. Childs 21.

70. Stegner vi.

71. J. W. Powell, *Report on the Arid Regions* 99.

72. J. W. Powell, *Report on the Arid Regions* 40.

73. Makower 137.

74. J. W. Powell, *Report on the Arid Regions* 54.

75. Stegner xiv.

76. Stegner 158–59.

77. Wild, *Desert Reader* 87.

78. Stegner 164.

79. Dutton 93.

80. Dutton 54–55.

81. Milton 10–11.

82. Milton 11.

83. Dutton 55.

84. Dutton 141.

Chapter 3. Imaginative Men

1. Remington, "A Few Words from Mr. Remington" 16.

2. Nevertheless, it should be noted that art critics such as Estelle Jussim, in *Frederic Remington, the Camera, and the Old West,* are willing "to state categorically that Remington's role was primarily to serve as an intermediary between the camera and the printed page until after the Spanish-American War" (3), thus implying that Remington wasn't as "imaginative" as he might have believed himself to be.

3. Horan 151.

4. Horan 152.

5. Horan 152.

6. Naef and Wood 12.

7. Naef and Wood 57.

8. Horan 152.

9. Limerick, *Desert Passages* 64.

10. Twain, "How to Tell a Story" 239.

11. Twain, *Roughing It* 29.

12. Rourke 212–13.

13. Twain, *Roughing It* 117.

14. Kinsey 4.

15. Kinsey 20–40.

16. I separate Remington's art from his fiction here. I discuss his fiction separately in the following chapter simply because Remington did not start publishing fiction until several years after he had worked through his initial reactions to the desert in his visual art.

17. Turner 1.

18. Turner 1.

19. Although many historians, geographers, and ethnographers have refined, refuted, or revised Turner's argument, the fact is that at the time about which I write, Turner's thesis provided the paradigm Americans employed to conceptualize the West. For responses to his frontier hypothesis, see Webb's *The Great Plains,* Limerick's *The Legacy of Conquest,* and Jordan and Kaups's *The American Backwoods Frontier.*

20. Turner 2–3.

21. Roosevelt, *The Strenuous Life* 1.

22. Lears 4–5.

23. Remington, *Pony Tracks* 61–62.

24. Quoted in Craven, *Sculpture in America* 533. This "dread background" consists of characters such as Deadwood Dick who, as Clarence Durham has shown, acted out the sort of white hat/black hat morality plays in the open spaces of the West with which present-day aficionados of grade B westerns and Saturday afternoon serials are familiar.

25. Frederic Remington, "A Few Words from Mr. Remington" 16.

26. Frederic Remington, "A Few Words from Mr. Remington" 16.

27. McCullough, "Remington the Man" 23.

28. Roosevelt, *Letters of Theodore Roosevelt* 749.

29. Ballinger 19.

30. Ballinger 20; Dutton 141.

31. Ballinger 20–21.

32. Baigell, *The Western Art of Frederic Remington* (1976) 24.

33. Ballinger 59.

34. Ballinger 35.

35. Weinberg, Bolger, and Curry, in the introduction to their *American Impressionism,* hold that "[m]uch of the most engaging American painting from the turn of the last century has been classified handily by style" (3). The term *Impressionist,* they observe, is used to describe the "lightly-brushed, high-key works that such artists as William Merritt Chase and Childe Hassam executed in the late 1800's" (3). Thus, although Remington's paintings are certainly not associated directly with the central canon of American Impressionism, his later work shows an affinity with the move-

ment, which "echoed and amplified" the work of "the entire circle of painters who constituted the avant-garde from the mid-1860's through the mid-1880's" in France (p. 3), and which, along with American Realism, represented one of the most influential visual arts movements of the turn of the century.

36. Ballinger 24.

37. Nemerov 289.

38. Quoted in Nemerov 290.

39. Nemerov 319.

40. Nemerov 290.

41. Ballinger 71.

42. Maxwell 407.

43. Coffin, "Remington's 'Bronco Buster'" 319.

44. Ballinger 66.

45. Ballinger 84.

46. Maxwell 407.

47. Levenson, introduction, *Tales of Adventure* xcii.

48. Mott 589.

49. Mott 592.

50. Crane, *Western Writings* 20.

51. Robertson 251.

52. Collins 142–43.

53. Crane, *Works,* vol. 8, 469.

54. Crane, *Works,* vol. 8, 447.

55. Crane, *Works,* vol. 8, 450.

56. MacMahon 486.

57. Levenson xxviii.

58. Crane, *Correspondence* 136.

59. Crane, *Correspondence* 242.

60. Goetzmann, *Exploration and Empire* xiii.

61. Slotkin, *The Fatal Environment* 41.

62. Crane, *Works,* vol. 5, 55–56.

63. Crane, *Works,* vol. 5, 180.

64. Crane, *Works,* vol. 5, 180.

65. Crane, *Works,* vol. 8, 449.

66. Crane, *Works,* vol. 5, 113.

67. Crane, *Works,* vol. 5, 111.

68. Webb County Heritage Foundation, *Walking Tour of Historic Laredo.*

69. Thompson, *Laredo: A Pictorial History* 46.

70. Marx 226.

71. It should also be noted, however, that this green grass must have been more pleasant to walk on than hot sand.

72. Crane, *Works,* vol. 5, 109.

73. Crane, *Works,* vol. 5, 110.

74. Crane, "The Bride Comes to Yellow Sky" (1898) 377, 384.

75. Crane, *Works,* vol. 5, 116.

76. Crane, *Works,* vol. 5, 117.

77. Crane, *Western Writings* 4.

78. McKibben 64.

Chapter 4. The Desert in the Magazines

1. Monroe 781.

2 Norwood 77.

3. Webb 492.

4. Worster 137.

5. J. W. Powell, "The Non-Irrigable Lands" 920.

6. J. W. Powell, "The Non-Irrigable Lands" 638.

7. Chielens xiv.

8. Levine, *Highbrow/Lowbrow* 223.

9. Levine 223.

10. Levine 224.

11. Robbins, "Scribner's Monthly" 364.

12. Mott 718.

13. Mott 44.

14. Perkins, "Harper's Monthly Magazine" 169.

15. Lukács 136.

16. Monroe 789.

17. Turner 1.

18. Nash 144.

19. Lutz 9.

20. Nash 145.

21. Muir et al., "A Plan to Save The Forests" 631.

22. The citizens of the Republic could not have helped but hope that Isaiah's prophecy for the nation of Israel would also hold true for them, that it would come to pass that "The wilderness and the solitary place shall be glad for them; and the desert shall rejoice, and blossom as the rose" (Isaiah 35:1).

23. White 502.

24. *McClure's* 25 (Sept. 1905): advertising supplement, 114.

25. A stylized, abstract desert recurs in Crane's poetry. Consider, for instance, two desert poems from *The Black Riders and Other Lines* (1895):

In the desert
I saw a creature, naked, bestial,
Who, squatting upon the ground
Held his heart in his hands,
And ate of it.

I said: "Is it good, friend?"
"It is bitter—bitter," he answered;
"But I like it
"Because it is bitter,
"And because it is my heart."

A second poem:

I walked in a desert.
And I cried:
"Ah, God, take me from this place!"
A voice said: "It is no desert."
I cried: "Well, but—
the sand, the heat, the vacant horizon."
A voice said: "It is no desert."

26. Conder 12.

27. Roosevelt, *The Spread of the English-Speaking Peoples* 23.

28. Quoted in Mitchell, "Naturalism and the Languages of Determinism" 528.

29. Smythe, "The Conquest of Arid America" 85.

30. Smythe, "The Conquest of Arid America" 85.

31. Smythe, "Ways and Means in Arid America" 758.

32. Smythe, "The Conquest of Arid America" 85.

33. Nemerov 300.

34. Roosevelt, *A Compilation of the Messages and Papers of the Presidents*, vol. 14, 6658, 6657.

35. Roosevelt, *Messages,* vol. 14, 6908. One of the projects would have been the Roosevelt Dam in Arizona, which was 280 feet high when completed in 1911, creating one of the largest artificial bodies of water in the world and enabling Arizona farmers to grow alfalfa, sugar beets, and fruit in the desert near the Salt River.

36. Austin, *The Land of Journey's Ending* 5.

37. Smythe, "Ways and Means in Arid America" 742.

38. R. S. Baker 216.

39. R. S. Baker 9.

40. R. S. Baker 9.

41. R. S. Baker 10.

42. Monroe 781.

43. Crane, *Western Writings* 227.

44. Smythe, "Ways and Means in Arid America" 749.

45. Smythe, "Real Utopias in the Arid West" 609.

46. Wister, "Where Fancy Was Bred" 574.

47. Janvier 929.

48. Remington, "Horses of the Plains" 337.

49. Remington, "Horses of the Plains" 337. This assessment of wild desert horses

as more "worthy" than the Mexican vaqueros who rode them deserves note, especially coming from a man who claimed to be enthusiastic about using his Winchester in "massacring" "Jews—inguns—chinamen—Italians—Huns, the rubbish of the earth I hate" (quoted in Samuels and Samuels 177).

50. Vorpahl, "Roosevelt, Wister, Turner, and Remington" 287, 290.

51. Vorpahl, "Roosevelt, Wister, Turner, and Remington" 288; Robert Murray Davis, introduction, *Owen Wister's West* 7–8.

52. Etulain 24.

53. Webb 492.

54. Wister, "The Evolution of the Cowpuncher" 603.

55. Wister, "The Evolution of the Cowpuncher" 603–4.

56. Wister, "The Evolution of the Cowpuncher" 604. Wister's use of the term *Baron Hirsch* is a bigoted reference to Jews.

57. Wister, "The Evolution of the Cowpuncher" 604.

58. Dary 308, 330.

59. Quoted in Vorpahl, *My Dear Wister* 39.

60. Wister, "The Evolution of the Cowpuncher" 617.

61. Wister, "The Evolution of the Cowpuncher" 615.

62. Wister, "The Evolution of the Cowpuncher" 617.

63. Veblen 41.

64. See entry for Nathaniel Southgate Shaler in *Cyclopedia of American Biography*, vol. 9, 315.

65. Shaler 777.

66. Shaler 777.

67. Porter 75–76.

68. Porter 77.

69. Porter 75.

70. Shaler 784.

71. Shaler 784–85.

72. Perkins 167.

73. Anonymous, "Man and Men in Nature" 541. It should be noted that these humans are not clearly averse to using new insights about the "cosmos" to enhance their material prosperity, for often these insights come in "the tangible form of immediately serviceable knowledge." Still, the anonymous author seems to prefer a noninstrumental, nature-for-its-own-sake approach to the nonhuman world, an approach which causes people "to dream and question concerning the fields which are to be the seat of their new life" (542).

74. Anonymous 542.

75. Reed 167.

76. Reed 167.

77. Reed 172.

78. Monroe 782.

79. Monroe 783.

80. Monroe 783.

81. Monroe 784.

82. White 503.

83. R. S. Baker 225.

84. Austin, "A Land of Little Rain" 97.

85. Austin, *The Land of Little Rain* 115.

86. Given her large contribution to the nation's desert literature, Mary Austin receives relatively brief treatment in this study. Although Austin is a major voice in the desert literature of the United States, and although she did publish *The Land of Little Rain* only two years after John C. Van Dyke's *The Desert* (see chapter 5), her approach to desert lands was, as scholars such as Sean O'Grady have established, much different from the rigid hierarchical one of the writers I treat here. Austin's was a more "ecological" worldview in that she was interested in living systems and cultural systems rather than in individual organisms and the supposed "superiority" to one another. Thus, although I do not think Austin's voice fits into precisely the same tradition as these writers and artists, nevertheless, her voice is closely related to theirs, a relationship whose outlines I have tried to define. See O'Grady 125.

87. Prudden 745.

88. Brooks 427.

89. Brooks 427.

90. Brooks 432.

91. Brooks 434.

92. Brooks 434.

93. Brooks 428.

94. Austin, "A Land of Little Rain" 99.

95. Austin, *The Land of Journey's Ending* 377.

96. Ronald 220.

97. R. S. Baker 215.

Chapter 5. A Desert Paradox

1. Van Dyke, *The Desert* 57.

2. Modern geographers refer to the region Van Dyke called the Colorado desert as the Colorado Plateau.

3. Lawrence Clark Powell, *Southwestern Classics* 315.

4. Ayer, "Second Part of Mr. Ayer's Journal for 1918," from the "Reminiscences," Edward Everett Ayer Papers, Newberry Library Archives, Newberry Library, Chicago.

5. Van Dyke, "Scrapbook," John C. Van Dyke Papers, courtesy of the Gardner A. Sage Library archives, New Brunswick, N.J.

6. Anonymous review of *The Desert*, by John C. Van Dyke, 1901 ed., *The Dial* 1 (1902): 22–23.

7. Anonymous review of *The Desert*, by John C. Van Dyke, 1918 ed., *The Dial* 19 (1918): 216.

8. Wild, "A Western Sun Sets in the East: The Five 'Appearances' Surrounding John C. Van Dyke's *The Desert*" 217.

9. Walker 185.

10. Wild, "A Western Sun Sets in the East" 217.

11. See, for instance, "J. C. Van Dyke Dead; Critic of Rembrandt Art."

12. Van Dyke, *The Desert* 169.

13. See Wild and Carmony's "The Trip not Taken," or Wild's introduction to the Van Dyke autobiography, xxvi–xxx.

14. These tearsheets are collected in the John C. Van Dyke Papers at the American Academy of Arts and Letters Library, New York City.

15. Lowenthal 61.

16. See especially Van Dyke's *Art for Art's Sake* 31, and his *Autobiography* 168–69.

17. Barrie, introduction, *Modern Painters,* by John Ruskin, xxxviii.

18. Bloom, *The Anxiety of Influence* 19.

19. Van Dyke [Van Dyck], "Artistic Nature" 220–21.

20. Van Dyke, *Art for Art's Sake* 21.

21. Van Dyke, *Art for Art's Sake* 18.

22. Van Dyke, *Nature for Its Own Sake* 256.

23. Wild, "Viewing America's Deserts" 308.

24. Van Dyke, *The Desert* ix.

25. Van Dyke, *The Desert* 232.

26. Van Dyke, *The Desert* 4.

27. Van Dyke, *The Desert* 5.

28. Van Dyke, *The Desert* 60.

29. Van Dyke, *The Desert* 61.

30. Van Dyke, *The Desert* 59.

31. Van Dyke, *The Desert* 26.

32. Van Dyke, *The Desert* 27.

33. Van Dyke, *The Desert* 27.

34. Van Dyke, *The Desert* 7.

35. Van Dyke, *The Desert* 12.

36. Porter 75–76.

37. Van Dyke, *The Desert* 143.

38. Van Dyke, *The Desert* 200.

39. Van Dyke, *The Desert* v.

40. Ingham and Wild make the case that A.M.C. is Andrew Carnegie in their essay "The Preface as Illumination."

41. Van Dyke, *The Desert* 77.

42. Van Dyke, "John Charles Van Dyke Correspondence with Charles Scribner's Sons, with Related Papers," Archives of Charles Scribner's Sons, box 160.

43. Ingham and Wild 335.

44. Ingham and Wild 334.

45. Wolff 29.

46. Wolff 27.

47. Butterfield, "Foreword," *Lockout* ix.

48. Slotkin, *The Fatal Environment* 41.

49. Van Dyke had what appears to have been a standing invitation to Frick's house, where Frick's butler, "Deacon," had been instructed to let him in any time. Van Dyke possessed various letters from Carnegie discussing mutual vacation plans, party plans, and miscellaneous social events (Van Dyke Scrapbook).

50. Van Dyke, *Autobiography* 77.

51. Carnegie 226.

52. Burgoyne 297.

53. Carnegie 227. Here, Van Dyke, who edited Carnegie's *Autobiography,* inserted into the text a letter he claims to have written Carnegie from Mexico in 1900. Thus they are Van Dyke's words as they appear in Carnegie's autobiography.

54. Carnegie 227.

55. Carnegie 228.

56. Carnegie 228–30.

57. Van Dyke Scrapbook.

58. Van Dyke, *Autobiography* 97.

59. The desert had already been treated rather harshly by the time Van Dyke got to it. There were, of course, railroads on it, along with copper and borax mines, irrigated farms, and towns. Some of this treatment had come at the hands of his brother Theodore, a successful and respected southern California land developer who owned a ranch in the Mojave Desert and whom Van Dyke visited on most of his trips west. See Dix Van Dyke, *Daggett.*

60. Reed 172.

61. Eco 7.

62. Eco 49.

63. Baudrillard 121.

Chapter 6. Early Voices

1. Saxton and Saxton 336.

2. The long American Indian oral literary tradition on the desert is, to a fair degree, accessible through the texts of the present. As Brian Swann asserts in his introduction to the *Harper's Anthology of 20th Century Native American Poetry,* this literature "grows out of a past that is very much a present." "More than most poetry being written today," he holds, "Native American poetry is the poetry of historic witness" (xviii). Nevertheless, although I do assume that the "poetry" of Silko's, Momaday's, and Anzaldúa's books indeed exhibits Swann's "historic witness," I would like to provide a brief introduction to past Native American figures of the arid western landscapes as a context for figures that have come after.

3. Critics such as Krupat and Vizenor, along with Brian Swann, Vine Deloria, Jr., Andrew Wiget, Nancy J. Parezo, Kelley A. Hays, Barbara F. Slivac, Patricia Clark Smith,

and Paula Gunn Allen, among others (see bibliography for complete references) have begun the arduous work of teaching contemporary Americans about this indigenous desert heritage.

4. As Arnold Krupat observes in *Ethnocriticism,* there are many prohibitive factors in the endeavors of Americans of the cultural mainstream to understand Native American literatures (see especially his introduction and chapter 5). For one, the apparatus of U.S. literary criticism is text oriented, while these narratives are oral. For another, the cultures in question are very different from one another, at times unrecognizable to each other as cultures (see Parezo, Hays, and Slivac 147). Finally, there is the question of language itself. As Gary Nabhan suggests in *The Desert Smells Like Rain,* the indigenous cultures of the deserts even tend to construct language about fairly objective physical occurrences differently from other Americans. Equally difficult for the typical Anglo literary critic to comprehend would be the Navajos, who, according to Barre Tolken, believe that language does not merely describe reality, it creates it. Telling stories and singing and narrating rituals are ways of actually creating the world in which the Navajos live (390). This is an unfamiliar concept to members of a culture who think of language as representational.

5. Bailey and Bailey 11–21.

6. Zolbrod 1–29.

7. Benedict 1.

8. Benedict 1.

9. Benedict 6.

10. Zolbrod 37.

11. Zolbrod 47.

12. Zolbrod 49.

13. Zolbrod 50.

14. Zolbrod 6.

15. Coulander 23.

16. Coulander 27.

17. Coulander 29–30.

18. Coulander 30.

19. Elaine Jahner calls such a reading not just standard but simplistic in her article "Metalanguages" (55).

20. Smith, with Allen, "Earthly Relations, Carnal Knowledge" 176.

21. Saxton and Saxton 333.

22. Saxton and Saxton 336.

23. Wild, *The Desert Reader* 7.

24. The nostalgia for the Pleistocene era that has lately become fashionable (as in Earth First!'s "Back to the Pleistocene") is not entirely well informed. Ancient and indigenous cultures failed to adapt to their arid environments just as modern Western ones have. As Dan Flores has concluded from Martin and Klein's monumental study *Quaternary Extinctions,* the Clovis people of the Southwest, as well as the Folsom and the Portales people who followed them, were likely deeply implicated in the ecological

disasters attending their cultures approximately 11,000 years ago. Later in history, too, there is the fall of the irrigated Southwest's Anasazi civilization, with which primitivists must come to terms.

25. As in the case of the preceding treatment of American Indian narratives, my survey of Hispanic responses to the deserts of the future United States is included as context for contemporary desert literature. For an authoritative treatment of the history I examine so briefly here, see David Weber's *The Spanish Frontier in North America*. For a literary history, see Raymond Paredes's "The Evolution of Chicano Literature" in Houston Baker's *Three American Literatures*. For a helpful study of the Chicana literature associated with the renaissance of the 1960s, see Tey Diana Rebolledo's "Tradition and Mythology: Signatures of Landscape in Chicana Literature." Alvina Quintana's *Home Girls* provides an excellent discussion of the relationship between the Chicana voice and the concept of place.

26. Regarding the word *Hispanic*, Carey McWilliams has asked, "How is one to characterize, in a phrase, a people so diverse in origin?" (7). In this book I have chosen to use the general term *Hispanic* to denote early writers of Spanish origin, because during the time in question, cultural distinctions among Spanish-speaking, Native, and English-speaking peoples were slightly less complex than they have become in recent years.

27. Weber 16.

28. Weber 24.

29. Weber 24.

30. As an example of the interrelatedness of exploration and narrative among Spanish conquistadors, Raymond Paredes reports that Capt. Marcus Farfán's drama describing the Spanish entrada into New Mexico was performed within two weeks of Juan de Oñate's arrival there in 1598. See Paredes, "The Evolution of Chicano Literature" 34.

31. Hallenbeck 16.

32. Hallenbeck 16.

33. Hallenbeck 35.

34. Castañeda 2, 82.

35. As David Weber has warned, the notion that "Spaniards came simply to plunder, whereas Englishmen and Frenchmen came to settle is a popular but false dichotomy" (64).

36. Weber 94.

37. Kino 184.

38. Kino 193.

39. Kino 191.

40. Kino 111.

41. Kino 113.

42. The Spanish explorers could not have approached the land as aggressively and imperialistically as Anglo explorers did, simply because they did not yet have the technology to do so. Nevertheless, many early Spanish explorers exhibited a concern with

the environmental viability of their behavior that those who followed would have done well to emulate.

43. Cabeza de Vaca 71.

44. Cabeza de Vaca 75.

45. Cabeza de Vaca 78.

Chapter 7. In Beauty It Is Finished

1. Momaday, *House Made of Dawn* 1.

2. Rudnick 10.

3. O'Grady 140.

4. O'Grady 141.

5. O'Grady 125.

6. Austin, *The Land of Little Rain* 103. The implications of Austin's work on gender go far beyond the scope of my discussion here, and indeed far beyond her desert writing. Lois Rudnick's essay in Monk and Norwood's *The Desert Is No Lady* provides a helpful starting point for a study of the relationship between her feminism and her nature writing.

7. Austin, *The Land of Journey's Ending* 437.

8. Austin, *The Land of Journey's Ending* 442–43.

9. Austin, *The Land of Journey's Ending* 438.

10. Austin, *The Land of Little Rain* 164.

11. Rudnick 25.

12. Abbey 42.

13. Abbey 54.

14. Goin has documented in photographs the convergence of phenomena that have made this part of the Great Basin Desert different from other deserts—in his words, "charged," "alien"—because on this radioactive landscape: "the physical threat, vague yet omnipresent, structures our response" (xix).

15. Abbey 54.

16. Intent in *Desert Solitaire* upon saving wild places so that people like himself could enjoy them, Abbey eventually came to blame Latino immigrants for having created "a poisoned environment" (Athanasiou 37) because he was unable to see that the very ways of seeing that had victimized the desert had also victimized the people he excoriated.

17. Momaday, "A First American Views His Land" 15; italics in original.

18. Momaday, "A First American Views His Land" 17.

19. Momaday, "A First American Views His Land" 18.

20. Momaday, "A First American Views His Land" 18.

21. Nabhan 8.

22. Silko, "Interior and Exterior Landscapes: The Pueblo Migration Stories" 155.

23. Silko, *Ceremony* 132.

24. Silko, *Ceremony* 258.

25. Aithal 170.

26. Rorty, *Contingency, Irony, and Solidarity* xvi. There is a logic to this dual convergence of traditions both in the physical place called the "desert" and in the conceptual place called the "novel." As Mikhail Bakhtin defines the novel, it must exist in a "heteroglot" world, a world in which society is unified at the level of language (Clark and Holquist 238–44, 246). This heteroglot world constitutes something like Jurgen Habermas' "ideal language situation," in which the voice of every inhabitant receives its due attention, and it is like Rorty's paradigm of a "conversational" society in which a perfect world order is brought about through informed conversation between human beings. The desert regions of the United States are conducive to such an ideal conversational culture precisely because for hundreds of years they have wreaked havoc on monolithic discourses *that* would monopolize conversation.

27. Silko, *Almanac of the Dead* 224–32.

28. Silko, *Almanac of the Dead* 177–79.

29. Silko, *Almanac of the Dead* 525–32.

30. Ross 10.

31. Baudrillard goes so far as to posit that, in the desert, human beings have murdered desire.

32. Paredes 61.

33. Anzaldúa 8–9.

34. Anzaldúa, author biography in *Borderlands/La Frontera* 205.

35. Anzaldúa 58.

36. Anzaldúa 55.

37. Anzaldúa 81.

38. Anzaldúa 91.

39. Williams 148.

40. Goin xix.

References

Abbey, Edward. *Desert Solitaire: A Season in the Wilderness*. New York: McGraw-Hill, 1968.

Aithal, S. K. "The Redemptive Return: Momaday's *House Made of Dawn*." *North Dakota Quarterly* 53 (Spring 1985): 160–72.

Anonymous. "Man and Men in Nature." *Atlantic* 74 (Oct. 1894): 541–47.

Anzaldúa, Gloria. *Borderlands/La Frontera*. San Francisco: Aunt Lute Books, 1987.

Aschmann, Homer. *Ibero-Americana 42: The Central Desert of Baja California; Demography and Ecology*. Berkeley: University of California Press, 1959.

Athanasiou, Tom. *Divided Planet: The Ecology of Rich and Poor*. New York: Little, Brown, 1996.

Austin, Mary. "The Basket Maker." *Atlantic* 91 (February 1903): 235–39.

———. "The Golden Fortune." *Atlantic* 92 (December 1903): 791–95.

———. "Jimville: A Bret Harte Town." *Atlantic* 90 (November 1902): 690–94.

———. *The Land of Journey's Ending*. 1924. New York: AMS Press, 1969.

———. "A Land of Little Rain." *Atlantic* 91 (January 1903): 96–99.

———. *The Land of Little Rain*. New York: Houghton Mifflin, 1903.

———. "The Last Antelope." *Atlantic* 92 (July 1903): 25–29.

———. "The Little Town of the Little Grape Vines." *Atlantic* 91 (June 1903): 822–25.

———. "A Shepherd of the Sierras." *Atlantic* 86 (July 1900): 54–58.

———. "Two Books on Western Birds." *Atlantic* 91 (February 1903): 269–70.

Ayer, Edward Everett. "Second Part of Mr. Ayer's Journal for 1918." 26 pp. (carbon). From the "Reminiscences." Edward Everett Ayer Papers, Newberry Library Archives, Newberry Library, Chicago.

Baigell, Matthew. *The Western Art of Frederic Remington*. New York: Ballantine Books, 1976.

Bailey, Garrick, and Roberta Glenn Bailey. *A History of the Navajos: The Restoration Years*. Santa Fe: School of American Research Press, 1986.

Baker, Houston A., ed. *Three American Literatures*. New York: Modern Language Association, 1982.

Baker, Ray Stannard. "The Great Southwest." *Century* 64 (May, June 1902): 5–15, 213–25.

Bakhtin, Mikhail. *The Dialogical Imagination*. Ed. Michael Holquist. Trans. Caryl Emerson and Michael Holquist. Austin: University of Texas Press, 1981.

Ballinger, James K. *Frederic Remington's Southwest*. Phoenix: Phoenix Art Museum, 1992.

Barrie, David. Introduction. *Modern Painters*. By John Ruskin. New York: Alfred A. Knopf, 1987. xvii–xliv.

Baudrillard, Jean. *America*. Trans. Chris Turner. London: Verso, 1988.

Benedict, Ruth. *Zuñi Mythology*. 1935. 2 vols. New York: AMS Press, 1969.

Berger, John. *Ways of Seeing*. New York: Viking Press, 1972.

Bjelajac, David. "The Boston Elite's Resistance to Washington Allston's *Elijah in the Desert*." *American Iconology: New Approaches to Nineteenth-Century Art and Literature*. Ed. David Miller. New Haven: Yale University Press, 1993. 39–57.

Bloom, Harold. *The Anxiety of Influence*. New York: Oxford University Press, 1973.

Bourdieu, Pierre. *Distinction: A Social Critique of the Judgment of Taste*. Trans. Richard Nice. Cambridge, Mass.: Harvard University Press, 1984.

Bowden, Charles. *Killing the Hidden Waters*. Austin: University of Texas Press, 1977.

Branch, Michael. "Ecocriticism: The Nature of Nature in Literary Theory and Practice." *Weber Studies*. 11.1 (Winter 1994): 41–55.

Bredahl, Carl A., Jr. *New Ground: Western Narrative and the Literary Canon*. Chapel Hill: University of North Carolina Press, 1989.

Brooks, Benjamin. "The Southwest from a Locomotive." *Scribner's* 34 (October 1903): 427–38.

Buell, Lawrence. *The Environmental Imagination: Thoreau, Nature Writing, and the Formation of American Culture*. Cambridge, Mass.: Harvard University Press, 1995.

Burgoyne, Arthur G. *The Homestead Strike of 1892*. 1893. London: Feffer and Simons, 1979.

Burke, Edmund. *A Philosophical Enquiry into the Origin of Our Ideas of the Sublime and Beautiful*. 1757. Ed. J. T. Boulton. Chicago: University of Notre Dame Press, 1968.

Burroughs, John. *Far and Near*. Vol. 13 of *The Complete Writings of John Burroughs*. New York: Wm. H. Wise and Co., 1924.

Butterfield, Roger. Foreword. *Lockout: The Story of the Homestead Strike of 1892; A*

Study of Violence, Unionism, and the Carnegie Steel Empire. By Leon Wolff. New York: Harper and Row, 1965. ix–xi.

Cabeza de Vaca, Alvar Núñez. *The Account: Cabeza de Vaca's Relación*. Trans. Martin A. Favata and José B. Fernández. Houston: Arte Público Press, 1993.

Carnegie, Andrew. *Autobiography of Andrew Carnegie*. Ed. John C. Van Dyke. Boston: Houghton Mifflin, 1920.

Castañeda, Pedro de. *The Journey of Coronado*. Trans. and ed. George Winship. 1902. New York: Allerton Book Co., 1922.

Chielens, Edward, ed. *American Literary Magazines: The Eighteenth and Nineteenth Centuries*. New York: Greenwood Press, 1986.

Childs, Elizabeth C. "Time's Profile: John Wesley Powell, Art, and Geology at the Grand Canyon." *American Art* 10.1 (Spring 1996): 7–35.

Clark, Katerina, and Michael Holquist. *Mikhail Bakhtin*. Cambridge, Mass.: Harvard University Press, 1984.

Coffin, William A. "Remington's 'Bronco Buster.'" *Century* 52 (June 1896): 318–19.

Collins, Michael J. "Realism and Romance in the Western Stories of Stephen Crane." *Under the Sun: Myth and Realism in Western American Literature*. Ed. Barbara Meldrum. Troy, N.Y.: Whitston Publishing Co., 1985. 138–49.

Commager, Henry Steele. *The American Mind: An Interpretation of American Thought and Character since the 1880's*. New Haven: Yale University Press, 1950.

Conder, John J. *Naturalism in American Fiction*. Lexington: University of Kentucky Press, 1984.

Coulander, Harold. *The Fourth World of the Hopis: The Epic Story of the Hopi Indians as Preserved in Their Legends and Traditions*. Albuquerque: University of New Mexico Press, 1971.

Crane, Stephen. *The Black Riders and Other Lines*. Boston: Copeland and Day, 1895.

———. "The Bride Comes to Yellow Sky." *McClure's* 10 (February 1898): 377–84.

———. *The Correspondence of Stephen Crane*. Ed. Stanley Wertheim and Paul Sorrentino. New York: Columbia University Press, 1988.

———. "A Man and Some Others." *Century* 53 (February 1897): 601–7.

———. *The University of Virginia Edition of the Works of Stephen Crane*. Ed. Fredson Bowers. 10 vols. Charlottesville: University Press of Virginia, 1969–76.

———. *The Western Writings of Stephen Crane*. Ed. Frank Bergon. New York: New American Classics, 1979.

Craven, Wayne. *Sculpture in America*. New York: Cornwall Books, 1984.

Dary, David. *Cowboy Culture*. New York: Alfred A. Knopf, 1981.

Davis, Mike. *City of Quartz*. New York: Verso, 1990.

Davis, Robert Murray. Introduction. *Owen Wister's West*. Ed. Robert Murray Davis. Albuquerque: University of New Mexico Press, 1987.

Deloria, Vine. *Red Earth, White Lies: Native Americans and the Myth of Scientific Fact*. New York: Scribner's, 1995.

DeVoto, Bernard. *The Year of Decision: 1846*. Boston: Little, Brown, 1943.

Dobie, J. Frank. *Coronado's Children: Tales of Lost Mines and Buried Treasures of the Southwest*. 1930. Austin: University of Texas Press, 1978.

Durham, Philip, ed. *Seth Jones and Deadwood Dick on Deck*. New York: Odyssey Press, 1966.

Dutton, Clarence. *Tertiary History of the Grand Cañon District*. 1882. Salt Lake City: Peregrine Smith, 1977.

Eco, Umberto. *Travels in Hyperreality*. Trans. William Weaver. San Diego: Harcourt Brace Jovanovich, 1986.

Emmons, David. "The Influence of Ideology on Changing Environmental Images." *Images of the Great Plains: The Role of Nature in Human Settlement*. Ed. Brian W. Blouet and Merlin P. Lawson. Lincoln: University of Nebraska Press, 1975. 125–36.

English, Paul Ward, and Robert C. Mayfield. "The Cultural Landscape." *Man, Space, and Environment: Concepts in Contemporary Human Geography*. Ed. English and Mayfield. New York: Oxford University Press, 1972. 3–9.

Etulain, Richard. *Owen Wister*. Boise State College Western Writers Series. Boise, Idaho: Boise State College, 1973.

"Eulogizes the Life of Dr. J. C. Van Dyke." *New York City Times*, December 9, 1932.

Evernden, Neil. *The Social Creation of Nature*. Baltimore: Johns Hopkins University Press, 1992.

Feltskog, E. N. "The Range of Vision: Landscape and the Far West, 1803 to 1850." *Landscape in America*. Ed. George F. Thompson. Austin: University of Texas Press, 1995. 75–92.

Flores, Dan. *Caprock Canyonlands: Journeys into the Heart of the Southwest*. Austin: University of Texas Press, 1990.

Foster, Edward Halsey. *Josiah Gregg and Lewis H. Garrard*. Boise State University Western Writers Series. Boise, Idaho: Boise State University, 1977.

Frémont, John Charles. *A Report on the Exploring Expedition to Oregon and North California in the Years 1843–44*. Vol. 1 of *The Expeditions of John Charles Frémont*. Ed. Donald Jackson and Mary Lee Spence. Urbana: University of Illinois Press, 1970.

Fryd, Vivian Green. *Art and Empire: The Politics of Ethnicity in the United States Capitol, 1815–1860*. New Haven: Yale University Press, 1992.

Gilpin, William. *Mission of the North American People: Geographical, Social, and Political*. Philadelphia: Lippincott, 1873.

Glotfelty, Cheryll, and Harold Fromm, eds. *Ecocriticism*. Athens: University of Georgia Press, 1996.

Goetzmann, William H. *Exploration and Empire: The Explorer and the Scientist in the Winning of the American West*. New York: Alfred A. Knopf, 1966.

———. "The Mountain Man as Jacksonian Man." *American Quarterly* 15 (Fall 1963): 402–15.

Goetzmann, William H., and Kay Sloan. *Looking Far North: The Harriman Expedition to Alaska*. New York: Viking Press, 1982.

Goin, Peter. *Nuclear Landscapes*. Baltimore: Johns Hopkins University Press, 1991.

Greeley, Horace. *An Overland Journey from New York to San Francisco in the Summer of 1859*. 1860. New York: Alfred A. Knopf, 1964.

Green, Stanley. *A History of Webb County*. Laredo, Tex.: Border Studies Center, 1992.

Gregg, Josiah. *Commerce of the Prairies*. 1844. Ed. David Freeman Hawke. Indianapolis: Bobbs-Merrill, 1970.

Habermas, Jurgen. *Philosophisch-politische Profile*. Frankfurt am Main: Suhrkamp Verlag, 1971.

Hallenbeck, Cleve. *The Journey of Fray Marcos de Niza*. Dallas: Southern Methodist University Press, 1987.

Higginson, Thomas Wentworth. "A World Literature." *Century* 39 (April 1890): 922–23.

Hobbs, Michael. "Living In-Between: Tayo as Radical Reader in Leslie Marmon Silko's *Ceremony*." *Western American Literature* 28 (Winter 1994): 301–12.

Hoffman, Katherine. *An Enduring Spirit: The Art of Georgia O'Keeffe*. Metuchen, N.J.: Scarecrow Press, 1984.

Horan, James D. *Timothy O'Sullivan: America's Forgotten Photographer*. Garden City, N.J.: Doubleday, 1966.

Horgan, Paul. *Great River: The Rio Grande in North American History*. In *Of America East and West: Selections from the Writings of Paul Horgan*. New York: Farrar, Straus, Giroux, 1984. 1–62.

Horkheimer, Max, and Theodor Adorno. *Dialectic of Enlightenment*. 1944. Trans. John Cumming. New York: Continuum, 1987.

Ingham, Zita, ed. *Association for the Study of Literature and Environment Bibliography, 1990–1993*. Jonesboro, Ark.: Association for the Study of Literature and Environment, 1994.

———, ed. *Association for the Study of Literature and Environment Bibliography, 1994*. Coos Bay, Ore.: Association for the Study of Literature and Environment, 1995.

———. "Reading and Writing a Landscape: A Rhetoric of Southwest Desert Literature." Diss. University of Arizona, 1991.

Ingham, Zita, and Peter Wild. "The Preface as Illumination: The Curious (If Not Tricky) Case of John C. Van Dyke's *The Desert*." *Rhetoric Review* 9 (Spring 1991): 328–39.

Irving, Washington. *The Rocky Mountains*. 2 vols. Philadelphia: Carey, Lea, and Blanchard, 1837.

———. *A Tour on the Prairies*. Philadelphia: Carey, Lea, and Blanchard, 1835.

"J. C. Van Dyke Dead; Critic of Rembrandt Art." *New York Herald Tribune* 6 December 1932.

"J. C. Van Dyke Dies; Authority on Art." *New York Evening Post* 6 December 1932.

Jahner, Elaine C. "Metalanguages." *Narrative Chance: Postmodern Discourse on Native American Indian Literatures*. Ed. Gerald Vizenor. Albuquerque: University of New Mexico Press, 1989. 155–85.

James, George Wharton. *The Wonders of the Colorado Desert*. 2 vols. Boston: Little, 1906.

Janvier, Thomas A. "Santa Fe Charley's Kindergarten." *Harper's* 111 (November 1905): 929–40.

Jones, Billy M. *Health Seekers in the Southwest*. Norman: University of Oklahoma Press, 1967.

Jordan, Terry G., and Matti Kaups. *The American Backwoods Frontier: An Ethnic and Ecological Interpretation*. Baltimore: Johns Hopkins University Press, 1989.

Jordan, Terry G., Jon T. Kilpinen, and Charles F. Gritzner. *The Mountain West: Interpreting the Folk Landscape*. Baltimore: Johns Hopkins University Press, 1996.

Jussim, Estelle. *Frederic Remington, the Camera, and the Old West*. Fort Worth: Amon Carter Museum, 1983.

Kant, Immanuel. *The Critique of Judgment*. 1790. Trans. Werner S. Pluhar. Indianapolis: Hackett Publishing Co., 1987.

Kinney, Abbot. "Forests and Streams." *Century* 40 (August 1890): 637–38.

Kino, Eusebio. *Kino's Historical Memoir of Pimería Alta*. Trans. and ed. Herbert Bolton. Cleveland: Arthur Clark Co., 1919.

Kinsey, Joni Louise. *Thomas Moran and the Surveying of the American West*. Washington, D.C.: Smithsonian Institution Press, 1992.

Kolodny, Annette. *The Land before Her: Fantasy and Experience of the American Frontiers, 1630–1860*. Chapel Hill: University of North Carolina Press, 1984.

———. *The Lay of the Land: Metaphor as Experience and History in American Life and Letters*. Chapel Hill: University of North Carolina Press, 1975.

Krupat, Arnold. *Ethnocriticism*. Berkeley: University of California Press, 1992.

———. "Post-Structuralism and Oral Literature." *Recovering the Word*: Essays on Native American Literature. Ed. Brian Swann and Arnold Krupat. Berkeley: University of California Press, 1987. 113–28.

Krutch, Joseph Wood. *The Desert Year*. New York: William Sloan Associates, 1952.

Lamar, Howard. Foreword. *Down the Santa Fe Trail and into Mexico*. By Susan Shelby Magoffin. 1926. Ed. Stella M. Drumm. New Haven: Yale University Press, 1962.

Lears, T. J. Jackson. *No Place of Grace: Antimodernism and the Transformation of American Culture, 1880–1920*. New York: Pantheon Books, 1981.

Leutze, Emmanuel. *Westward the Course of Empire Takes Its Way (Westward Ho!)*. U.S. Capitol, Washington, D.C. 1861–62.

Levenson, J. C. Introduction. *Tales of Adventure*. Vol. 5 of *The University of Virginia Edition of the Works of Stephen Crane*. Ed. Fredson Bowers. Charlottesville, University of Virginia Press, 1970.

Levine, Lawrence W. *Highbrow/Lowbrow*. Cambridge, Mass.: Harvard University Press, 1988.

Limerick, Patricia Nelson. *Desert Passages*. Albuquerque: University of New Mexico Press, 1985.

———. *The Legacy of Conquest: The Unbroken Past of the American West*. New York: W. W. Norton, 1987.

Love, Glen. "Revaluing Nature: Toward an Ecological Criticism." *Western American Literature* 25 (Fall 1990): 201–15.

Lowenthal, David. "The American Scene." *Geographical Review* (January 1968): 61–88.

Lukács, Georg. *History and Class Consciousness*. Trans. Rodney Livingstone. Cambridge, Mass.: MIT Press, 1988.

Lutz, Tom. *American Nervousness*. Ithaca, N.Y.: Cornell University Press, 1991.

Lyon, Thomas J. "Beyond the Frontier Mind." *Old Southwest/New Southwest: Essays on a Region and Its Culture*. Ed. Judy Nolte Lensink. Tucson: Tucson Public Library, 1987. 119–30.

———. "The Nature Essay in the West." *A Literary History of the American West*. Ed. Thomas J. Lyon. Sponsored by the Western Literature Association. Fort Worth: Texas Christian University Press, 1987. 221–65.

MacMahon, James A. *Deserts*. New York: Alfred A. Knopf, 1985.

Magoffin, Susan Shelby. *Down the Santa Fe Trail and into Mexico*. 1926. New Haven: Yale University Press, 1962.

Makower, Joel, ed. *The Map Catalog*. New York: Random House, 1990.

Manje, Juan Mateo. *Luz de Tierra Incógnita*. Trans. Harry J. Karns. Tucson: Arizona Silhouettes, 1954.

Manly, William Lewis. *Death Valley in '49*. 1894. Ann Arbor: University Microfilms, 1966.

Martin, Paul S., and Richard B. Klein, eds. *Quaternary Extinctions: A Prehistoric Revolution*. Tucson: University of Arizona Press, 1984.

Marx, Leo. *The Machine in the Garden: Technology and the Pastoral Ideal in America*. New York: Oxford University Press, 1964.

Maxwell, Perriton. "Frederic Remington, Most Typical of American Artists." *Pearsons* 18 (1907): 395–407.

McCullough, David. "Remington the Man." *Frederic Remington: The Masterworks*. Ed. Michael Edward Shairo. New York: Harry N. Abrams, 1988. 14–37.

McKibben, Bill. *The End of Nature*. New York: Random House, 1989.

McKinsey, Elizabeth. *Niagara Falls: Icon of the American Sublime*. Cambridge: Cambridge University Press, 1985.

McWilliams, Carey. *North from Mexico: The Spanish-Speaking People of the United States*. 1948. New York: Greenwood Press, 1968.

Meeker, Joseph M. *The Comedy of Survival: Studies in Literary Ecology*. New York: Scribner's, 1974.

Meinig, D. W. Introduction. *The Interpretation of Ordinary Landscapes*. Ed. D. W. Meinig. New York: Oxford University Press, 1979. 1–7.

———. *Southwest: Three Peoples in Geographical Change, 1600–1970*. New York: Oxford University Press, 1971.

Merwin, Henry Childs. "Books about Nature." *Scribner's* 33 (April 1903): 430–37.

Milton, John. *Paradise Lost*. New York: W. W. Norton, 1975.

Mitchell, Lee Clark. "Naturalism and the Languages of Determinism." *Columbia Literary History of the United States*. Ed. Emory Elliot. New York: Columbia University Press, 1988. 525–45.

Momaday, N. Scott. "A First American Views His Land." *National Geographic* 150 (July 1976): 13–18.

———. *House Made of Dawn*. New York: Harper and Row, 1968.

Monroe, Harriet. "Arizona." *Atlantic Monthly* 89 (June 1902): 780–89.

Mott, Frank Luther. *A History of American Magazines*. Vol. 4: *1885–1905*. Cambridge, Mass.: Belknap Press/Harvard University Press, 1957.

Muir, John. "The Grand Canyon." *Southwest Stories*. Ed. John Miller and Genevieve Morgan. San Francisco: Chronicle Books, 1993.

Muir, John, Gifford Pinchot, Nathaniel Shaler, et al. "A Plan to Save the Forests." *Century* 49 (February 1895): 626–34.

Nabhan, Gary Paul. *The Desert Smells Like Rain: A Naturalist in Papago Indian Country*. San Francisco: North Point Press, 1982.

Naef, Weston J., in collaboration with James N. Wood. *Era of Exploration: The Rise of Landscape Photography in the American West, 1860–1885*. Boston: New York Graphic Society, 1975.

Nash, Roderick. *Wilderness and the American Mind*. New Haven: Yale University Press, 1967.

Nelson, George. *How to See: Visual Adventures in a World God Never Made*. Boston: Little, Brown, 1977.

Nemerov, Alex. "Doing the 'Old America.'" *The West as America*. Ed. William Treuttner. Washington, D.C.: Smithsonian Institution Press, 1991. 285–343.

Norris, Frank. *McTeague*. 1899. New York: Penguin, 1982.

Norwood, Vera. "Crazy-Quilt Lives: Frontier Sources for Southwestern Women's Literature." *The Desert Is No Lady: Southwestern Landscapes in Women's Writing*. Ed. Vera Norwood and Janice Monk. New Haven: Yale University Press, 1987. 74–95.

Novak, Barbara. *American Painting of the Nineteenth Century*. New York: Praeger, 1969.

———. *Nature and Culture: American Landscape Painting, 1825–1875*. New York: Oxford University Press, 1980.

O'Grady, John P. *Pilgrims to the Wild*. Salt Lake City: University of Utah Press, 1993.

Paredes, Raymond A. "The Evolution of Chicano Literature." *Three American Literatures*. Ed. Houston A. Baker. New York: Modern Language Association, 1982. 33–79.

Parezo, Nancy J., Kelley A. Hays, and Barbara F. Slivac. "The Mind's Road: Southwestern Indian Women's Art." *The Desert Is No Lady: Southwestern Landscapes in Women's Writing*. Ed. Vera Norwood and Janice Monk. New Haven: Yale University Press, 1987. 146–73.

Pérez Castillo, Susan. "Postmodernism, Native American Literature and the Real: The Silko-Erdrich Controversy." *Massachusetts Review* 32 (Summer 1991): 285–94.

Perkins, Barbara M. "Harper's Monthly Magazine." *American Literary Magazines: The Eighteenth and Nineteenth Centuries*. Ed. Edward Chielens. New York: Greenwood Press, 1986. 166–71.

Pike, Zebulon Montgomery. *Exploratory Travels through the Western Territories of North America*. 1811. Chicago: W. H. Lawrence and Co., 1889.

Pollitzer, Anna. *A Woman of Paper: Georgia O'Keeffe*. New York: Simon and Schuster, 1988.

Porter, Joseph C. *Paper Medicine Man*. Norman: University of Oklahoma Press, 1986.

Potter, David M. *People of Plenty: Economic Abundance and the American Character*. Chicago: University of Chicago Press, 1954.

Powell, John Wesley. "The Cañons of the Colorado." *Scribner's* 9 (January-March 1875): 293–310, 395–409, 523–37.

———. *The Exploration of the Colorado River*. 1875. Chicago: University of Chicago Press, 1957.

———. "Institutions for the Arid Lands." *Century* 40 (May 1890): 111–16.

———. "The Irrigable Lands of the Arid Region." *Century* 39 (March 1890): 766–76.

———. "The Non-Irrigable Lands of the Arid Region." *Century* 39 (April 1890): 915–22.

———. "The Physical Features of the Colorado Valley." *Popular Science Monthly* 7 (August–October 1875): 385–99, 531–41, 670–80.

———. *Report on the Lands of the Arid Regions of the United States*. 1878. Ed. Wallace Stegner. Cambridge, Mass.: Belknap Press/Harvard University Press, 1962.

Powell, Lawrence Clark. *Southwest Classics: The Creative Literature of the Arid Lands— Essays on the Books and Their Writers*. Los Angeles: Ward Ritchie Press, 1974.

"Prof. J. C. Van Dyke, Art Authority, Dies." *New York Times*, December 6, 1932.

Prudden, T. Mitchell. "Glimpses of the Great Plateau." *Harper's* 103 (October 1901): 745–50.

Quintana, Alvina. *Home Girls: Chicana Literary Voices*. Philadelphia: Temple University Press, 1996.

Raymond, Elizabeth. "Desert/Paradise: Images of Nevada Landscape." *Nevada Public Affairs Review* 1988, no. 1: 12–18.

———. "Geographic Purgatory: Sense of Place in the Great Basin." *Halcyon 88* 10: 187–200.

Rebolledo, Tey Diana. "Tradition and Mythology: Signatures of Landscape in Chicana Literature." *The Desert Is No Lady: Southwestern Landscapes in Women's Writing*. Ed. Vera Norwood and Janice Monk. New Haven: Yale University Press, 1987. 96–124.

Reed, Verner Z. "The Desert." *Atlantic* 90 (August 1902): 166–72.

Reisner, Marc. *Cadillac Desert: The American West and Its Disappearing Water*. New York: Penguin Books, 1993.

Remington, Frederic. "The Essentials at Fort Adobe." *Harper's* 96 (April 1898): 727–35.

———. "A Few Words from Mr. Remington." *Collier's* 18 (March 1905): 16.

———. "Horses of the Plains." *Century* 37 (January 1889): 332–43.

———. *Pony Tracks*. 1895. Norman: University of Oklahoma Press, 1989.

Rev. of *The Desert*. By John C. Van Dyke. 1901 ed. *The Dial* 1 (January 1902): 22–23.

Rev. of *The Desert*, by John C. Van Dyke. 1918 ed. Photographs by J. Smeaton Chase. *The Dial* 19 (September 1918): 216.

Robbins, Fred. "Scribner's Monthly." *American Literary Magazines*. Ed. Edward E. Chielens. New York: Greenwood Press, 1986. 364–69.

Robertson, Jamie. "Stephen Crane, Eastern Outsider in the West and Mexico." *Western American Literature* 13 (1978): 243–57.

Ronald, Ann. "Why Don't They Write about Nevada?" *Western American Literature* 24 (Fall 1989): 213–23.

Roosevelt, Theodore. *A Compilation of the Messages and Papers of the Presidents*. Prepared under the Direction of the Joint Committee on Printing of the House and Senate. Vol. 14. n.d.

———. *Letters of Theodore Roosevelt*. Ed. Elting E. Morrison et al. Cambridge, Mass.: Harvard University Press, 1951.

———. *The Spread of the English-Speaking Peoples*. 1899. New York: G. P. Putnam's Sons, 1900. Vol. 1 of *The Winning of the West*. 6 vols.

———. *The Strenuous Life*. New York: Century Co., 1901.

Rorty, Richard. *Contingency, Irony, and Solidarity*. Cambridge: Cambridge University Press, 1989.

———. *Essays on Heidegger and Others*. Cambridge: Cambridge University Press, 1991.

Rosenberg, Harold. *The Tradition of the New*. New York: Horizon Press, 1959.

Ross, Andrew. *The Chicago Gangster Theory of Life: Nature's Debt to Society*. London: Verso, 1994.

Rourke, Constance. *American Humor*. 1931. Tallahassee: University Presses of Florida, 1986.

Rudnick, Lois. "Re-Naming the Land: Anglo Expatriate Women in the Southwest." *The Desert Is No Lady: Southwestern Landscapes in Women's Writing*. Ed. Vera Norwood and Janice Monk. New Haven: Yale University Press, 1987. 10–26.

Ruppert, James. "Dialogism and Mediation in Leslie Marmon Silko's *Ceremony*." *Explicator* 51 (Winter 1993): 129–34.

Ruskin, John. *Modern Painters*. Ed. David Barrie. New York: Alfred A. Knopf, 1987.

Russell, Frank. "The Pima Indians." *Bureau of Ethnology Annual Report*. Vol. 25. Washington, D.C.: U.S. Government Printing Office, 1904–5. 3–389.

Samuels, Peggy, and Harold Samuels. *Frederic Remington: A Biography*. Garden City, N.Y.: Doubleday, 1982.

Saxton, Dean, and Lucille Saxton. *O'otham Hoho'ok A'agitha: Legends and Lore of the Papago and Pima Indians*. Tucson, University of Arizona Press, 1973.

Schuyler, David. "The Sanctified Landscape: The Hudson River Valley, 1820 to 1850." *Landscape in America*. Ed. George F. Thompson. Austin: University of Texas Press, 1995. 93–109.

Sessions, George, and Bill Devall. *Deep Ecology: Living as if Nature Mattered*. Salt Lake City: Peregrine Smith, 1985.

Shaler, Nathaniel. "The Landscape as a Means of Culture." *Atlantic* 82 (December 1898): 777–85.

Shelton, Richard. Introduction. *The Desert*. By John C. Van Dyke. Layton, Utah: Gibbs Smith, 1980. xi–xxix.

Silko, Leslie Marmon. *Almanac of the Dead*. New York: Penguin Books, 1991.

——. *Ceremony*. New York: Viking Press, 1977.

——. "Here's an Odd Artifact for the Fairy-Tale Shelf." Rev. of *The Beet Queen,* by Louise Erdrich. *Impact/Albuquerque Journal* 8 (October 1986): 10–11.

——. "Interior and Exterior Landscapes: The Pueblo Migration Stories." *Landscape in America*. Ed. George F. Thompson. Austin: University of Texas Press, 1995. 155–69.

——. *Storyteller*. New York: Seaver Books, 1981.

Slotkin, Richard. *The Fatal Environment*. New York: Atheneum, 1985.

——. *Regeneration Through Violence*. Middletown, Conn.: Wesleyan University Press, 1973.

Smith, Catherine. Letter to the author. 24 January 1994.

Smith, Henry Nash. *Virgin Land: The American West as Symbol and Myth*. New York: Random House, 1950.

Smith, Patricia Clark, with Paula Gunn Allen. "Earthly Relations, Carnal Knowledge: Southwestern American Indian Women Writers and Landscape." *The Desert Is No Lady: Southwestern Landscapes in Women's Writing*. Ed. Vera Norwood and Janice Monk. New Haven: Yale University Press, 1987. 174–98.

Smythe, William E. "The Conquest of Arid America." *Century* 50, May 1895, 85–99.

——. "Real Utopias in the Arid West." *Atlantic* 79 (May 1897): 599–609.

——. "Ways and Means in Arid America." *Century* 51 (March 1896): 742–58.

Spicer, Edward H., and Raymond Thompson. *Plural Society in the Southwest*. New York: Interbook, Inc., 1972.

Stegner, Wallace. *Beyond the Hundredth Meridian*. Cambridge, Mass.: Riverside Press, 1954.

Swann, Brian. Introduction. *Harper's Anthology of 20th Century Native American Poetry*. Ed. Duane Niatum. New York: Harper and Row, 1988. xii–xxxii.

Tatum, Charles. Introduction. *New Chicana/Chicano Writing 1*. Ed. Charles Tatum. Tucson: University of Arizona Press, 1992. xi–xiv.

Thacker, Robert. *The Great Prairie Fact and Literary Imagination*. Albuquerque: University of New Mexico Press, 1989.

Thompson, Jerry. *Laredo: A Pictorial History*. Norfolk, Va.: Donning Company, 1986.

Tolken, Barre. "Life and Death in the Navajo Coyote Tales." *Recovering the Word*. Ed. Brian Swann and Arnold Krupat. Berkeley: University of California Press, 1987. 388–401.

Tuan, Yi-Fu. *Topophilia: A Study of Environmental Perception, Attitudes, and Values*. Englewood Cliffs, N.J.: Prentice Hall, 1974.

Tuckerman, H. T. *Book of the Artists*. New York: G. P. Putnam and Son, 1867.

Turner, Frederick Jackson. "The Significance of the Frontier in American History." *The Frontier in American History*. 1920. New York: Henry Holt and Co., 1962. 1–38.

Twain, Mark. "How to Tell a Story." *Selected Shorter Writings of Mark Twain*. Ed. Walter Blair. Boston: Houghton Mifflin, 1962. 239–43.

——. *Roughing It*. 1872. New York: Viking Press, 1984.

Van Dyke, Dix. *Daggett: Life in a Mojave Frontier Town*. Ed. Peter Wild. Baltimore: Johns Hopkins University Press, 1997.

Van Dyke, John C. *Art for Art's Sake: Seven University Lectures on the Technical Beauties of Painting*. New York: Scribner's, 1893.

———. [Van Dyck]. "Artistic Nature." *The Studio* 17 (November 1883): 219–21.

———. *The Autobiography of John C. Van Dyke*. Ed. Peter Wild. Salt Lake City: University of Utah Press, 1993.

———. *The Desert: Further Studies in Natural Appearances*. New York: Scribner's, 1901.

———. *The Desert: Further Studies in Natural Appearances*. Photographs by J. Smeaton Chase. New York: Scribner's, 1918.

———. *The Grand Canyon of the Colorado: Recurrent Studies in Impressions and Appearances*. New York: Scribner's, 1920.

———. *How to Judge of a Picture: Familiar Talks in the Gallery with Uncritical Lovers of Art*. New York: Chautauqua, 1888.

———. "John Charles Van Dyke Correspondence with Charles Scribner's Sons, with Related Papers." The Archives of Charles Scribner's Sons, Box 160. Manuscripts Division, Department of Rare Books and Special Collections, Princeton University Libraries. Published with permission of the Princeton University Library.

———. "John Ruskin." *Library of the World's Best Literature*. Vol. 21. Ed. Charles Dudley Warner. New York: International Society, 1897. 12509–12516.

———. *The Mountain: Renewed Studies in Impressions and Appearances*. New York: Scribner's, 1916.

———. *Nature for Its Own Sake: First Studies in Natural Appearances*. New York: Scribner's, 1898.

———. "Old English Masters—Cole's New Series: William Hogarth." *Century* 54 (July 1897): 323–29.

———. *Old English Masters, Engraved by Timothy Cole*. New York: Century, 1902.

———. "Old English Masters: Sir Joshua Reynolds." *Century* 54 (October 1897): 815–22.

———. *Old English Masters* tearsheets. John C. Van Dyke Papers. American Academy of Arts and Letters Library, New York City.

———. "Recent American Sculpture." [Open Letter] *Century* 52 (June 1896): 158–59.

———. Scrapbook. John C. Van Dyke Papers. Archives, Gardner A. Sage Library, New Brunswick, N.J. Published with permission.

———. "Titian's Flora." [Open Letter] *Century* 51 (December 1895): 318–19.

Veblen, Thorstein. *The Theory of the Leisure Class*. 1899. New York: Random House, 1934.

Vizenor, Gerald. "A Postmodern Introduction." *Narrative Chance: Postmodern Discourse on Native American Indian Literatures*. Ed. Gerald Vizenor. Albuquerque: University of New Mexico Press, 1989. 3–16.

Vorpahl, Ben Merchant. *My Dear Wister: The Frederic Remington–Owen Wister Letters*. Palo Alto: American West Publishing Co., 1972.

————. "Roosevelt, Wister, Turner, and Remington." *A Literary History of the American West*. WLA. Fort Worth: Texas Christian University Press, 1987. 276–94.

Walker, Franklin. *A Literary History of Southern California*. Berkeley: University of California Press, 1950.

Warkentin, John. "The Desert Goes North." *Images of the Plains*. Ed. Brian W. Blouet and Merlin P. Larson. Lincoln: University of Nebraska Press, 1975. 149–63.

Webb, Walter Prescott. *The Great Plains*. Boston: Ginn and Co., 1931.

Webb County Heritage Foundation. *Walking Tour of Historic Laredo*. n.d.

Weber, David J. *The Spanish Frontier in North America*. New Haven: Yale University Press, 1992.

Weinberg, H. Barbara, Doreen Bolger, and David Park Curry. Introduction. *American Impressionism and Realism: The Painting of Modern Life, 1885–1915*. Ed. Weinberg, Bolger, and Curry. New York: Metropolitan Museum of Art, 1994. 3–34.

White, William Allen. "On Bright Angel Trail." *McClure's* 25 (September 1905): 502–15.

Wiget, Andrew. *Critical Essays on Native American Literature*. Boston: G. K. Hall, 1985.

Wigglesworth, Michael. "God's Controversy with New England." 1662. *Proceedings of the Massachusetts Historical Society, 1871–1873*.

Wild, Peter. *George Wharton James*. Western Writers Series. Boise: Boise State University Press, 1990.

————. Introduction. *The Autobiography of John C. Van Dyke*. Ed. Peter Wild. Salt Lake City: University of Utah Press, 1993.

————. "Viewing America's Deserts." *Puerto del Sol* 21.1 (1992): 303–21.

————. "A Western Sun Sets in the East: The Five 'Appearances' Surrounding John C. Van Dyke's *The Desert*." *Western American Literature* 25 (Fall 1990): 217–31.

————, ed. *The Desert Reader*. Salt Lake City: University of Utah Press, 1991.

Wild, Peter, and Neil Carmony. "The Trip Not Taken: Our Foremost Desert Wanderer as Flimflam Man." *Journal of Arizona History* (Spring 1993): 65–80.

Williams, Raymond. *The Country and the City*. Oxford: Oxford University Press, 1973.

Williams, Terry Tempest. *Refuge: An Unnatural History of Family and Place*. New York: Random House, 1991.

Wister, Owen. "The Evolution of the Cowpuncher." *Harper's* 91 (September 1895): 602–17.

————. "La Tinaja Bonita." *Harper's* 90 (May 1895): 859–79.

————. "Where Fancy Was Bred." *Harper's* 92 (March 1896): 574–84.

Wolff, Leon. *Lockout: The Story of the Homestead Strike of 1892; A Study of Violence, Unionism, and the Carnegie Steel Empire*. New York: Harper and Row, 1965.

Worster, Donald. *Rivers of Empire: Water, Aridity, and the Growth of the American West*. New York: Oxford University Press, 1985.

Zimmer, Carl. "How to Make a Desert." *Discover* 16.2 (February 1995): 50–56.

Zolbrod, Paul G. *Diné bahanè: The Navajo Creation Story*. Albuquerque: University of New Mexico Press, 1984.

Index

Note: Page numbers in italics indicate illustrations.

Abbey, Edward: *Desert Solitaire,* 142, 161–62
Alden, Henry Mills, 107
Almanac of the Dead (Silko), 166–68
Anaya, Rudolfo, 3
Anglo-Saxon conquest. *See* desert, racism and
Anzaldúa, Gloria, 3, 4, 10; *Borderlands/ La Frontera,* 168–70
"Arizona" (Monroe), 95, 103, 118–19
Art for Art's Sake (Van Dyke), 132
Atlantic Monthly Magazine, 93–94
Austin, Mary, 3, 49; in *Atlantic Monthly,* 119; definition of desert, 5; on descriptions of desert, 10–11, 13; on desert culture, 8, 159–61; *The Land of Little Rain,* 160–61; racial views of, 101

Autobiography (Carnegie), 139
Ayer, Edward Everett, 128

Bacheller News Syndicate, 75
Baker, Ray Stannard, "The Great Southwest," 102–3, 119, 127
Borderlands/La Frontera (Anzaldúa), 168–70
Bowden, Charles, 3
"Bride Comes to Yellow Sky" (Crane), 9, 74, 75, 78, 79, 80–88, *84*
Brooks, Benjamin: "The Southwest from a Locomotive," 120

Cabeza de Vaca, Alvar Núñez, 155–56
"Cañons of the Colorado" (Powell), *38, 39*
Carnegie, Andrew, 98, 136–40; *Autobiography,* 139
Castañeda, Carlos, 153–54
Cavalryman's Breakfast on the Plains (Remington), 62, *63,* 72

Century Illustrated Magazine, 92–94
Ceremony (Silko), 164–65
Cibola, 153
Clemens, Samuel, 52, 54–57; *Roughing It*, 54–57
Commerce of the Prairies (Gregg), 26–29
"Conquest of Arid America" (Smythe), 96, 99–100
Coronado, Francisco, 152–53
cowboy, myth of, 9, 70, 121
Crane, Stephen, 4, 74–88; "The Bride Comes to Yellow Sky," 9, 74, 75, 78, 79, 80–88; initial illustration from "The Bride Comes to Yellow Sky," *84*; "A Man and Some Others," 74, 78–79; "Moonlight on the Snow," 74, 79–80; *The Red Badge of Courage*, 75
Critic, The, 128

Death Valley in '49 (Manley), 23–24
de Niza, Fray Marcos, 153
desert: as aesthetic object, 127; awareness of ecological distinctiveness, 121; and comic voice, 54; conceptual definition of, 5; as corrective for problems of civilization, 117; as deadly, 13; as democratizing linguistic field, 166–70, 187n; as geographical celebrity, 54; in Judeo-Christian thought, 6; and local color, 54; moral associations, 14; and new vocabularies, 10–11, 17; paradoxical perceptions of, 120, 125, 126; as psychological obstacle, 14; racism and, 99–104, 106–11; reclamation of, 97; as stage, 52–53, 57, 58, 61, 73, 80–88, 103; and the sublime, 28–30, 31, 38, 47; and transcendental aesthetics, 34; and visual literacy, 16–17, 49; as wasteland, 9; as Wild West, 52, 71, 75, 76, 78, 80
"Desert" (Reed), 141
Desert (Van Dyke), 9, 127–44

Desert Smells Like Rain (Nabhan), 163
Desert Solitaire (Abbey), 142, 161–62
Dial, The, 128–29
Down the Santa Fe Trail and into Mexico (Magoffin), 21–22
Dutton, Clarence, 43–49, 66; *Tertiary History*, 46–49

environmental doublethink, 9
"Essentials at Fort Adobe" (Remington), 105
"Evolution of the Cowpuncher" (Wister), 107–11
Exploration of the Colorado River of the West (Powell), 33–40, *36*
Exploratory Travels through the Western Territories of North America (Pike), 20

"First American Views His Land" (Momaday), 163
Foote, Mary Hallock: illustration for Smythe's "Ways and Means in Arid America," 123, *124*
Frémont, John C., 21

geography, U.S., as bifurcated, 78, 138
geological catastrophism, theory of, 52, 53
Ghost Riders (Remington), 71
Gilder, Richard Watson, 96
Goin, Peter, 170; *Nuclear Landscapes*, 162
Great American Desert, 5; Josiah Gregg on, 27; Zebulon Pike on, 6
Greeley, Horace: *An Overland Journey from New York to San Francisco*, 30–32
Gregg, Josiah: *The Commerce of the Prairies*, 26–29

Harper's Magazine, 93–94
Hillers, Jack, 51; *Side Cañon*, 41, *42*
Homestead, Pennsylvania, 137, 141

Hopi Emergence Story, 149
"Horses of the Plains" (Remington), 106
The Horse Thief (Remington), 70, 71
House Made of Dawn (Momaday), 165–66
Hudson River School, 15

"Interior and Exterior Landscapes" (Silko), 164
Irving, Washington: *A Tour on the Prairies*, 25; *Rocky Mountains*, 25

James, William, 98
Janvier, Thomas: "Santa Fe Charley's Kindergarten," 105
Jefferson, Thomas, and agrarian myth, 8

King, Clarence, 51
Kinney, Abbot, 92
Kino, Father Eusebio Francisco, 154
Krutch, Joseph Wood, 3

Land of Little Rain (Austin), 160–61
"Landscape as a Means of Culture" (Shaler), 113–15
Leutze, Emmanuel: *Westward the Course of Empire Takes Its Way*, 16, *18–19*
literary naturalism, 97–98

MacMonnies, Frederick, 66
Magoffin, Susan Shelby: *Down the Santa Fe Trail and into Mexico*, 21–22
"A Man and Some Others" (Crane), 74, 78–79
Manifest Destiny, 14, 101
Manley, William Lewis: *Death Valley in '49*, 23–24
Marching in the Desert (Remington), 66
Martin, E. S., 110
Mather, Cotton, 6
McClure's Magazine, 74, 93
McLuckie, John, 138–40

Momaday, N. Scott, 3, 4, 159; "A First American Views His Land," 163; *House Made of Dawn*, 165–66
Monroe, Harriet, 112; "Arizona," 95, 103, 118–19
"Moonlight on the Snow" (Crane), 74, 79–80
Moran, Thomas: *The Chasm of the Colorado*, 41, *44–45*, 57
Muir, John, 3, 9, 10, 96

Nabhan, Gary: *The Desert Smells Like Rain*, 163
Nature for Its Own Sake (Van Dyke), 132
Navajo Creation Story, 147–49
Nuclear Landscapes (Goin), 162

Olmsted, Frederick Law, 96
"On Bright Angel Trail" (White), 97, 119
On the Southern Plains in 1860 (Remington), 67, *67*, 71, 72, 73
O'Sullivan, Timothy, 51; *Rhyolite Columns*, *53*
Outlaw (Remington), 71
Outlier (Remington), 71–72
Overland Journey from New York to San Francisco (Greeley), 30–32

Pike, Zebulon, 4, 6, 17, 66; *Exploratory Travels through the Western Territories of North America*, 20
Pinchot, Gifford, 96
"Plan to Save the Forests" (Sargent), 96
Powell, John Wesley, 32–43; in *Chicago Tribune*, 33; detail from topographic map by, *46*; *Exploration of the Colorado River of the West*, 33–40, *36*; illustrations from "The Cañons of the Colorado," *38*, *39*; "The Non-Irrigable Lands of the Arid Region," 92, 93; in *Popular Science Monthly*, 40; *Report on the Arid Regions*, 40–43; in *Scribner's Magazine*, 35–38

prairie ocean. *See* prairie sea
prairie sea, 22, 26
progressivism, 99–104, 113–25, 135
Pueblo Creation Story, 148

"Rain Goes Away" (Tohono O'odham),
    147, 149–52
Rattlesnake (Remington), 70
reclamation: Reclamation Act of 1902,
    8, 101. *See also* desert, reclamation
    of
Red Badge of Courage (Crane), 75
Red Men and White (Wister), 107
Reed, Verner: "The Desert," 141
Remington, Frederic, 4, 52, 57–73;
    Cavalryman's Breakfast on the Plains,
    62, *63*, 72; "The Essentials at Fort
    Adobe," 105; *Ghost Riders,* 71;
    "Horses of the Plains," 106; *The
    Horse Thief,* 70, 71; illustrations for
    "La Tinaja Bonita," 105; *Marching in
    the Desert,* 66; *On the Southern Plains
    in 1860,* 67, *67,* 71, 72, 73; *The
    Outlaw,* 71; *The Outlier,* 71–72; and
    pursuit of Geronimo, 61, 65; *The
    Rattlesnake,* 70; on sculpture, 68–69;
    Shoshonie—Prairie, Blue Sky, 65; *The
    Stampede,* 70, *71*; *Untitled (Prairie and
    Rimrocks),* 72; *The Wounded Bunkie,*
    68, *69*
Report on the Arid Regions (Powell), 40–
    43
Rhyolite Columns (O'Sullivan), *53*
Rocky Mountains (Irving), 25
Roosevelt, Theodore, 8, 59, 96, 98; first
    address to Congress, 101; opinion of
    Remington, 60; response to Crane's
    "A Man and Some Others," 104
Roughing It (Clemens), 54–57

Salvatierra, Juan María, 154
"Santa Fe Charley's Kindergarten"
    (Janvier), 105

Sargent, Charles: "A Plan to Save the
    Forests," 96
Scribner's Magazine, 93–94
Shaler, Nathaniel, 96, 112; "The
    Landscape as a Means of Culture,"
    113–15
Shoshonie—Prairie, Blue Sky
    (Remington), 65
Side Cañon (Hillers), 41, *42*
"Significance of the Frontier in American
    History" (Turner), 58
Silko, Leslie Marmon, 3, 4; *Almanac of
    the Dead,* 166–68; *Ceremony,* 164–65;
    "Interior and Exterior Landscapes,"
    164
Smythe, William: "The Conquest of Arid
    America," 96, 99–100; "Ways and
    Means in Arid America," 123
social Darwinism, 78, 79, 80, 98, 100–
    104, 113, 134
"Southwest from a Locomotive"
    (Brooks), 120
Stampede (Remington), 70, *71*
strenuous life, 59, 99, 102, 112, 119
sublime, desert as. *See* desert, and the
    sublime

Tertiary History (Dutton), 46–49
"Tinaja Bonita" (Wister), 105
Tohono O'odham, 163; "Rain Goes
    Away," 147, 149–52
Tour on the Prairies (Irving), 25
Turner, Frederick Jackson: and 1890
    census, 9; "The Significance of the
    Frontier in American History," 58
Twain, Mark. *See* Clemens, Samuel

Untitled (Prairie and Rimrocks)
    (Remington), 72

Van Dyke, John C., 10, 127–44; *Art for
    Art's Sake,* 132; *Nature for Its Own
    Sake,* 132

visual literacy. *See* desert, and visual literacy

wasteland. *See* desert, as wasteland
"Ways and Means in Arid America" (Smythe), 123
Westward the Course of Empire Takes Its Way (Leutze), 16, *18–19*
"Where Fancy Was Bred" (Wister), 105
White, William Allen: "On Bright Angel Trail," 97, 119

Wigglesworth, Michael, 6
Wild West. *See* desert, as Wild West
Williams, Terry Tempest, 3, 170
Winchell, Benjamin, 128
Wister, Owen, 52; "Evolution of the Cowpuncher," 107–11; *Red Men and White,* 107; "La Tinaja Bonita," 105; "Where Fancy Was Bred," 105
Wounded Bunkie (Remington), 68, *69*

Zuñi Emergence Story, 148

About the Author

David Warfield Teague was born in 1964 in Lafayette, Indiana, and was raised in Conway, Arkansas. He received a bachelor's degree in English literature, with honors and distinction, from Hendrix College and completed his master's and doctoral degrees in English literature at the University of Virginia. His short story "A Singing Cowboy" received the 1995 *Redneck Review of Literature* Western Fiction Prize, and his scholarly entries on Edward Hoagland and William Least Heat-Moon appeared in the anthology *American Nature Writers,* edited by John Elder. He also edited *The Secret Life of John C. Van Dyke: Selected Letters* with Peter Wild. Teague teaches English and American literature in the University Parallel Program at the University of Delaware in Wilmington.